Lecture Notes in Computer Science 10371

Commenced Publication in 1973
Founding and Former Series Editors:
Gerhard Goos, Juris Hartmanis, and Jan van Leeuwen

Editorial Board

David Hutchison
  Lancaster University, Lancaster, UK
Takeo Kanade
  Carnegie Mellon University, Pittsburgh, PA, USA
Josef Kittler
  University of Surrey, Guildford, UK
Jon M. Kleinberg
  Cornell University, Ithaca, NY, USA
Friedemann Mattern
  ETH Zurich, Zurich, Switzerland
John C. Mitchell
  Stanford University, Stanford, CA, USA
Moni Naor
  Weizmann Institute of Science, Rehovot, Israel
C. Pandu Rangan
  Indian Institute of Technology, Madras, India
Bernhard Steffen
  TU Dortmund University, Dortmund, Germany
Demetri Terzopoulos
  University of California, Los Angeles, CA, USA
Doug Tygar
  University of California, Berkeley, CA, USA
Gerhard Weikum
  Max Planck Institute for Informatics, Saarbrücken, Germany

More information about this series at http://www.springer.com/series/7408

Yoshinori Hara · Dimitris Karagiannis (Eds.)

Serviceology
for Services

5th International Conference, ICServ 2017
Vienna, Austria, July 12–14, 2017
Proceedings

 Springer

Editors
Yoshinori Hara
Graduate School of Management
Kyoto University
Kyoto
Japan

Dimitris Karagiannis
Research Group Knowledge Engineering
University of Vienna
Vienna
Austria

ISSN 0302-9743   ISSN 1611-3349 (electronic)
Lecture Notes in Computer Science
ISBN 978-3-319-61239-3   ISBN 978-3-319-61240-9 (eBook)
DOI 10.1007/978-3-319-61240-9

Library of Congress Control Number: 2017946066

LNCS Sublibrary: SL2 – Programming and Software Engineering

© Springer International Publishing AG 2017
This work is subject to copyright. All rights are reserved by the Publisher, whether the whole or part of the material is concerned, specifically the rights of translation, reprinting, reuse of illustrations, recitation, broadcasting, reproduction on microfilms or in any other physical way, and transmission or information storage and retrieval, electronic adaptation, computer software, or by similar or dissimilar methodology now known or hereafter developed.
The use of general descriptive names, registered names, trademarks, service marks, etc. in this publication does not imply, even in the absence of a specific statement, that such names are exempt from the relevant protective laws and regulations and therefore free for general use.
The publisher, the authors and the editors are safe to assume that the advice and information in this book are believed to be true and accurate at the date of publication. Neither the publisher nor the authors or the editors give a warranty, express or implied, with respect to the material contained herein or for any errors or omissions that may have been made. The publisher remains neutral with regard to jurisdictional claims in published maps and institutional affiliations.

Printed on acid-free paper

This Springer imprint is published by Springer Nature
The registered company is Springer International Publishing AG
The registered company address is: Gewerbestrasse 11, 6330 Cham, Switzerland

Preface

The 5th International Conference on Serviceology (ICServ) was the latest in the ongoing conference series, building on the success of four previous events held in Tokyo, Japan (ICServ 2016), San Jose, CA, USA (ICServ 2015), Yokohama, Japan (ICServ 2014), and AIST Tokyo Waterfront, Japan (ICServ 2013). Initiated by the Society for Serviceology in Japan, it aims to build a community of researchers, academics, and industry leaders following a common goal: the (co)-creation of services in a sustainable society.

This year's event was held in Vienna, the capital and largest city of Austria, and the primary center for culture, economics, and politics. ICServ 2017 was hosted by the University of Vienna at the Faculty of Computer Science. The university, one of the oldest and biggest in the German-speaking area, was founded in 1365 by Duke Rudolph IV and has been the academic home of 15 Nobel Prize winners and many leaders of academic and historical importance.

ICServ 2017 received a total of 75 submissions from 20 countries, around the world. The Program Committee together with external reviewers contributed 225 reviews. As a result, with a competitive acceptance rate of only 28%, 21 full papers were selected to be included in these proceedings. The accepted papers can be classified under the main areas of human-centered services, customer satisfaction, service innovation and marketing, and service design. The research comprises case studies, strategies, risk analysis, reports, as well as prototypes, modeling methods, and tools. Consequently, empirical research, behavioristic research, and design-science research contributions were accepted.

The ICServ 2017 program also included keynotes, one podium discussion, four special sessions, and one tutorial. Each special session addressed a specific topic related to services and had between four to eight papers presented. The organizers of the special sessions were responsible for attracting and reviewing submissions. Special Session 1, "Meaningful Technology for Seniors," was organized by Dr. Kentaro Watanabe (AIST, Japan) and Prof. Marketta Niemela (VTT, Finland). It addressed the importance of service providing technologies for elderly-care and elderly-nursing systems. Special Session 2, entitled "Holistic Approach of Service Modeling," was organized by Prof. Yoshinori Hara (Kyoto University, Japan), Joaquin Iranzo (Atos, Spain), and Prof. Dimitris Karagiannis (University of Vienna, Austria). This session included a set of talks addressing holistic approaches in contrast to silo solutions towards service modeling and service design. Prof. Patrik Strom (University of Gothenburg, Sweden) and Dr. Mitsutaka Matsumoto (AIST, Japan) organized Special Session 3 entitled "Services and Green Economy." The presentations focused on environmental friendly issues like recycling in correlation with services. "Design and Support Technology" was Special Session 4, which was organized by Prof. Takashi Tanizaki (Kindai University, Japan) and Prof. Nobutada Fuji (Kobe University, Japan). Key aspects of services for customer satisfaction improvement in the food and tourism industry were addressed by numerous papers.

ICServ 2017 would not have been possible without the involvement of a large scientific community. We thank our authors for showing interest and being willing to submit their work to ICServ 2017. We sincerely appreciate the valuable amount of time and knowledge that the Program Committee members, members of four special sessions, and supportive additional reviewers invested in carefully reviewing the submitted papers. Furthermore, we would like to express our gratitude to the honorary general conference chair, Prof. Shoji Yamamoto (Kwansei University, Kobe, Japan) and to the Steering Committee chair, Prof. Tamio Arai (Shibaura Institute of Technology, Japan). We also want to thank our industrial sponsors Fujitsu, Hilti, NEC, and ADOxx (www. adoxx.org) as well as our affiliated communities, the Society for Serviceology (www. serviceology.org) and the Open Models Laboratory (OMiLAB, www.omilab.org), without which such an event would not have been possible. We are also very grateful to the Springer team led by Alfred Hofmann for making the publication of these proceedings possible.

Last but not least we like to thank the organization team for their hard work and dedication in making ICServ 2017 a success. Our thanks go to Iulia Cristina Hatiegan, Iulia Vaidian, Shihoko Murakami, Junko Kozakai, Eriko Nakashima, Simon Doppler, Franz Staffel, and Elena Miron.

May 2017
Yoshinori Hara
Dimitris Karagiannis

Organization

Organizing Committee

Honorary General Conference Chair

Shoji Yamamoto   Kwansei University, Kobe, Japan

Steering Committee Chair

Tamio Arai,   Shibaura Institute of Technology, Japan

Program Chair

Dimitris Karagiannis   University of Vienna, Austria

Program Committee

Jürgen Anke	Hochschule für Telekommunikation Leipzig, Germany
Daniel Beverungen	Paderborn University, Germany
Dominik Bork	University of Vienna, Austria
Xavier Boucher	Ecole des Mines de Saint Etienne, France
Christoph Breidbach	The University of Melbourne, Australia
Robert Andrei Buchmann	Babes-Bolyai University Cluj, Romania
Sergio Cavalieri	University of Bergamo, Italy
Houn-Gee Chen	National Taiwan University, Taiwan
Ja-Shen Chen	Yuan Ze University, Taiwan
Eng K. Chew	University of Technology Sydney, Australia
Valentin Cristea	University Politehnica of Bucharest, Romania
Edward Crowley	Photizo Group and Manchester University, UK
Monica Dragoicea	University Politehnica of Bucharest, Romania
Eman El-Sheikh	University of West Florida, USA
Xiucheng Fan	Fudan University, China
Louis Freund	San Jose State University, USA
Nobutada Fujii	Kobe University, Japan
Yoshinori Fujikawa	Hitotsubashi University, Japan
Ken Fukuda	AIST, Japan
Walter Ganz	Fraunhofer IAO, Germany
Aditya Ghose	University of Wollongong, Australia
Tatsunori Hara	University of Tokyo, Japan
Yoshinori Hara	Kyoto University, Japan
Kazuyoshi Hidaka	Tokyo Institute of Technology, Japan
San-Yih Hwang	National Sun Yat-sen University, Taiwan
Lakhmi C. Jain	University of Canberra, Australia

Julia M. Jonas	Friedrich Alexander University of Erlangen-Nürnberg, Germany
Toshiya Kaihara	Kobe University, Japan
Koji Kimita	Tokyo Metropolitan University, Japan
Axel Korthaus	Victoria University, Australia
Michitaka Kosaka	JAIST, Japan
Natalia Kryvinska	University of Vienna, Austria
Stephen Kwan	San Jose State University, USA
Moon Kun Lee	Chonbuk National University, Korea
Jan Marco Leimeister	University of St. Gallen, Switzerland
Eldon Y. Li	National Chengchi University, Taiwan
Mattias Lindahl	Linköping University, Sweden
Ruqian Lu	Chinese Academy of Sciences, China
Leszek A. Maciaszek	Wroclaw University of Economics, Poland
Birgit Mager	Köln International School of Design, Germany
Hisashi Masuda	JAIST, Japan
Heinrich C. Mayr	Alpen-Adria Universität Klagenfurt, Austria
Kyrill Meyer	University of Leipzig, Germany
Chieko Minami	Kobe University, Japan
Lasse Mitronen	Aalto University, Finland
Hiroyasu Miwa	AIST, Japan
Masaaki Mochimaru	AIST, Japan
Yoichi Motomura	AIST, Japan
Hideyuki Nakashima	University of Tokyo, Japan
Andy Neely	University of Cambridge, UK
Satoshi Nishimura	AIST, Japan
Nariaki Nishino	University of Tokyo, Japan
Taiki Ogata	University of Tokyo, Japan
Takashi Okuma	AIST, Japan
Lia Patricio	University of Porto, Portugal
Christoph Peters	University of St. Gallen, Switzerland
Martin Petry	Hilti AG, Schaan, Liechtenstein
Manuele Kirsch Pinheiro	University of Paris 1 Pantheon Sorbonne, France
Dimitris Plexousakis	University of Crete, Greece
Jens Poeppelbuss	University of Bremen, Germany
Anca Purcarea	University Politehnica of Bucharest, Romania
Jolita Ralyte	University of Geneva, Switzerland
Shai Rozenes	Afeka Tel Aviv Academic College of Engineering, Israel
Yuriko Sawatani	Tokyo University of Technology, Japan
Satoshi Shimada	Kyoto University, Japan
Yoshiki Shimomura	Tokyo Metropolitan University, Japan
Jim Spohrer	IBM, USA
Rudi Studer	Karlsruhe Institute of Technology, Germany
Satoko Suzuki	Kyoto University, Japan
Takeshi Takenaka	AIST, Japan
Takashi Tanizaki	Kindai University, Japan

Marja Toivonen   VTT Technical Research Centre of Finland, Finland
Keiko Toya   Graduate School of Global Business Meiji University,
                            Japan
Vivek K. Velamuri   HHL Leipzig Graduate School of Management,
                            Germany
Kentaro Watanabe   AIST, Japan
Takahira Yamaguchi   Keio University, Japan
Yukata Yamauchi   Kyoto University, Japan
Alfred Zimmermann   Reutlingen University, Germany

Additional Reviewers

Marina Bitsaki   University of Crete, Greece
Sissy-Josefina Ernst   University of Kassel, Germany
Christian Grotherr   University of Hamburg, Germany
Kyriakos Kritikos   University of Crete, Greece
Vimal Kunnummel   University of Vienna, Austria
Richard Larson   Massachusetts Institute of Technology, USA
Mahei Manhai Li   University of Kassel, Germany
Jan Martin Persch   University of Kassel, Germany
Nikolaos Tantouris   University of Vienna, Austria
Chrysostomos Zeginis   University of Crete, Greece

Special Sessions

Special Session I: Meaningful Technology for Seniors

Organizers

Kentaro Watanabe   AIST, Japan
Marketta Niemelä   VTT, Finland

Special Session II: Holistic Approach of Service Modelling

Organizers

Yoshinori Hara   Kyoto University, Japan
Joaquin Iranzo   Atos, Spain
Dimitris Karagiannis   University of Vienna, Austria

Special Session III: Services and Green Economy

Organizers

Patrik Ström   University of Gothenburg, Sweden
Mitsutaka Matsumoto   AIST, Japan

Special Session IV: Design and Support Technology for Value Co-creation

Organizers

Takashi Tanizaki   Kindai University, Japan
Nobutada Fujii   Kobe University, Japan

Organizing Committee

Iulia Cristina Hatiegan
Iulia Vaidian
Simon Doppler
Franz Staffel
Elena Miron

Affiliated Communities

Society for
Serviceology
www.serviceology.org

OMiLAB®

www.omilab.org

Industrial Sponsors

We thank all our sponsors for supporting the ICServ2017 conference.

www.adoxx.org

Contents

Service Innovation and Marketing

Service Design

Human-Centered Service

Analysing and Computing the Risk of Customer Integration for a Service Provider

Wolfgang Seiringer

[1] Institute of Software Technology and Interactive Systems,
Vienna University of Technology, Vienna, Austria
wolfgang.seiringer@gmail.com

Abstract.
The active customer participation during service co-production means risks and also chances for a service provider. Without knowledge about the risks, it is difficult for a service provider to benefit from customer integration. Risk factors of the mandatory customer integration are the active or passive role of the customer, quantity and quality of the provided resources and experience. In this paper we analyse the risk of customer integration and present a risk based approach to measure the potential loss for a service provider due to unexpected customer performance. Our paper provides a detailed analysis of concepts related to customer integration and a risk based method suitable as extension for existing service performance and costings methods. Such a costing method is Activity-Based Costing (ABC).

Keywords: customer integration, risk based service costing, service production, service performance

1   Introduction

Up to a certain level customer integration is mandatory during service production to get the desired service outcome [1]. For a service provider customer integration means risks and chances. Shifting the workload to the customer is a chance to reduce the own costs, but unskilled and not motivated customers are an economic risk for service providers [2]. To participate in service production a customer must have the willingness and also the ability. The willingness can be expressed by a price reduction, which is possible when assembling furniture at home [3]. Without the required skills, the willingness, time and resources are not enough [4]. Customer participation can be defined "... *as the degree of, consumers effort and involvement, both mental and physical, necessary to participate in production and delivery, of services.*" [5]. Customer participation can be exploited to increase productivity, to add additional values, to reach new customers, to motivate customers and to intensify customer relationship [6], [4]. From another perspective customer participation predominantly means risks and uncertainties for a service provider. Trying to isolate the own business activities from the customer is one possible reaction not to lose control over service production and consequently the service quality [1].

© Springer International Publishing AG 2017
Y. Hara and D. Karagiannis (Eds.): ICServ 2017, LNCS 10371, pp. 3–14, 2017.
DOI: 10.1007/978-3-319-61240-9_1

In order to make a customer's implications on service performance and costs manageable, the risks and consequences of customer integration must be considered [3]. This will help service providers to decide when and which tasks should be isolated from the customer not to lose control over the service production and the associated costs. Also which actions and trainings can help to improve service experience for provider and customer [7].

The total service costs of a service are the result of the invested resources during coproduction of provider and customer. During service production, service provider and service customer are part of a service system. A service system can be characterized as a changing configuration of technologies and resources (including human resources) organized with the goal to jointly create the demanded service [8]. Both parties have to invest resources such as knowledge, information, technologies, experience, human resources or infrastructure capabilities in the service system. To improve the efficiency of service systems, to create new services and to systematize service innovation, such service systems are addressed by service science [9], [10], [11]. Research results from service science are required to demonstrate the economic importance of services. Compared to other economic sectors such as automotive or manufacturing, the service sector is often regarded as less productive [12]. Overall, however, the economic importance of the service sector constantly increases. Most employment growth, for example, originates in the service sector, and about 70% of the people in OECD countries are currently working in companies related to it [13]. Regarding the economic importance, the financial crisis, which started in 2007, and the ensuing economic crisis of the early 21st century showed, that the service sector can also experience economic problems [14], [15].

Since "… *the customer is a coproducer of service* …" [16], the concept of service-dominant (S-D) logic additionally motivates investigations concerning performance measurements in service systems. Especially as the customer is regarded as an integral component of service co-production. In S-D logic, the most important resources of a service system are knowledge and competencies. The knowledge and competencies of a customer are of particular interest for service costing. Responding to individual levels of competencies and knowledge can be a competitive advantage and can help to compute service costs more accurate.

Cost analyses are performed by companies to achieve pre-defined goals of the corporate strategy [17]. This requires solid information to support leadership decisions. In general, are companies analysing costs to gain higher margins compared to competitors by lowering production and distribution costs [18]. Two existing costing methods used for services costing are activity-based costing (ABC) and time-driven activity-based costing (TDABC) [19], [20]. However, neither ABC nor TDABC cover customer input and the associated uncertainties for service performance. The amount of required human resources, and time to produce a service, depends directly on a customer's input and how efficient it can be integrated into service production. This implies that without their integration, a major cost-influencing factor is not being taken into account, which decreases the reliability and the value of service cost information. With our paper we also address the missing customer perspective in service costing.

The concept of customer participation in the context of services and cost analysis is also investigated by other researchers. Several works have been published on this topic. In the thesis of [21], the relation of customer involvement to product complexity and production costs is examined based on interviews and a survey via e-mail. The research work in [22] examines customer engagement and tries to provide a concept to improve a customer framework based on the Total Economic Impact (TEI) methodology. A survey and interviews were used as input and to develop the proposed methodology. Customer participation and the impact on customer satisfaction and quality of service delivery are investigated in [7].

The above considerations inspired us to analyse possible benefits and risks a service provider is confronted with during customer integration and the implications on service costing. A main target is to find customer input factors expressing the risk of customer input on service production which can be used as basis to add a customer perspective to service costing [23].

Customer participation is regarded as a key characteristic for sustain service management. Concrete risk factors can improve decision making in the context of service management. Thus, the selected research question and associated hypothesis is: *Which customer associated risk factors influence service performance?* Our hypothesis claims: *Customer associated risk factors can help to make service performance more controllable.*

To answer the research question and hypothesis, we have defined a method to compute a customer-risk factor. These risk factor should further on be the basis for a risk based costing approach. Such a costing approach can be used to integrate customer associated risks into service costing.

The contribution of this paper will be an in-depth analysis of customer integration from provider's perspective. A company can use our work to gain a deeper insight into the level of customer participation and its consequences to service performance and costs. Furthermore, a company can use the customer-risk factors to improve an organization's strategy in terms of capacity and human resource planning.

In this this article at first, literature dealing with customer involvement and service production is presented. Afterwards our method to compute a customer-risk factor is described. Finally, our results are discussed and conclusions are drawn to give an outlook for subsequent research activities.

2 Customer Integration during Service Production

To benefit from customer integration a service company needs a clear understanding what services are and how they are produced and how the customer participates and has to be integrated. This is necessary not to lose control of service production and the outcome [24]. A service provider has to integrate a customer into service production. This is independent if we talk about end consumers or business consumers. During the production process a customer participates by providing input expressed by information, effort, time, labour, property, knowledge, physically presence or physical possessions [1], [2], [25]. Customers are an inexpensive resource, as they are experts of their own domain. Customer integration provides the chance to develop new services and to increase service performance [26]. But customer integration is also getting more difficult, as service providers have to offer more customizable services [25]. The complexity of customer integration strongly depends on the active or passive role a customer wants to obtain. Active customer participation can increase service productivity and also customer satisfaction [7].

A distinction between customer involvement and customer participation is possible. Customer involvement describes how psychologically related a customer is to a service. It is argued, that a customer can be longer involved than actively participating in service production [4], [27]. In this paper we use these two concepts interchangeable as we are focused on the concept of customer integration during service production, independent if a customer participates or is involved.

Compared to goods production, service production is characterized by the mandatory customer participation. Production in general means to create performance as it is done in manufacturing companies by finishing or extracting raw materials or also in service companies [28]. Service production is a customer-dominated process and depends on customer input [3]. For effective service co-production three key factors are perceived clarity of the task, ability or competence and motivation [3]. All three factors will increase the likelihood for good service performance and a customer's service experience. Customer integration usually takes place at the visible part of a service organizations production system. The invisible part is represented by the management and support system which supplies the necessary resources for the visible part, where customer integration takes place [29]. For service production customer input has a control function by defining the necessary production processes and business activities. Consequently, this affects a provider's service costs and it can also be argued that "… *a customer wish to control the process of service production and delivery thus reduce risk and increasing revenue*" [30].

For participating in a production process a customer can have different motivations and can occupy different roles with varying importance. Described motivations are an intrinsic motivation to actively influence service production [5], getting control over the situation, human contact, doing it oneself [23], try to control the efficiency of the process, control the efficacy of the outcome, emotional benefits, maximize the outcome, psychological benefits, personal interaction, information exchange, affective commitment, unique experience, self-serving bias, encouragement of creative participation, self-efficacy or interaction fairness [4]. Personal interaction and information exchange have the "… *highest relation with customer participation …*" [30] and personal interaction is strongly related to the integrative nature of service production [30]. The integrative nature of service production forces a service provider to supply capacity also without a customer, which leads to an ongoing information exchange between the provider and customer.

2.1 Customer roles

Possible roles for a customer are, the customer as the advocate, customer as the innovator, customer as the source of competences, customer as the human resource, customer as the partial employee, customer as the productive resource, customer as a co-producer, customer as an instructor, customer as promoter, customer as a human resource, customer as organizational consultant, the customer as contributor to quality, satisfaction and value, the customer as competitor to the service organization and customer as auditor. A customer's role should be clear to overcome problems during customer integration and not to get into "..."*blaming culture" where each side blame the other side for the problems that occur...*" [1], [7], [26].

2.2 Types and Levels of Customer Involvement

Different levels of customer involvement (low, moderate and high) can be identified depending on the service type. On all three levels active participation of the customer is required. If only low level participation is required, only customer presence is required, because the service provider is doing all the work. The levels of customer involvement has different consequences for the service provider. If a customer purchases a service for the first time, active participation can be higher compared to if the customer has purchased a service several times in the past. Low customer involvement also means that the customer's presence is only required during service delivery and that the process of service provision is highly standardized and not intended to be customizable. Customer involvement is moderate when customer input is required during the production of a standardized service. A haircut or a full-service restaurant are B2C examples, for B2B examples are transportation and payroll services. Customer involvement is high when active customer participation is required during service production and the customer co-creates the outcome. High customer involvement is required when it is difficult to standardize a service. An example for the B2C area is personal training, for the B2B sector consulting is such a service. High customer involvement is also required in education and health services [1], [2], [7], [31].

3 Risks of Customer Integration

Customer integration can lead to problems during service production and is a source for uncertainty. When customers provide specifications, which are technically insufficient, and change often or claim additional price discounts, an undesired service output may be produced [2], [7]. Problems during customer integration can result in role conflicts when a customer's expectations cannot be met by the service provider [2]. Drawbacks of customer involvement are decreasing service performance and customer satisfaction due to unskilled customers. Problems of customers to carry out their associated tasks which affects the motivation of the involved employees and can result in a useless service production output. This can lead to economic uncertainties for the whole service provider and increases customer contact frequency and the duration of the service production process. Customer who actively participate in service production may be less satisfied compare to passive customers [7]. An increasing customer participation requires also employees which are capable und flexible to react on changing customer involvement [3]. Reducing its own risk can be a reason for a customer to be an efficient co-producer [5].

Customer involvement during production can result in uncertainty between provider and customer in the areas of planning, integration and production. Provider as well as customer can be the source of these three elements of uncertainty [32]. *Planning uncertainty* occurs on the provider's side when the customer knows under which conditions (location, time, quantity and quality) the external factors are necessary, but the provider does not know whether the customer is able to supply them. *Integration uncertainty* relates to the existing knowledge of provider and customer of how to integrate the external factors into the process of service production. Integration uncertainty occurs when the customer lacks the information under which conditions (location, time, quantity and quality) external factors are required. *Production uncertainty* depends on integration uncertainty and affects provider and customer. For the customer, production uncertainty is related to an uncertainty of the ability to create the required external factors. Internal production factors are required to create external production factors. The provider is confronted with an uncertainty regarding how these external factors must be combined with the own internal factors. Especially during the process of factor combination in order to co-create the demanded service.

The *financial risk* is related to the immateriality of services and the promised performance (commitment). As a result, it is difficult to define an adequate ratio between price and performance or an adequate service cost calculation. For the customer, a promised service is associated with the uncertainty of making a profit or an unexpected deficit. For the service provider, the customer is one main source of financial uncertainty. A customer's direct impact on service production requires additional considerations of which resources are required and which are affected by customer involvement. Apart from supplying sufficient personnel capacity, it can be necessary to invest into systems and machinery. The financial risk could be reduced by the usage of an exact service-oriented costing method.

Physical risk occurs when the customer can suffer a physical damage because of service consumption. Examples are the use of public transportation, medical treatments or services related to sports. Psychological risk is mainly associated with the immateriality of services and can occur before, during or after consumption. If the customer expects negative consequences to his social environment, this is called *social risk* which occurs when the customer behaves differently to his/her habit in the selection and consumption of service offerings. Visiting a political event of a prohibited party or a sect is associated with a social risk.

The usually intangible service output and the inseparability of service production and consumption, complicates the tasks of quality check and error correction prior to service production. If a customer supplies an incomplete service specification, this complicates delivering the demanded service. One main reason for uncertainty during service production is the dependency on customer input [33].Until the customer provides the required input, it is difficult to exactly schedule the required resources. This means capacity planning is also affected by the customer input, which increase performance uncertainty for a service provider. Therefore, a service provider is additionally confronted with uncertainty in terms of capacity planning.

4 An Approach for Customer Integration Risk Computation

Customer integration means risks and chances for a service provider. To benefit from it the associated risk must be known. Consequently, the risk event we observe is customer integration.

Customer integration can be a long-lasting process with a varying customer input. Due to the nature of services a service provider is forced to integrate it into service production. Customer input is extreme heterogenic and often difficult to identify. This makes it difficult to measure its impact on service performance. Every customer input which must be integrated and handled by a service provider causes effort and is a potential risk factor. Customers provide these input in tangible and intangible form. A tangible customer input is for example, the personal presence during a project meeting or a defect car with a flat tire, which needs a repair service in a garage. Intangible input is experience or information in form of a problem description.

For approach development, we used the input of our above literature study and a detailed analysis of two different services. The first service was software engineering from a software company and the second was a maintenance service for medical devices. From both companies, we got access to service related data and experienced employees were interviewed by us. From the data, we could derive the actual practice to store and operate with service related business data. Based on this input a detailed description of the service processes and the effects of customer integration could be created.

We have analysed the service from the customer integration perspective. This means, to select the relevant service activities, software engineering is viewed from the perspective of a service provider which is forced to integrate customer input during the process of software development. For our example, we have used the service activities requirements analysis, implementation, testing, deployment and maintenance. For each of these activities customer contact with different intensity is necessary and a varying importance of the input categories exist. For requirements engineering the experience and availability of domain experts have a high impact on service performance. During implementation, a customer's IT infrastructure influences service performance. Because a bad infrastructure can increase implementation time. Also for testing the IT infrastructure and employees which are necessary for acceptance tests are important. For deployment and maintenance, the IT infrastructure has a high impact and for deployment especially a customer's experience.

Our proposed approach consists of two steps. The first step is to estimate the Customer Integration Level (CIL) and the second step is to use the CIL to determine the associated customer integration risk. In the following both steps are described in detail.

4.1   Step 1: Customer Integration Level (CIL)

We could identify three general categories for customer input. These are *co-production (Co)*, *resources (Re)* and *experience (Ex)*. These three categories are necessary to compute the Customer Integration Level (CIL). The calculated CIL value represents the quality of *Co*, *Re* and *Ex* and the positive or negative impact on service performance. A high *CIL* implies a high input factor quality and potentially a lower risk during customer integration and consequently on service performance.

Co-production represents a customer's varying presence (low, moderate, high) during service production. With *resources*, the various tangible and intangible resources of a customer are meant, e.g. only information and/or physical presence. Finally, *experience* describes a customer's experience with the demanded service. For a service provider, it makes a difference if a customer knows a service or not. These three categories are always present in a service scenario, while the importance and impact on service performance can vary between services.

Each of the three input categories covers several risks a service provider is confronted with. Co-production covers risk concerning the customer contact. Was a high number of customer contact necessary? How was the customer behaviour during the contact phase e.g. cooperative and motivated? Did the customer provide prompt answers to questions?

Resources covers risk of the committed resources like knowledge and technologies. Relevant questions from provider perspective are: Are the qualifications of the responsible persons at the customer sufficient to perform the required tasks? Is the provided information detailed enough to solve the service tasks?

Experience covers the risk an unexperienced customer may imply. For a service provider, this means to answer questions like: Is bad experience with that customer known from past service productions or business partners. How was the performance of the past service productions?

4.1.1   CIL Computation

To compute the Customer Integration Level (CIL) for an individual service S_i, first the CIL for each service activity SA_i of S_i must be computed. A service consists of one or several individual service activities. Service activities can be identified, as they are necessary to produce an individual service, require customer input and provide output for subsequent service activities. The structure of service and service activities can be compared to the concepts of business process and activities, which are know from Business Process Modelling (BPM). Splitting up a service into different service activities can increase the manageability of a service and shows which service activities are also required for other services.

The CIL_{SA_i} is computed by multiplying the three previously identified customer input categories Co-Creation (Co), Resources (Re) and Experience (Ex) with the associated weighting factors Co_w, Re_w and Ex_w. The weighting is used to consider service scenarios where the impact of the three input categories on service production is different, compare to Equation 1.

To calculate the CIL for a service it is only necessary to sum up and compute the average of the CIL per sevice activity and if necessary to group it by customers, compare to Equation 2. For the rating and numeric value computation of the input categories we decided to use three categories 1 for low quality and risky, 2 for moderate quality and an acceptable risk level and 3 for high quality and low risk potential. We applied this categorization with low, medium and high for CIL_{SA_i} and CIL_{S_i}. This type of classification, which can be compared to a Likert Scale, supports the understanding of our model and corresponds with the described levels of customer integration in our state of the art section. The usage of a more granular scaling is possible if it fits to the analysed service scenario.

$$CIL_{SA_i,Cust_n} = Co * C_w + Re * R_w + Ex * E_w, \text{with } Co, Re, Ex$$
$$\in \{1 \ (low), 2 \ (moderate), 3 \ (high)\} \quad and \quad Co_w + Re_w + Ex_w$$
$$= 1$$

Equation 1: CIL computation for service activity SA_i and customer $Cust_n$

$$CIL_{S_i,Cust_n} = \frac{\sum_i^n CIL_{SA_i,Cust_n}}{n}, with \ n = number \ of \ different \ SA_i$$

Equation 2: CIL computation for a service S_i and customer $Cust_n$

4.2 Customer Risk Factor (Step 2)

The second step in our model is to compute the concrete risk for customer integration. The computed customer integration risk $Risk_{SA_i,Cust_n}$ expresses the probability of having problems during customer integration which leads to a loss for the service provider. The $Risk_{SA_i,Cust_n}$ is computed based on the previously determined $CIL_{SA_i,Cust_n}$ and is derived from predefined severity classes for each CIL level, compare to Equation 3 and Equation 4. The identified severity classes can subsequently be used for risk computations e.g. integrate $Risk_{SA_i,Cust_n}$ into cost or resource forecasting. This can be done by multiplying $Risk_{SA_i,Cust_n}$ with costs or ressources. Each severity class has a numeric boundary which represents the acceptable loss for this severity class e.g. 20% difference between forecasted and actual costs or capacity. We have used the severity classes insignificant up to 20%, significant 60%, or severe 100%. Depending on the service scenario other boundaries and severity classes are also possible.

To identify the correct severity class for each $CIL_{SA_i,Cust_n}$ we currently use the maximum likelihood classification to have an insignificant, significant or severe loss with the given $CIL_{SA_i,Cust_n}$. Where $LK_{SA_i,Cust_n}$ is the maximum posteriori probability of $CIL_{SA_i,Cust_n}$ belonging to one of the three severety classes (insignificant, significant or severe).

$$Risk_{SA_i,Cust_n} = 1 + \begin{cases} 0.2_{insignifi.} \ if \ max(LK_{SA_i,Cust_n,insignifican}) \\ 0.6_{signifi.} \ if \ max(LK_{SA_i,Cust_n,significant}) \\ 1_{severe} \ if \ max(LK_{SA_i,Cust_n,severe}) \end{cases}$$

$$LK(CIL_{SA_i,Cust_n}, SeveretyLevel_i) = \frac{n}{N}, with \ n$$
$$\in SeveretyLevel_i \ and \ N \ number \ ob \ past \ observed \ service \ activities$$

Equation 3: Risk computation for service activity SA_i and customer $Cust_n$

$$Risk_{S_i,Cust_n} = \frac{\sum_{i=1}^{n} Risk_{SA_i,Cust_n}}{n}, with \ n \ is \ the$$
$$number \ of \ different \ service \ activities \ SA_i$$

Equation 4: Risk computation for a complete service S_i and customer $Cust_n$

5   Conclusions

For a service provider, it is vital to know which factors influence service performance. We identified customer integration as one main source for uncertainty of service performance. Consequently, we analysed the concept und risks of customer integration during service production. To make the customer associated risks more controllable, we have presented an approach to compute a customer integration level and a provider's risk during customer integration. Such a risk value can be integrated into service performance measurement and especially into service cost management to get more reliable service costs forecasts. With our approach at first, the Customer Integration Level (CIL) is computed to evaluate the quality of customer participation. The CIL is subsequently part of the Customer Risk Factor (CRF) which represents the risk level by the given CIL. At the moment, our approach is a model which requires a validation with actual business data and a benchmark with existing methods. Consequently, the next step of our research activities will be the evaluation with actual business data and to find out how exact our risked based cost forecasting performs.

References

[1]   M. Bitner, W. Faranda, A. Hubbert and V. Zeithaml, "Customer contributions and roles in service delivery," *International Journal of Service Industry Management,* pp. 193-205, 1997.

[2]   A. Hsieh, C. Yen and K. Chin, "Participative customers as partial employees and service provider workload," *International Journal of Service Industry Management,* pp. 187-199, 2004.

[3]   S. Auh, S. J. Bell, C. S. McLeod and E. Shih, "Co-production and customer loyalty in financial services," *Journal of Retailing,* no. August, 2007.

[4]   R. A. Risch and K. S. Schultz, "Customer Participation in Service Production and Delivery," in *Handbook of Service Marketing & Management*, Sage Publications, 2000, pp. 111-126.

[5]   P. R. Silpakit, "Participatizing the Service Encounter: A Theoretical Framework," *Services Marketing in a Changing Environment*, pp. 117-121, 1985.

[6]   Z. J. Lynne, "Conceptualizing Involvement," *Journal of Advertising*, no. June, pp. 4-14, 1986.

[7]   H. Dadfar, S. Brege and S. Sarah Ebadzadeh Semnani, "Customer involvement in service production, delivery and quality: the challenges and opportunities," *International Journal of Quality and Service Sciences*, no. 5:1, pp. 46-65, 2013.

[8]   J. Cardoso, C. Pedrinaci, T. Leidig, P. Rupino and P. D. Leenheer, "Open semantic service networks," *in The International Symposium on Services Science (ISSS)*, pp. 1-15, 2012.

[9]   K. Hidaka, "Trends in Service Sciences in Japan and Abroad," *Quarterly Review*, pp. 35-47, 2006.

[10]   L. Paulson, "Services Science: A New Field for Today's Economy," in *IEEE JNL*, 2006.

[11]   J. Spohrer, P. Maglio, J. Bailey and D. Gruhl, "Steps Toward a Science of Service Systems," *IEEE Computer*, pp. 71-77, 2007.

[12]   U. Nations, "Implications of the Global Economic Cirsis on India's Service Sector," in *United Nations Conference on Trade and Development (UNCTAD)*, New York and Geneva, 2012.

[13]   OECD, "Enhancing the Performance of the Services Sector," 2005.

[14]   L. Elliott, "Three myths that sustain the economic crisis," 2012. [Online]. Available: http://www.theguardian.com/business/economics-blog/2012/aug/05/economic-crisis-myths-sustain. [Accessed 05 2014].

[15]   M. N. Baily and J. Elliott D., "The US Financial and Economic Crisis: Where Does It Stand and Where Do We Go From Here?," in *Business and Public Policy*, 2009.

[16]   S. Vargo and R. Lusch, "Evolving to a new Dominant Logic for Marketing," *Journal of Marketing 68*, pp. 1-17, 2004.

[17]   P. Morris and J. Ashley, in *Translating Corporate Strategy into Project Strategy: Realizing Corporate Strategy Through Project Management*, Project Management Institute, 2004.

[18]   M. Reimann, O. Schilke and J. Thomas, "Customer relationship management and firm performance: the mediating role of business strategy," *J. of the Acad. Mark. Sci*, pp. 326-346, 2010.

[19]   R. Cooper and R. Kaplan, "Measure Costs Right: Make the Right Decisions," *Havard Business Review*, 1988.

[20]   S. R. Anderson and R. S. Kaplan, "Time-Driven Activity-Based Costing: A Simpler and More Powerful Path to Higher Profits," Mcgraw-Hill Professional, 2007.

[21]   E. Wendel, "Does high product complexits & production cost drive high customer involement in product development? (Master Thesis) (http://www.diva-portal.org/smash/get/diva2:653301/FULLTEXT01.pdf)," 2009.

[22]   R. Forrester, Measuring The Total Economic Impact Of Customer Engagement, 2008.

[23]   L. Nachum, "The Productivity of Intangible Factors of Production: Some Measurement Issues Applied to Swedish Management Consulting Firms," *Journal of Service Research,* no. November, pp. 123-137, 1999.

[24]   J. Anisa, "Services Marketing Theory Revisited: An Empirical Investigation into Financial Services Marketing," *Journal of Business and Management,* no. Volume 4, Issue 4, pp. 36-45, 2012.

[25]   P. Maglio and J. Spohrer, "Fundamentals of service science," *Journal of the Academy of Marketing Science,* no. July, pp. 18-20, 2007.

[26]   A. Bettencourt Lance, "Customer voluntary performance: Customers as partners in service delivery," *Journal of Retailing,* no. Volume 73, Issue 3, pp. 383-406, 1997.

[27]   J. A. Muncy and S. D. Hunt, "Consumer Involvement: Definitional Issues and Research Directions," no. Volumne 11, pp. 193-196, 1984.

[28]   G. Fandel and S. Blaga, "Elements of the production of services," in *Modern Concepts of the Theory of the Firm – Managing Enterprises of the New Economy*, Springer, 2004, pp. 175-190.

[29]   A. Chea, "Activity-Based Costing System in the Service Sector: A Strategic Approach for Enhancing Managerial Decision Making and Competitiveness," *International Journal of Business and Management,* vol. 6, no. 11, 2011.

[30]   L. Ying and W. Haiying, Research on the Motivation of the Customer Participation Based on Gray Relational Analysis, 2011.

[31]   P. Chathotha, L. Altinayb, R. J. Harringtonc, F. Okumusd and E. S. Chane, "Co-production versus co-creation: A process based continuum in the hotel service context," *International Journal of Hospitality Management,* no. Volume 32, pp. 11-20, 2013.

[32]   J. Erkoyuncu, R. Rajkumar, E. Shehab and K. Cheruvu, "Understanding service uncertainties in industrial product-service system cost estimation," *The International Journal of Advanced Manufacturing Technology,* vol. Volume 52, no. Numbers 9-12, 2010.

[33]   B. Edvardsson, A. Gustafsson and I. Roos, "Service portraits in service research: a critical review," *International Journal of Service Industry Management,* vol. Vol. 16, no. No. 1, pp. 107-121, 2006.

Shift Scheduling to Improve Customer Satisfaction, Employee Satisfaction and Management Satisfaction in Service Workplace where Employees and Robots Collaborate

Takashi Tanizaki[1*], Takeshi Shimmura[2], and Nobutada Fujii[3]

[1]Faculty of Engineering, Kindai University, Hiroshima, Japan
tanizaki@hiro.kindai.ac.jp
[2]Ritsumeikan University, Shiga, Japan
t-shinmura@gankofood.co.jp
[3]Graduate School of System Informatics, Kobe University, Hyogo, Japan
nfujii@phoenix.kobe-u.ac.jp

Abstract. In this paper, shift scheduling method to improve customer satisfaction (CS), employee satisfaction (ES) and management satisfaction (MS) in service workplace where employees and robots collaborated is proposed. In service industry, it is important to introduce the labor force created as a result of operations efficiency improvement to the other business that creates added value. For this purpose, in recent years, it has been researched to introduce robots to service workplace. In restaurant business, it is necessary to improve CS, ES and MS together, because of increasing customers' repeat and improving profitability. Therefore we started to research mentioned at the beginning. Since there are a trade-off relationship among CS, ES and MS, it is required to make a balanced plan. Therefore shift scheduling problem is modeled as multi-objective optimization problem so as to improve CS, MS, ES and formulated as a set cover problem. Finally, relationship of CS, ES, MS and method to create shift schedule to improve them are discussed based on numerical experiments.

Keywords: shift scheduling, customer satisfaction, employee satisfaction, management satisfaction, set cover problem

1 Introduction

In order to improve service satisfaction, it is important to introduce the labor force created as a result of the efficiency of operations to the other business that creates added value. For this purpose, in recent years, it has been researched to introduce robots to service workplace, assign low-value-added tasks to robots, and assign high-value-added tasks to employees. In addition to the above, restaurant business, increasing customer repeat and improving profitability are required. In order to achieve this objective, it is necessary to improve CS, ES and MS together. Therefore, we have

© Springer International Publishing AG 2017
Y. Hara and D. Karagiannis (Eds.): ICServ 2017, LNCS 10371, pp. 15–25, 2017.
DOI: 10.1007/978-3-319-61240-9_2

been researching a method to create shift scheduling that can improve CS, ES and MS in restaurants where employees and robots collaborate. Since these are in a trade-off relationship, it is required to make a balanced plan.

As a preceding study, a method to solve this problem by modeling as a multi-objective optimization problem that can improve ES and MS, and a solution method that balances both ES and MS was proposed, and its effectiveness was confirmed [1]. However, in this research, CS was expressed in constraint formulas, and research that can simultaneously improve CS, ES, and MS was not conducted. Therefore, we started to research a method which creates a shift schedule aiming at the above three improvements.

In this paper, shift scheduling problems in service workplaces where employees and robots collaborated is modeled as multi-objective optimization problems so as to improve CS, ES, MS, it is formulated as set cover problem and relationship of them are discussed based on numerical experiments.

2   Modeling of Shift Scheduling for Restaurant Employees

Based on the results of discussions with eating and drinking establishments offering cuisine at reasonable prices, we make following modeling.

1. Make employee type part-time, full-time, and manager. These and robots have different cost per hour.
2. Classify work place of the restaurant into the front work with the contact operation of customers and the backyard work without that of customers.
3. The work content of each task is two tasks, simple task and complicated task. Ability of employees shall be "Workable" or "Impossible to work" for each work place and work content. Robots can only work for simple task of backyard work and simple task of front work outside business hours. Assume the desire degree of employees for each day and time zone is to be "Work permitted", "Not work permitted", "Desirably not to work".
4. Set necessary capabilities for each work place and work content by time zone.
5. Concepts for evaluation of CS, ES, and MS are as follows.
   - CS improves as employees work for front work. It further improves if employees work for complicated task.
   - ES improves as employees work for time zone, work place and work content of "Work permitted". It declines as employees work for time zone, work place and content of "Desirably not to work".
   - MS declines as employees work hours increase. It improves as robots work hours increase, since managers want to operate many robots that are not costly for working.

In this model, based on time zone, work place and work content desired by each employee, those of employees and robots are determined so that CS, ES and MS will be the highest while satisfying minimum necessary capabilities and employee's "Not work permitted" time zone, work place and work content.

3   Formulation

This problem is formulated as set cover problem [2].

3.1   Set cover problem

In the set covering problem, when a set M and a subset group S_j of M and a weight c_j corresponding to S_j are given, subset families are selected so as to cover all elements of the set maximizing sum of weights c_j corresponding to S_j. The formulation is shown below.

1. Notation

   M : Element set ($i \in M = \{1, 2, \cdots, m\}$)

   S_j : Subset family of M ($i \in N = \{1, 2, \cdots, n\}$)

   $a_{i,j}$: 1 if S_j covers element i, 0 otherwise

   c_j : Weight corresponding to S_j

   x_j : 1 if S_j is a solution, 0 otherwise

2. Formulation

   <Objective function>

$$Minimize \sum_{j \in N} C_j x_j \tag{1}$$

Expression (1) shows minimization of sum of weights c_j.

   <Constraint expression>

$$\sum_{j \in N} a_{i,j} x_j \geq 1, \ \forall i \in M \tag{2}$$

Expression (2) shows that one or more elements i of the element set M must be covered.

3.2   Shift scheduling method

Before shift scheduling, it is made all work schedule patterns (i.e. subset family) that can be worked based on desired work plan of each employee. Shift scheduling is determined by selecting from subset family so as to maximize total of CS, ES and MS satisfying constraints on the minimum necessary capability and employee's "Not work permitted" time zone, work place and work content.

3.3 Formulation of shift scheduling problem

1. Notation

m : Employee ($m = 1, 2, \cdots, M$)

n : Robot ($n = 1, 2, \cdots, N$)

d : Planning period (day) ($d = 1, 2, \cdots, D$)

t : Planning period (hour) ($t = 1, 2, \cdots, T$)

p : Work place ($p = front, backyard$)

v : Work content ($v = simple, complicated$)

T_{max} : Maximum working hours per day

T_{min} : Minimum working hours per day

$g_{m,d}$: Work schedule pattern ($g_{m,d} = 1, 2, \cdots, G_{md}$)

    Work schedule pattern is made based on desired work plan of each employee

$a_{m,d,g_{m,d},t}$: Desire degree of employees for time zone

        Desire degree of Employee m on day d , work schedule pattern $g_{m,d}$ and time t is as follows:

$$a_{m,d,g_{m,d},t} = \begin{cases} -1 & \text{"Work permitted"} \\ 0 & \text{"Not work permitted"} \\ 1 & \text{"Desirably not to work"} \end{cases}$$

$C_{m,p,v}$: Ability of employees

        Ability of employee m on work place p and work content v is as follows:

$$C_{m,p,v} = \begin{cases} 0 & \text{"Im possible to work"} \\ 1 & \text{"Workable"} \end{cases}$$

$L^{min}_{d,t,p,v}$: Necessary capabilities on work place p , work content v , day d and time t

e_m : Unit price of employee m

r : Unit price of robot

$q_{m,p,v}$: Desire degree of employees m on work place p and work content v

$x_{m,d,t,p,v}$: 0-1 integer variable which denotes whether employee m works or not on day d , time t , work place p and work content v

$$x_{m,d,t,p,v} = \begin{cases} 1 & \text{Work} \\ 0 & \text{Not work} \end{cases}$$

$y_{m,d,t,p,v}$: 0-1 integer variable which denotes whether robot n works or not on day d , time t , work place p and work content v

$$y_{m,d,t,p,v} = \begin{cases} 1 & \text{Work} \\ 0 & \text{Not work} \end{cases}$$

$z_{m,d,g_{m,d}}$: 0-1 integer variable which denotes whether employee m select work schedule pattern $g_{m,d}$ or not on day d

$$z_{m,d,g_{m,d}} = \begin{cases} 1 & Select \\ 0 & Not\ select \end{cases}$$

2. Formulation

<Objective function>

$$Maximize \quad \alpha CS + \beta ES + \gamma MS \quad (3)$$
$$(\alpha + \beta + \gamma = 1)$$

Expression (3) shows the weighted sum of CS, ES and MS. CS, ES and MS is as follows:

$$CS = \sum_{m=1}^{M} \sum_{d=1}^{D} \sum_{t=s.b.}^{c.b.} \left\{ 3x_{m,d,front,complicated} + x_{m,d,fromt,simple} \right\} \quad (4)$$
$$(s.b.\ is\ start\ bu\sin ess,\ c.b.\ is\ close\ bu\sin ess)$$

$$ES = \sum_{m=1}^{M} \sum_{d=1}^{D} \sum_{g_{m,d}=1}^{G_{m,d}} \sum_{t=1}^{T} a_{m,d,g_{m,d},t} z_{m,d,g_{m,d}} + \sum_{m=1}^{M} \sum_{d=1}^{D} \sum_{t=1}^{T} \sum_{p=front}^{backyard} \sum_{v=simple}^{complicated} q_{m,p,v} x_{m,d,t,p,v} \quad (5)$$

$$MS = -\sum_{m=1}^{M} \sum_{d=1}^{d} \sum_{t=1}^{T} \sum_{p=front}^{back yard} \sum_{v=simple}^{complicated} e_m x_{m,d,t,p,v} + \sum_{n=1}^{N} \sum_{d=1}^{D} \sum_{t=1}^{T} \sum_{p=front}^{backyard} \sum_{v=simple}^{complicated} ry_{n,d,t,p,v} \quad (6)$$

Expression (4) shows CS. If employee works for simple task of front work, CS improves by 1, if he works for complicated task of front work, it improves by 3. Expression (5) shows ES. If employee works on "Work permitted" time zone, ES improves by 1, if he works on "Desirably not to work" time zone, it declines by 1. If employee works on "Work permitted", work place and work content, ES improves by $q_{m,p,v}$, if he works on "Desirably not to work" work place and work content, it declines by $q_{m,p,v}$. Expression (6) shows MS. If employee m works, MS decline by e_m. If robot works, MS improves by r.

<Constraint expression>

$$\sum_{g_{m,d}=1}^{G_{m,d}} z_{m,d,g_{m,d}} \leq 1 \quad (\forall m, \forall d) \quad (7)$$

$$\sum_{p=front}^{backyard} \sum_{v=simple}^{complicated} x_{m,d,t,p,v} = \sum_{g_{m,d}=1}^{G_{m,d}} a_{m,d,g_{m,d},t}^2 z_{m,d,g_{m,d}} \quad (\forall m, \forall d, \forall t) \quad (8)$$

$$\sum_{m=1}^{M} x_{m,d,t,p,complicated} + \sum_{n=1}^{N} y_{n,d,t,p,complicated} \geq L_{d,t,p,complicated}^{min} \quad (\forall m, \forall t, \forall p) \quad (9)$$

$$\sum_{m=1}^{M} x_{m,d,t,p,simple} + \sum_{n=1}^{N} y_{n,d,t,p,simple} \geq L_{d,t,p,simple}^{min} \quad (\forall m, \forall t, \forall p) \tag{10}$$

$$\sum_{d=1}^{D} \sum_{t=1}^{T} x_{m,d,t,p,v} = 0 \quad \left(if \ C_{m,p,v} = 0 \right) \quad (\forall m, \forall p, \forall v) \tag{11}$$

$$\sum_{p=front}^{backyard} \sum_{v=simple}^{complicated} y_{n,d,t,p,v} \leq 1 \quad (\forall n, \forall d, \forall t) \tag{12}$$

$$\sum_{n=1}^{N} \sum_{d=1}^{D} \sum_{t=1}^{T} \sum_{p=front}^{backyard} y_{n,d,t,front,complicated} = 0 \tag{13}$$

$$\sum_{n=1}^{N} \sum_{d=1}^{D} \sum_{t=s.b.}^{c.b.} y_{n,d,t,front,complicated} = 0 \tag{14}$$

$$T_{min} \leq \sum_{t=1}^{T} a_{m,d,g_{m,d},t}^{2} \leq T_{max} \quad \left(\forall m. \forall d, \forall g_{m,d} \right) \tag{15}$$

Expression (7) shows that each employee's work schedule pattern for each day is one or none. Expression (8) shows that each employee works for time zone of the selected work schedule pattern. Expression (9) and (10) shows that each complicated tasks and simple tasks requires more than minimum necessary capability. Expression (11) shows that employees cannot work for "Impossible to work" work place and "Impossible to work" work content. Expression (12) shows that each robot's work schedule pattern for each day is one or none. Expression (13) shows that robots can't work for complicated task. Expression (14) shows that the robot can't work for simple task of front work during business hours. Expression (15) shows the maximum and minimum working hours for a day.

4   Results of numerical experiment and discussion

4.1   Numerical experiment condition

Numerical experiments are conducted using parameters related to employees and robots shown in Tables 1 to 4. Employee No.1 to No.9 is part-time, No.10 to No.14 is full-time, and No.15 is manager. Each part-time has a high desire degree for simple tasks, each full-time and manager has a high desire degree for complicated tasks in Table 2. Each part time has a desire of time zone, each full-time and manager desires all time zones in Table 3. Employee 2 and employee 7 cannot work for complex task.

Table 1. Experiment setting

the number of employees	15
the number of robots	1~3
plan period (day)	1
plan period (time)	15
maximum working hours	3
minimum working hours	8
business hours	3~14

Table 2. Parameter for employee and robot

		number	cost/hour	desire degree			
				fron/simple	front/complicated	back/simple	back/complicated
employee	part-time	9	1	0	-1	1	-0.5
	full time	5	1.5	-0.5	1	-1	0
	manager	1	2.5	-0.5	1	-1	0
robot		1~3	0.3				

Table 3. Desired work plan of each employee

employee	time zone of working hours														
	1	2	3	4	5	6	7	8	9	10	11	12	13	14	15
1	-1	-1	-1	-1	1	1	1	1	1	1	1	1	1	0	0
2	0	0	0	0	0	0	0	0	-1	-1	-1	1	1	1	1
3	1	1	1	1	-1	-1	-1	-1	1	1	1	1	1	0	0
4	0	0	0	1	1	1	1	1	-1	-1	-1	-1	-1	0	0
5	0	0	0	-1	-1	-1	-1	1	1	1	1	1	1	-1	-1
6	1	1	1	1	1	1	1	1	0	0	0	0	0	0	0
7	0	0	0	0	0	0	0	1	1	1	-1	-1	-1	-1	-1
8	1	1	1	1	1	-1	-1	-1	-1	-1	0	0	0	0	0
9	0	0	0	1	1	1	1	1	-1	-1	-1	-1	-1	0	0
10	1	1	1	1	1	1	1	1	1	1	1	1	1	1	1
11	1	1	1	1	1	1	1	1	1	1	1	1	1	1	1
12	1	1	1	1	1	1	1	1	1	1	1	1	1	1	1
13	1	1	1	1	1	1	1	1	1	1	1	1	1	1	1
14	1	1	1	1	1	1	1	1	1	1	1	1	1	1	1
15	1	1	1	1	1	1	1	1	1	1	1	1	1	1	1

Table 4. Necessary capabilities

work place	work content	time zone of working hours														
		1	2	3	4	5	6	7	8	9	10	11	12	13	14	15
front	simple	1	1	1	2	2	2	2	2	2	2	2	2	2	1	1
	complicated	1	1	1	2	2	2	2	2	2	2	2	2	2	1	1
back	simple	2	2	2	2	3	3	2	2	2	2	3	3	2	2	2
yard	complicated	2	2	2	2	2	2	2	2	2	2	2	2	2	2	2

4.2 Results of numerical experiment and discussion

Numerical experiments are conducted in which the coefficients of expression (3) are changed to increments of 0.01 within the range satisfying $\alpha + \beta + \gamma = 1$, and the relationship between CS, ES, and MS is discussed. Results of three robots cases are mainly discussed.

As shown in Fig.1, the relationship between CS and ES stratifies according to MS. When MS is low to moderate, CS and ES are in a trade-off relationship. In order to raise CS, trade-offs with ES occur to select employees who do not want to work for

"Desirably not to work" time zone. When MS is high, CS is constant regardless of the ES's high or low, because it will be the minimum necessary capability of front work must be maintained.

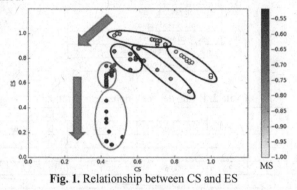

Fig. 1. Relationship between CS and ES

As shown in Fig.2, the relationship between ES and MS stratifies according to CS. When CS is low, ES and MS are in a trade-off relationship with MS being high. The reason for this is that when the CS is low, employees' front work is decreased and MS improves. As CS goes up, employees' front work hours increase, so MS and ES are in a trade-offs relationship as ES declines. When CS is high, the work place is limited, so there is no trade-off between ES and MS, which is almost one point.

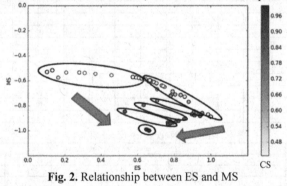

Fig. 2. Relationship between ES and MS

As shown in Fig.3, the relationship between CS and MS stratifies according to ES. When ES is low, CS and MS are in a trade-off relationship with MS being high. Full-time and managers have a high degree of desire for complicated tasks of front work, and also have high degree of desire to work. Therefore, as CS increases, ES also increases, so CS does not become high when ES is low. As the ES increases, the number of employees who desire front work increases, CS is a high value, MS is a low value, CS and MS are in a trade-off relationship. When the ES becomes high, since the work is limited to the time and places that employee's desire, the trade-off relationship between CS and MS disappears and it becomes almost one point.

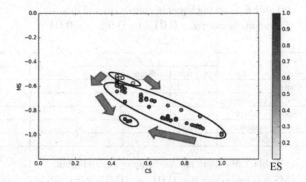

Fig. 3. Relationship between CS and MS

Next, working hours of employees and robots ware disucussed in case of emphasizing CS, ES and MS, respectively. As shown in Table 5, in the case of CS emphasis, the total of working hours of employees is 86 hours. In order to improve CS, the most employees work for the front work. As shown in Table 6, in the case of ES emphasis, part-times work 16 hours for simple task of backyard work. In other words, part-times work a lot for highly desire degree work. On the other hand, since part-times work on simple task of backyard work, work place of the robot was reduced. As a result, working hours of robots is 21 hours, which is the smallest compared with others. As shown in Table 6, in the case of MS emphasis, the total working hours of employees is 77 hours, which is the smallest as compared with others. In addition, the working hours of robots is 37 hours, which is the largest compared with others. Further more, the total time required for each work place and work content at each time in this experiment is 114 hours. In other words, this plan is created to operate with the necessary minimum capability.

From above discussion, in the case of CS emphasis, many robots work to maximize CS, and the maximum number of employees work for complicated task of front work. In the case of ES emphasis, in order to make ES the highest, all employees don't work for "Desirably not to work" time zone, work place and work content. In the case of MS emphasis, in order to maximize MS, working hours of employee are the minimum of the range that satisfies the minimum required capability.

Table 5. Working hours of employees and robots
(CS emphasis case; $\alpha =0.98$, $\beta = 0.01$, $\gamma = 0.01$)

work place	work content	employee				robot
		part-time	full-time	manager	total	
front	simple	22	0	0	22	3
	complicated	19	37	8	64	0
back	simple	1	0	0	1	33
yard	complicated	27	3	0	30	0
total		89	40	8	117	36

Table 6. Working hours of employees and robots
(ES emphasis case; $\alpha = 0.01$, $\beta = 0.98$, $\gamma = 0.01$)

work place	work content	employee				robot
		part-time	full-time	manager	total	
front	simple	22	0	0	22	3
	complicated	0	24	5	29	0
back	simple	16	0	0	16	18
yard	complicated	11	16	3	30	0
total		49	40	8	97	21

Table 7. Working hours of employees and robots
(MS emphasis case; $\alpha = 0.01$, $\beta = 0.01$, $\gamma = 0.98$)

work place	work content	employee				robot
		part-time	full-time	manager	total	
front	simple	22	0	0	22	3
	complicated	16	9	0	25	0
back	simple	0	0	0	0	34
yard	complicated	28	2	0	30	0
total		66	11	0	77	37

Finally, the relationship between the number of robots and the objective function value is discussed. CS, ES and MS with the maximum objective function value in the case of one robot, two robots and three robots is shown in Table8. Total satisfaction improves as the number of robots increases. Among CS, ES and MS, CS is the most improved and its contribution to total satisfaction is high. Furthermore, MS also improves, so that total satisfaction improves without increasing costs. Meanwhile, although ES declines, it is not big. From above discussion, it is better to have many robots work so as to improve total satisfaction although ES declines.

Table 8. CS,ES and MS with the maximum objective function

category	The number of robots		
	1	2	3
CS	133.0	148.0	154.0
ES	127.5	125.5	124.5
MS	-141.5	-127.0	-121.2
Total	119.0	146.5	157.3

5   Conclusions

In this research, shift scheduling method for service workplace where employees and robots collaborated is proposed. For above purpose, shift scheduling problem is modeled as multi-objective optimization problem so as to improve CS, MS, ES and formulated as set cover problem. Furthermore, the relationship of CS, ES, MS and the work scheduling plan with the highest satisfaction is disucssed by numerical experiments. As a result, the following is confirmed.

- CS, ES, and MS have trade-off relationships and parts where there is no trade-off relationship. When MS is high, the ES declines low, and CS keeps required minimum capability. When ES is high, both MS and CS decline. When MS is high, MS decline and CS is moderate.
- Total satisfaction is improved by increasing the number of robots.

In the future, we would like to apply this method to real restaurants and to do a demonstration experiment to improve satisfaction.

Acknowledgments

This study is supported by JSPS KAKENHI (16H02909).

References

1. Nobutada, F., Junpei, O., Toshiya, K., Takeshi, S.: A Study on Co-creative Staff Shift Planning Method in Food and Drink Industry, Proceedingd of 3rd Domestic Conference for Servisology, pp.294-298 (2015)
2. Masahiro, K., Mutsunori, Y., Toshihide, I.:Local Search Method for Set Cover Probrem, Continuous and Discrete Mathematics for Optimization RIMS Kokyuroku 1114 pp.211-220 (1999)

Application-Driven Product-Service System Configuration: Customer-Centered Strategy

Alexander Smirnov[1,2], Nikolay Shilov[1,2],
Andreas Oroszi[3], Mario Sinko[3], Thorsten Krebs[4]

[1] SPIIRAS, 14 Line 39, 199178 St. Petersburg, Russia
[2] ITMO University, Kronverkskiy pr. 49, 197101 St. Petersburg, Russia
[3] Festo AG & Co. Ruiter Straße 82, Esslingen, 73734, Germany
[4] encoway GmbH, Buschhöhe 2, Bremen, 28357, Germany
{nick, smir}@iias.spb.su;
{oro, sni}@de.festo.com; krebs@encoway.de

Abstract. Companies are currently forced to implement new production and marketing paradigms because modern markets are getting more and more saturated and commoditized. One of the trends is orientation to services. The paper investigates the problem of product-service system configuration in a customer-centered way and discusses how it has been solved. The paper shares the authors' vision of required improvements in business processes and information systems at the considered company related to life cycle management for product-service system configurations. Though the research results are based on the analysis of one company, the presented work can give significant input to achieve benefits for component manufacturers that tend to become system vendors in general.

Keywords: Product-service system, customer view, application view, information management, business process, information system

1   Introduction

Companies are currently forced to implement new production and marketing paradigms because modern markets are getting more and more saturated and commoditized [1, 2]. This equally applies to markets with long histories regarding type of products. There are many product manufacturers and vendors what results in extremely small rooms for new products. The markets are shrinking and companies striving for attracting and retaining customers see service provision as a new path towards profits and growth. As a result, they have to be very innovative in order to survive.

One of the trends is orientation to services. This opens a completely new world of business models allowing companies to transform from product suppliers to service providers or even to virtual companies acting as brokers. For example, Rolls-Royce instead of selling aircraft engines now charges companies for hours that engines run and takes care of servicing the engines [3]. Another famous example is Uber, that does not only provides taxi services, but it does this without actually owning cars and acts

© Springer International Publishing AG 2017

Y. Hara and D. Karagiannis (Eds.): ICServ 2017, LNCS 10371, pp. 26–37, 2017.
DOI: 10.1007/978-3-319-61240-9_3

just as a connecting link between the taxi drivers and passengers. Timely changed business model can provide for a significant competitive advantage (e.g., the current capitalisation of Uber is about $68 billion, which is $20 billion higher than that of GM [4]).

Automation equipment production is not an exception. The carried out analysis of the business and information management processes related to an automation equipment producer shows that instead of offering separate products, the company now tends to offer complex products (which may consist of several other products), whole integrated systems and also software units using different services [5, 6]. Product-Service Systems (PSS) assume orientation on combination of products and services (often supporting the products) instead of focusing only on products. This paradigm fits well automation equipment producers, for which tight relationships with customers are of high importance. These tight relationships enable the possibility to get valuable equipment usage statistics, analyse use cases and get direct customer's feedback [7-9].

Besides the products themselves and services as standalone "products", a good way to create additional customer value is to provide the customer with PSS configuration possibilities. Both physical and software components are not used individually but in a greater context at the customer's site what means that integrated products, systems, and services as well as their valid combinations have to be considered all together. Running a set of components from an automation equipment manufacturer, for example, for the customer, it is of high value that the components do not fail. Service contracts for maintenance on a regular basis and maybe also on spare parts are only a few examples of how the product manufacturers can give added value to their customers.

The paper is based on the analysis and modification of the information management processes related to PSS configuration at the automation equipment producer Festo AG & Co KG. Festo is a worldwide provider of automation technology for factory and process automation with wide assortments of products (more than 30 000 – 40 000 products of approximately 700 types, with various configuration possibilities) ranging from simple products to complex systems (fig. 1).

Around the world, 61 Festo national companies and 250 regional offices in 176 countries ensure that advice, service, delivery quality and reliability precisely meet customer needs in all global industrial regions. Today, more than 300,000 industrial customers in 200 industry segments worldwide rely on Festo's problem-solving competency. It produces pneumatic and electronic automation equipment and products

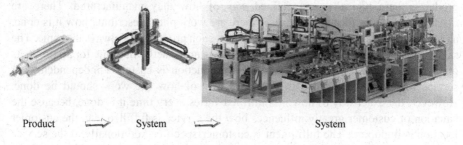

Product ⟹ System ⟹ System

Fig. 1. Assortment range: from simple products to complex systems

for various process industries in 11 Global Production Centers and 28 National Service Centers.

The paper investigates the problem of PSS configuration information management in a customer-centered way and the way it has been solved. Implementing such an application-system view addresses the problem of designing the customer view on PSS selection, configuration and usage, i.e. defining customer's experience by "talking in a customer-understandable language" and addressing his/her application problems.

The paper shares the vision of the authors of required improvements in business processes and information systems at the considered company related to life cycle management for PSS configurations. Though the research results are based on the analysis of one company, the presented work can give significant input to achieve benefits for component manufacturers that tend to become system vendors in general.

The remaining part of the paper is structured as follows. The next section presents some ideas regarding modularization and configuration of services. Then, the approach is described followed by the pilot case study. Main findings of the carried out research are discussed in sec. 5. Some summarizing remarks are presented in the Conclusion.

2   Modularization And Configuration of Services

The fist, obvious difference when talking about selling products and services is that a product can only be sold once. Of course, you can make a contract for a larger number of that one product from which the customer gets a few on a regular basis. However, each individual product is manufactured and sold once. Services, on the other hand, can be recurring and rather long lasting. Basically, there are two different types of services:

- Point-of-sale (POS), which means that a service is a stand-alone product or is sold together with components or systems in a single quotation (as a PSS), and
- Contracts, which are long-term services for components or systems that are already in place at a customer site. Such long-term services are typically based on maintenance, which lowers the customer's risk of component or system failure. Maintenance contracts can also be agreed on for whole production environments, i.e. a running set of components and / or machines from potentially different vendors.

Next, there is a difference in how products and services are "produced". For tangible products, there typically is a defined way of how they manufactured. There are machines available for manufacturing, there are work plans describing how it is done, and there is a defined outcome. This means that such products are always the same. The same resources are used and the production costs are exactly the same for all products of the same product variant [10, 11]. The production is customer-independent. For service fulfillment there also is a defined way of how the work should be done. However, the exact way of how it is fulfilled varies every time it is done, because the situation of customer greatly influences how the service is fulfilled, e.g. the customer location is important. The fulfillment is customer-specific. Additionally, if the service is part of a PSS, then it belongs to some components or systems. The service itself will be different depending on the relevant products, their age, their usage, and so on.

These differences between product manufacturing and service fulfillment lead to different pricing strategies (fig. 2). For tangible products, the price is typically based on the production costs plus some margin. The price may also be country-specific, leading to a number of list prices, probably different because of currency rates or on the competition in the regarding countries. It is a rather new trend to use the value a product has for the customer as a source for pricing, e.g. leading to value-based pricing strategies. Still, usually specific characteristics of customers are used to group them, not to identify a single customer. Such groups may be the location, the time or the type of device used for product search. For services, the individual customer is also put into a group of persons that are similar in the sense of a list of characteristics. Regarding a Pareto-optimal approach, this can be an efficient approach since some customers are really similar in their behavior.

Car insurances are a good example of doing this: they group persons into groups based on their location and their history of previous accidents. However, when the car itself comes into play, the combination of customer and car is really individual.

The same holds for components and systems that are installed and running on customer sites. How old is that system? How frequently is it used? All these factors make pricing for service offers really difficult. Next to the service tasks themselves, additional information about serviced products/systems, their usage and about the customer are needed for a good calculation. When a company deals with the same customers over longer periods, it is thus a good idea to collect information about the "installed base" and about the planned and current usage. When well motivated, customers will accept a price that is based on measuring their individual behavior.

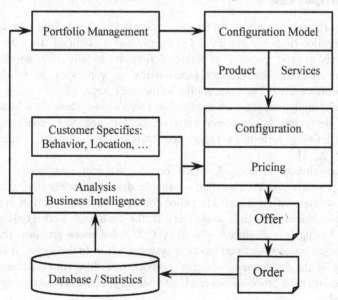

Fig. 2. PSS configuration and pricing specifics

3   Approach

The used gap analysis methodology was implemented through the following steps. First, the analysis of the current organisation of the information management was carried out. Then, the expert estimation of the company benchmark was done. Based on this, the comparison of the present and future business process and information management organisation was done resulting in creating corresponding process matrixes. This has made it possible to identify major gaps between the present and the future business organization, analyse these and define strategies to overcome these gaps.

Research efforts in the area of information management show that information and knowledge needs of a particular employee depend on his/her tasks and responsibilities. Different stages of the product lifecycle management processes in the company are associated with different roles like product managers, sales personnel and even customers. The representatives of different roles have different needs when interacting with an application like a PSS configurator. Product managers or a sales representatives, for example, know about the products and are able to configure by deciding on technical facts. A customer, on the other hand, may not know about the technical details of the company's products or even what kind of product he/she may use to solve his/her application problem. This is the reason why technical product details should be hidden from the customer under the application layer.

3.1   Application view

The complex PSS view comes from the application side. After defining the application area, configuration rules and constraints to the product are defined. They are followed by characteristics and product structure definition. Finally, the apps (software applications) enriching the product functionality or improving its reliability and maintenance are defined. The same applies to the sales stage.

As a result, implementing such application-constraints-system view addresses the problem of designing the customer view on product selection, configuration and processing (defining customer's experience, "talking in a customer-understandable language") [12, 13].

As it was already mentioned, based on the different complexity levels, the company's products can be classified as simple discrete components, configurable products or system configurations. The major goals are reducing the effort in producing products and reducing the time-to-delivery to the customer. Both goals should be reached by having less engineering activity (ETO) but more products that can be assembled based on a pre-defined modular system (ATO). In this sense, it is intended to make use of the "economies of scale". Products of different complexity require distinct handling in the process from request to delivery. Three levels of complexity are differentiated:

- **PTO – pick to order:** A product is order-neutrally pre-fabricated and sold as a discrete product. This means that no configuration is necessary to identify the correct combination of components. The different combinations already exist and for the customer it is a selection process rather than a configuration process. No order-specific production is required.

- **ATO – assemble to order:** The different components a product can be composed of are pre-fabricated but the correct combination of components is left open for order clearing process. The product itself is order-specifically produced from these existing components.
- **ETO – engineer to order:** A product is based on a known set of pre-fabricated components (like in the ATO scenario) but the specific customer need requires additional engineering activity. In this case new components need to be engineered, constructed and fabricated in order to fulfil a customer order and product the order-specific product.

Of course, the selection and configuration of these different types needs to be addressed accordingly. However, the customer should not be aware of this distinction. To the customer, the sales process should always "feel" the same.

As it was mentioned, different information needs of different roles (product managers, sales personnel, customers, etc.) are the reason to hide the technical product and service details under the application layer. In addition, the selection of the right product for solving the application problem can be based on a mapping between the application layer and a (hidden) technical product layer. In the optimal case, a customer does not notice whether he/she is selecting a discrete product, configuring a complex system, and so on.

As a result, the overall concept of customer-centric view on the products has been formulated as shown in fig. 3. It includes the introduced above new role of "System architect" responsible for the holistic view to the system and its configuration, description of its functionality and applications, and designing a customer view to it.

3.2   Changes in information systems

The changing requirements on business processes also induce changing requirements on information systems.

In today's world, most companies do product specification with word documents or similar approaches. These documents are handed over to construction. Construction hands over other data, e.g. technical characteristics via PDM systems or CAD files, to manufacturing, and so on. At the time a sales channel is set up for the new product, the initial data from product specification is lost. Thus, a new requirement for effectively setting up sales configurators and after-sales support is a continuous database. Knowledge about the product's application domain should be formally acquired already in the early phases of new product development. In this case, the data is available whenever needed in later steps of the product lifecycle process.

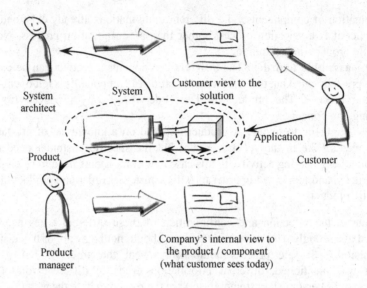

System architect

System

Customer view to the solution

Product

Application

Customer

Product manager

Company's internal view to the product / component (what customer sees today)

Fig. 3. The shift from the product view to the application view

Typically, the new product development process is structured in several milestones, such as design approval, technical approval or sales approval. During the entire life cycle, different roles work on product-centred data: product managers, engineers, controllers, marketing, sales personnel, and so on. Thus, either the relevant product data needs to be handed over – and potentially transformed – from a phase of the life cycle to later phases, or there is a single information system with which all the different roles carry out their daily work; every role on their specific view on a portion of the product data. In both cases, one of the major benefits for all concerned roles would be a seamless integration of all product life cycle phases within a comprehensive workflow.

A product-modelling environment must be capable of configuring modular product architecture. This means that using such an environment, it must be possible to reuse single product models in the scope of system configurations and assign product or system models to application knowledge. This requires the definition of well-formed product model interfaces to allow for modularity. Such interfaces enable a black-box approach, in which all products or modules implementing this interface can be chosen for the complex product / system; i.e. they become interchangeable. For the customer the complex details of product models on lower levels of the system architecture remain invisible. The customer decides based on the visible characteristics of the black-box.

Finally yet importantly, it is also important to support multi-user activities on the different parts of product, system and application models without losing track of changes and implication that such changes have.

4   Pilot case study implementing the developed approach

The developed approach has been verified on a pilot case for the Control cabinet product for selected customers. This is a complex product consisting of the cabinet itself housing a large number of different control elements, some of which are also complex products. Due to variety of components, its functionality is significantly defined by the software control system. Control cabinets are usually configured individually by company's product managers based on the customer requirements since their configurations are tightly related to the equipment used by the customer.

Before the change, the customer together with the product manager had to compile a large bill of materials by deciding individually for every single component, in order to get the control cabinet. The customer would not be able to do this alone without assistance of the company's representative who is an expert in the product range. Now, with a holistic customer-centric view to the control cabinet as to a single complex product including corresponding apps and software services, it can be configured and ordered as one product by the customer usually without assistance.

At the first stage, based on the demand history, the main requirements and components are defined at the market evaluation stage.

Then, at the engineering stage the components, baseline configurations based on branch specific applications as well as possible constraints are defined. The result of this is a source data for creating a cabinet configurator tool that makes it possible for the customers to configure cabinets based on their requirements online. At this stage, such specific characteristics are taken into account as components used, characteristics and capabilities of the cabinet, as well as resulting lead time and price (fig. 4).

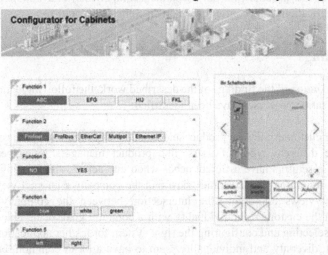

Fig. 4. Control cabinet configurator: an interface example

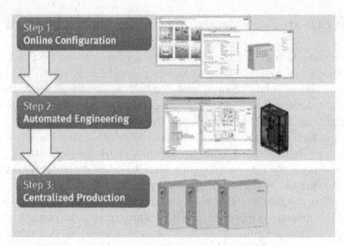

Fig. 5. Control cabinet: from online configuration to production

Based on the customer-defined configuration the engineering data is generated in an automatic (in certain cases – semi-automatic) way, which is used for the production stage. As a result, the centralized production of cabinets is based on the automatically generated engineering file (fig. 5).

The new business process made it possible to reduce the time from configuration to delivery from several weeks to few days (depending on the required components). The product maintenance is also significantly simplified due to the system-based view. All the data about this product (not only separated components) is available and can be used for modification of its configuration on customer's demand.

5   Findings

As a summarization of the findings of the described work, the following main strategies of the servitization processes have been identified:

1. Designing customer view on product selection, configuration and processing.

There are different types of users, like product managers, sales personnel or customers. These users have different needs when interacting with an application like a product configurator. The customer view and the company's internal view describe two contrary views addressing the intersection between the company's product diversity and the customer's individuality with a common goal: being able to guide a customer in selecting and configuring the right system for his/her application problem. At first sight, diversity and individuality seem to have a lot in common, but the goal behind each is rather distinct. It is important to analyse the customer's context (especially for offering services): system usage, customer's industry, who does the maintenance, country-specific regulations, etc.

2. Increasing system modularity / reusability in the context of PSS.

The structure of product combinations and systems needs to modularized. Comparable modules have the key ability to be used in multiple configuration contexts. This concerns not only products and components, but also product combinations and whole PSSs assuming building a multilevel PSS configuration model. Thus, a general PSS model architecture needs to be set up.

3. From business processes to IT and vice versa.

Though it is reasonably considered that the changes of business processes are the driver to changes in the corresponding IT systems, the experience has shown that it is not always the case. Having defined a general strategy, the company can try to implement some pilot particular IT solutions to support existing business processes or parts of them. If such solutions turn out to be successful, they could be extended and will cause changes in the business processes.

Besides the above strategies, some more particular findings with impacts on business processes and information systems can be identified as well.

The impacts on business processes include:
1. Aligning the business processes (improving interoperability and avoiding redundant tasks). When building a new configurator platform, it is important to align business processes like new PSS configuration together with the desired outcome. Doing so can help improving interoperability and avoiding redundant tasks e.g. in data maintenance.
2. Setting up sales and pricing strategies. While for tangible products, the price is typically based on the production costs plus some margin, pricing for services and PSS is difficult and requires development of new sales strategies.

The impacts on information systems include:
3. Homogenizing and standardizing master data (increasing master data quality; e.g. for being able to compare components, which are necessary to build partially defined combinations and PSSs).
4. Implementing tool support for the changed processes (supporting the improved business processes).
5. PSS needs to be defined. This includes data about components / machines, data about services, and about valid combinations of components and services.
6. Configuration of services needs additional knowledge sources.
7. Statistics need to be recorded and interpreted.

Impacts 6 and 7 are tightly related. Since software services are dealing with information, one has to provide such optimized and up-to-date information in order for services to operate efficiently as well as collect usage information to use it for further improvements and optimization. For a hardware system, the customer can tune parameters individually based on the particular usage. For services, if an extensive usage statistics is collected, some specific parameters can be offered to the customers in order to improve their production processes. The statistics can also be used for improvement of the company products and PSS. For example, a strategy that brings companies and their customers in a closer collaboration is innovation democratisation [14] standing for involvement of customers into the process of creating new products and services. This makes it possible for companies to better meet the needs of their customers.

6   Conclusions

The paper is concentrated on improving customer's experience in configuring and ordering for configurable PSS. The core idea is the change from the convenient for the company view of the products to the customer-friendly view from the system application perspective, which required an introduction of a new PLM role of "System architect". The developed business process and supporting information systems made it possible to implement the scenario of the automated production of the customer-configured control cabinet.

The presented work is an ongoing joint research, which is still in an intermediary step of implementation. So far, a pilot case for the control cabinet product has been implemented together with the CPQ (configure – price – quote) software vendor encoway GmbH. This configuration application is already in use for selected customers. The future work will include achieving automated production of other customer-configured PSS. The research is based on the company Festo AG&Co KG, however, the results can give significant input to achieve benefits for component manufacturers that tend to become system vendors in general.

Acknowledgements. The research was supported partly by project funded by grant # 16-07-00375 of the Russian Foundation for Basic Research and research Program I.5 of the Presidium of the Russian Academy of Sciences (State Research no.0073-2015-0006). This work was also partially financially supported by Government of Russian Federation, Grant 074-U01.

References

1. M.-R. Zhang, C.-C. Yang, S.-Y. Ho, C. H. Chang. A study on enterprise under globalization competition knowledge management and creation overhead construction. J of Interdisciplinary Mathematics, Vol. 17, No. 5-6, 2014, pp. 423-433.
2. K. Erdener, S. Hassan. Globalization of consumer markets: structures and strategies. Routledge, 2014.
3. J. R. Bryson, P. W. Daniels (eds.), Handbook of Service Business: Management, Marketing, Innovation and Internationalisation. Edward Elgar Publishing, 2015.
4. The Wall Street Journal, 2016. URL: http://www.wsj.com/.
5. F. Ceschin. Product-Service System Innovation: A promising approach to sustainability. Sustainable Product-Service Systems. Springer International Publishing, 2014, pp. 17-40.

6. J. Wallin, V. Parida, O. Isaksson. Understanding product-service system innovation capabilities development for manufacturing companies. J of Manufacturing Technology Management Vol. 26, No. 5, 2015, pp. 763-787.

7. H. Baumeister. Customer relationship management for SMEs. Proceedings of the 2nd Annual Conference eBusiness and eWork e2002, Prague, Czech Republic, 2002.

8. J. Fjermestad, N. C. Romano Jr. An Integrative Implementation Framework for Electronic Customer Relationship Management: Revisiting the General Principles of Usability and Resistance. Proceedings of the 36th Hawaii International Conference on System Sciences (HICSS'03), Big Island, HI, USA, 2003.

9. F. Piller, C. Schaller. Individualization Based Collaborative Customer Relationship Management: Motives, Structures, and Modes of Collaboration for Mass Customization and CRM. Working Paper No. 29 of the Dept. of General and Industrial Management, Technische Universität München, 2004.

10. O. Saidani, S. Nurcan. Business process modeling: a multi-perspective approach integrating variability. Enterprise, Business-Process and Information Systems Modeling. Springer, Lecture Notes in Business Information Processing, Vol. 175, 2014, pp. 169-183.

11. G. Rock, K. Theis, P. Wischnewski. Variability Management. Concurrent Engineering in the 21st Century: Foundations, Developments and Challenges. Springer, 2015, pp. 491-519.

12. A. Smirnov, A. Kashevnik, N. Shilov, A. Oroszi, M. Sinko, T. Krebs. Changing business information systems for innovative configuration processes. R. Matulevičius, F. M. Maggi, P. Küngas, eds. Joint Proceedings of the BIR 2015 Workshops and Doctoral Consortium co-located with 14th International Conference on Perspectives in Business Informatics Research (BIR 2015). CEUR, Vol. 1420, 2015, pp. 62-73.

13. A. Smirnov, N. Shilov, A. Oroszi, M. Sinko, T. Krebs. Towards Life Cycle Management for Product and System Configurations: Required Improvements in Business Processes and Information Systems. Procedia CIRP, Vol. 48, 2016, pp. 84-89.

14. E. von Hippel. Democratizing innovation, The MIT Press, Cambridge, Massachussets, USA, 2006.

Consumers' Responses to Service Failures and Recoveries

Julie A. Edell

Fuqua School of Business, Duke University, Durham, NC 27708-0120, USA

julie.edell@duke.edu

Abstract. This paper presents the results of a study examining the nature of consumers' emotional reactions following a significant service failure. In addition to measuring consumers' feelings about the outcome that occurred (including the remedy), the emotional response to the service provider and the emotional response about the decision makers own choice to use that provider were captured separately. Consumers regretted their decision to use a provider if the provider only offers them compensation and not an apology when there was a delay in the service. Negative emotions focused toward the self and toward the provider played significant roles in the continuation intentions of the consumers. Offering a small amount of compensation ($10) for a delay with an apology was as effective as offering a large amount of compensation ($350) without an apology. An apology was significantly related to all of the feelings and to the continuation behavior. The level of compensation, however, was only related to greater satisfaction and continuation intentions. The mediating role of these emotional responses on satisfaction and continuation intentions showed that the emotions experienced were important mediators of satisfaction with the handling of the failure and with continuation intentions.

Keywords: Emotional responses, Apology, Compensation, Service failure

1   Introduction

Much of the previous research on consumers' responses to service failures has included multiple measures of emotion but without specifying the focus of these emotions. Consumers may regret their decision to use the particular provider, be disappointed with the outcome, or be angry with the provider. If a participant is only asked how disappointed they are after a bad experience, without specifying the focus of that disappointment, it is not possible to discern with whom the disappointment is directed. The purposes of this research are to examine 1) the emotional responses directed to the consumer, the provider and the outcome after a service failure and 2) consumers' responses to remedies offered.

© Springer International Publishing AG 2017

Y. Hara and D. Karagiannis (Eds.): ICServ 2017, LNCS 10371, pp. 38–45, 2017.
DOI: 10.1007/978-3-319-61240-9_4

2   Literature

Service recovery research has often examined restitution or compensation to the customer who has experienced a service failure and the role that an apology may play in the recovery [1-3]. Wirtz and Mattila investigated a service delay in a restaurant and found that both a twenty percent discount and an apology were significantly related to satisfaction, though the interaction was not. An apology was also related to continuation behaviors. Other researchers [4-6] have found that compensation was strongly related to customer satisfaction following a service failure.

3   Methods

3.1   Design

This study used a mixed between subject design with two factors, compensation level ($10, $100, or $350) and apology (yes or no). Participants were randomly assigned to one of the six conditions.

3.2   Participants

Participants were recruited from Amazon Turk and responded to a solicitation that "asked them to read a service scenario (see Appendix) and respond to a set of questions indicating their reactions to the scenario." One hundred and fifty people participated in the study and were paid $0.50.

3.3   Procedure

Participants were told that this was a study investigating people's responses to service encounters where the outcome is less than desirable. Participants read the scenario and were asked to respond to all questions as if they were the person in the scenario. The scenario is in the Appendix. It had six versions – crossing the three levels of compensation with an apology or no apology. The first question was a free response asking for the person's thoughts and feelings about the scenario. The next six measures were scaled questions in which the participant was asked to reveal their emotional reactions (both positive and negative) towards the provider, the outcome, and the decision they had made. Having both free response and scaled questions provides multiple measures of the feelings. Participants were then asked how satisfied they were with the way the airline handled the situation, for their likelihood of using the provider again and their likelihood of recommending the provider to a friend. A second open-ended question was then asked what the airline should have done to make up for the delay. Finally, participants were asked how much it would matter to you that the airline was delayed, since the perception of the severity of the delay may have differed across participants.

4   Measures

4.1   Free response

Participants were asked, "What thoughts and feelings would you be having if you were Sam (the person experiencing the airline delay)?" Participants' feelings and thoughts were coded by two people blind to the research hypotheses. The responses relevant to these results are: regret, disappointment, and anger. The coders also recorded whether the thoughts were self, outcome or provider focused. The intercoder correlation was no less than.88 percent on any of the categories and disagreements were resolved through discussion.

4.2   Emotional response, satisfaction and continuation

The scaled emotion measures consisted of items with either a positive or a negative valence for each of three foci - the self, the provider or the outcome. Participants were asked to "Please put yourself in Sam's place and indicate how well each of the following phrases describes the way you would feel." The positive valenced item of each question appears in parentheses. For each focus, the two items were added together, reverse coding the positive emotion. The provider-focused emotions were "Angry (Happy) with the airline'." The outcome-focused emotions were "Disappointed (Delighted) with what happened." The self-focused phrases were "Regretful about (Satisfied with) my decision to use this airline."   These were answered on 5-point Likert scales anchored by "Describes Extremely Well (5)" and by "Describes Not Well At All (1)."

Overall satisfaction was measured by asking respondents, "Please put yourself in Sam's place and indicate your responses if you experienced what Sam experienced. How satisfied are you with the way the airline handled the situation?" This was answered on 5-point Likert scales anchored by "Extremely Satisfied (5)" and by "Not At All Satisfied (1)."

Two measures of continuation intent were captured by asking the participants, "How likely would you be to use this airline again?" and "How likely are you to recommend this airline to your friends?" Continuation measures were answered on 5-point Likert scales anchored by "Very Likely (5)" and by "Not At All Likely (1)" and summed.

4.3   Service recovery

Participants were also asked an open-ended question to explore how participants felt service providers should have responded. Participants were asked, "What should the airline have done to make up for the delay?" These comments were coded to indicate whether the comment was about compensation, apology, another remedy or nothing else.

4.4   Severity

Finally, to determine the severity of the service failure, participants were asked, "How much would it matter to you that the airline was delayed?" This was also answered on a 5-point Likert scale anchored by "Matters Extremely Much (5)" and by "Doesn't Matter At All (1)."

5   Results

Scaled data were analyzed with an ANCOVA with the perception of the severity of the delay as a covariate and compensation level, apology and their interaction as between subject factors. The means of the scaled dependent variables for each of the six apology by compensation conditions are given in Table 1. The measure of severity of the service failure was significant in all of the analyses, with the more severe the delay was perceived to be, the more negative (or less positive) was the response. Due to the zero/one nature of the free response data (1 if mentioned and 0 if not), the free response data were analyzed using a chi-square test.

5.1   Emotions

There was a significant effect of apology on provider-focused emotions ($F_{(1,129)} = 11.12$, $p < .005$). Neither the main effect of compensation ($F_{(1,129)} < 1$) nor the interaction of apology by compensation level ($F_{(1,129)} < 1$) was significant. At each level of compensation, the presence of an apology resulted in less negative emotions toward the airline, than when no apology was given. There is no difference ($F_{(1,129)} = 2.14$, $p > .14$) in the negative emotions toward the provider whether the consumer was offered compensation of \$10 with an apology rather than \$350 with no apology.

The results for the self-focused emotions are similar. Participants felt significantly less negative self-focused emotions for having selected this airline ($F_{(1,130)} = 8.44$, $p < .005$) when an apology was given than when it was not. Neither the main effect of compensation level ($F_{(1,130)} = 1.76$, $p > .15$) nor the interaction of apology by compensation level ($F_{(1,130)} < 1$) was significant. At every level of compensation, the self-focused emotions were less negative when an apology was given than when it was not. There is no difference ($F_{(1,130)} < 1$) in the negative self-focused emotions whether the consumer was offered compensation of \$10 with an apology or \$350 without an apology.

Examining the outcome-focused emotions, the effect of an apology is also significant here ($F_{(1,130)} = 4.65$, $p < .05$). In addition, the main effect of compensation level ($F_{(1,130)} = 2.56$, $p < .10$) is marginally significant, with higher compensation associated with less negative emotions about the outcome. The interaction of apology with compensation level ($F_{(1,130)} < 1$) was not significant. Again, there is no difference ($F_{(1,130)} < 1$) in the negative outcome-focused emotions whether the consumer was offered compensation of \$10 with an apology rather than \$350 but with no apology.

While the open-ended response show a pattern similar to the measured emotions, the average numbers of feelings expressed is quite small (.21 for self-focused feelings, .38 for provider-focused feelings and .46 for outcome-focused feelings) and were not analyzed.

This study shows that an apology after a service delay has a major impact. Consumers experience less negative feelings about the provider, about their decision to use that provider and about the outcome itself if they receive an apology.

Do these feelings impact the customers' satisfaction with the way the service provider handled the delay, the likelihood of using the provider again and recommending the provider to others? These measures will be examined next.

5.2   Satisfaction

Both an apology ($F_{(1,128)}$ = 11.38, p < .001) and the level of compensation given ($F_{(2,128)}$ = 5.16, p < .01) had a significant impact on the satisfaction with the way the provider handled the service failure. Compensation of $350 resulted in great satisfaction than compensation of $100 or $10 (which were not different). The presence of an apology resulted in a greater satisfaction for every level of compensation. Again, there is not a significant difference in this evaluation ($F_{(1,128)}$ < 1) between those receiving $10 with an apology and those receiving $350, but no apology.

5.3   Continuation

Perhaps even more important than the satisfaction with the way the airline handled the situation, is the whether or not the customer would use the airline again and recommend it to others. The presence of an apology ($F_{(1,130)}$ = 16.28, p < .0001) had a significant impact on the intentions of the customer to using the airline again and recommend it to others. The apology by compensation interaction was marginally significant, though the positive continuation intentions were higher in the presence of an apology for all levels of compensation. As with the other measures, those receiving an apology and the lowest compensation had intentions as positive as those receiving $350, but no apology.

5.4   Mediation Analyses

Another goal of this research was to examine the extent to which the emotions experienced mediated the effects of compensation and an apology. Table 2 contains the regression coefficients and model summaries for the mediation analyses. To examine the extent to which the variously focused emotions mediate the effects of the apology and compensation on Satisfaction, the parallel multiple mediator model (Process model 4) of Hayes [7] was used. The effect of apology on satisfaction was mediated by the emotional responses to the delay. While only the provider-focused emotions had a significant direct effect on satisfaction, the total effect of apology on satisfaction was significant (t = 3.41, p < 0.0005). The level of compensation (as a continuous variable) on satisfaction was not fully mediated by the emotional responses. Rather, the effect of compensation on satisfaction operated directly.

To examine whether satisfaction mediates the effects of compensation and apology on the continuation intentions after accounting for their impact through the emotions, the serial multiple mediator model (Process model 6) was used [7]. Here the findings show that the effects of apology and compensation on the continuation intentions is fully mediated by their impact on satisfaction and the emotional responses.

5.5   Service Recovery

A second-opened question asked respondents to indicate what the airline should have done to make up for the delay. Remedy responses were coded into four categories – apologize, compensate more, something else, and nothing more. These responses were analyzed using chi square tests. Apology had a significant relationship with remedy response Chi-square$_{(4)}$ = 11.39, p < .05). Fewer (26.15%) of those receiving an apology felt the airline should have provided more compensation versus 53.42% of those not receiving an apology. More of those receiving an apology (52.31%) thought the airline did not need to do anything more compared to 34.25% for those not receiving an apology.

The amount of compensation also had a significant relationship with remedy (Chi-square$_{(8)}$ = 20.54, p < .01). Fewer (22.22%) of those receiving the $350 voucher felt the airline should have provided more compensation versus 61.70% of those receiving the $10 voucher. More of those receiving the $350 voucher (62.22%) thought the airline did not need to do anything more compared to 23.40% for those receiving the $10 voucher. At every level of compensation, those receiving an apology were less likely to feel the airline should offer higher compensation than those at the same level of compensation but not receiving an apology.

6   Conclusions

Consumers regret their decision to use a provider if the provider only offers them compensation and not an apology when there is a delay in the service. Negative emotions focused toward the self and toward the provider played significant roles in the continuation intentions of the consumers. Offering a small amount of compensation ($10) for a delay with an apology was as effective as offering a large amount ($350) without an apology. An apology was significantly related to all of the feelings and to the continuation behavior. The level of compensation, however, was only related to greater satisfaction and continuation intentions.

The mediating role of the emotional responses on satisfaction and continuation intentions showed that the emotions experienced were important mediators of satisfaction with the handling of the failure and with continuation intentions.

Table 1. Cell Means

	No Apology	Apology
$10 Compensation	Negative Self-Focused=8.08 Negative Outcome-Focused=9.42 Negative Provider-Focused=8.27 Satisfaction=2.31 Continuation Intentions=4.15	Negative Self-Focused=6.33 Negative Outcome-Focused=8.24 Negative Provider-Focused=6.62 Satisfaction=3.33 Continuation Intentions=6.67
$100 Compensation	Negative Self-Focused=6.79 Negative Outcome-Focused=8.79 Negative Provider-Focused=7.83 Satisfaction=2.79 Continuation Intentions=5.46	Negative Self-Focused=6.14 Negative Outcome-Focused=8.05 Negative Provider-Focused=7.05 Satisfaction=3.09 Continuation Intentions=6.05
$350 Compensation	Negative Self-Focused=7.00 Negative Outcome-Focused=8.23 Negative Provider-Focused=7.50 Satisfaction=3.14 Continuation Intentions=5.59	Negative Self-Focused=6.55 Negative Outcome-Focused=8.32 Negative Provider-Focused=7.00 Satisfaction=3.76 Continuation Intentions=6.64

Table 2. Regression Coefficients and Model Summary of the Mediation Effects

	Negative Self-Focused Emotions Coefficient (SE)	Negative Provider-Focused Emotions Coefficient (SE)	Negative Outcome-Focused Emotions Coefficient (SE)	Satisfaction Coefficient (SE)	Continuation Intentions Direct Effect Coefficient (SE)	Continuation Intentions Total Effect of each Variable alone Coefficient (SE)
Level of Compensation	-0.0014 (0.0011)	-0.0011 (0.001)	-0.0016* (0.0009)	0.0017*** (0.0005)	-0.0002 (0.0009)	0.0025* (0.0012)
Apology	-0.9308*** (0.3243)	-1.0261**** (0.2879)	-0.6614** (0.269)	0.2453 (0.1611)	0.4129 (0.2592)	1.3584*** * (0.3468)
Importance	0.9564**** (0.212)	0.9635**** (0.1883)	0.9745**** (0.1759)	0.0489 (0.1148)	-0151 (0.1833)	
Negative Self-Focused Emotions				-0.0374 (.0546)	-0.2113** (.0872)	- 0.2512** * (.1045)
Negative Provider-Focused Emotions				-0.3719**** (0.0653)	-0.0495 (0.1166)	- 0.4417*** * (.1251)
Negative Outcome-Focused Emotions				-0.0304 (0.0557)	-0.0188 (0.089)	- 0.0059 (.1042)
Satisfaction					1.0687**** (0.1409)	
Constant	3.2734** (0.969)	3.7961**** (0.8606)	4.7906**** (0.8042)	5.2165**** (.5221)	4.3132**** (1.1107)	
R2	0.1877	0.2371	0.2306	0.4698	0.6028	
	F(3,131)= 10.09****	F(3,131)= 13.57****	F(3,131)= 13.09****	F(6,128)= 18.91***	F(7,127)= 27.54****	

* p<.10, ** p<.05, *** p<.01, **** p<.001

Appendix

Scenario - Sam is flying to New York to meet with some new business clients. He boards the flight on his regular carrier at 6:45 am and is scheduled to depart at 7:15 am and arrive at LaGuardia airport in New York City at 8:45 am. At 7:20 the flight attendant announces that there will be a delay in departing. At 7:45, the attendant announces that there is a mechanical issue with the plane and the flight is now scheduled to depart at 8:45. At 9:00 am the flight finally departs with a scheduled arrival in New York at 10:30 am. Because of the delay, the flight attendant gives everyone on board a $10 voucher that they can use to buy food or drink on that flight or a later one (or $100 or $350 voucher that they can use toward a ticket on another flight). (Apology is "Then the pilot comes on and says he is very sorry for the delay and realizes that this delay will cause people to miss connections and important events. He reminds the passengers that his number one job is their safety and asks them to please fly with the airlines again.")

References

1. Levesque TJ, McDougall GHG (2000) Service problems and recovery strategies: an experiment. Canadian Journal of Administrative Sciences 17(1): 20-37.
2. Mattila AS (2001) The impact of relationship type on customer loyalty in a context of service failures. Journal of Service Research 4(2): 91-101.
3. Wirtz J, Mattila AS (2004) Consumer responses to compensation, speed of recovery and apology after a service failure. Journal of Service Industry Management 15(2): 150-166.
4. Darida T, Levesque T, McDougall G (1996) Service problems and recovery strategies: an exploratory investigation in the hospitality sector. In: Berneman C (ed) Proceedings of the Administrative Sciences Association Conference 1997. Administrative Sciences Association, Montreal, pp. 101-110.
5. Smith AK., Bolton RN, Wagner J (1999) A model of customer satisfaction with service encounters involving failure and recovery. Journal of Marketing Research 36: 356-372.
6. Webster E, Sundaram DS (1998) Service consumption criticality in failure recovery. Journal of Business Research 41: 153-159.
7. Hayes AF (2013) Introduction to mediation, moderation and conditional process analysis: a regression-based approach. Guilford Press, New York.

Analyzing an Ecosystem for Complex Consumer Services

Mirjana Radonjic-Simic[1], Frank Wolff[1],
and Dennis Pfisterer[2]

[1] Baden-Wuerttemberg Cooperative State University Mannheim, Germany
{mirjana.radonjic-simic, frank.wolff}@dhbw-mannheim.de,
[2] Institute of Telematics, University of Lübeck, Germany
pfisterer@itm.uni-luebeck.de

Abstract. Complex consumer services denote an arbitrary combination of services that fulfil a particular need based on consumer-defined context and requirements. While contemporary service environments are predominately supply-oriented and focused on the provision of single services, complex consumer services require dynamic and co-evolving networked structures (i.e., business ecosystems) to support consumers requesting and transacting such complex services. This paper outlines a consumer-oriented business ecosystem by describing its actors, primary roles, and the value exchanges between them, as well as, illustrates the structural leverage points relevant for the development and growth of such an ecosystem.

Keywords: Business Ecosystem, Complex Consumer Services, Value Networks

1 Introduction

The recent technological developments toward an interconnected world are opening up new opportunities for commercial exchange and give rise to a novel type of products and services that have not been possible before [7]. These can be combined and personalized in a way to satisfy the individual needs and contextual requirements of the consumer emphasizing the primacy of customer experience and the distributed co-creation of value [4].

Consider a tourist who wants to visit a concert and a mountaintop close to the city using the mountain railway; this includes reservation of tickets and searching for parking close to it. Also the mountain railway is only attractive if the weather is good and the queue is short. As a consumer, our tourist is asking for a *complex service* that can be satisfied with service providers offering distinct parts of the complex service. We define a *complex consumer service as any arbitrary combination of single services that fulfil a particular need based on the consumer-defined context.* This context is seen as a richer description of the demand – for our tourist including, e.g., schedule and environmental constraints like weather, location or other state-related data.

© Springer International Publishing AG 2017
Y. Hara and D. Karagiannis (Eds.): ICServ 2017, LNCS 10371, pp. 46–52, 2017.
DOI: 10.1007/978-3-319-61240-9_5

Contemporary service environments are predominately supply-oriented and focused on the provision of single services or a pre-defined combination of them. And thus, limited to support consumers to compose different cross-domain services in one complex service to fulfil a particular consumer-defined context, and to transact it in one single enclosing transaction to avoid switching costs. Our previous work [9], [5] addressed those issues from the technological perspective and proposes Distributed Market Spaces (DMS) – an exchange environment supporting consumers and providers in making transactions of complex products and services in a decentralized, peer-to-peer manner. We argue that the DMS architecture can serve as a technical infrastructure for dynamic structures of interconnected actors, i.e., business ecosystems, required to support complex consumer services. Yet, for a business ecosystem to be created an enabling infrastructure is necessary but not sufficient as it cannot cover the mechanisms by which the different actors interact to create and share value, nor how those interactions impact the business ecosystem during its life cycle.

The main contribution of this paper is to outline such a consumer-oriented ecosystem for complex consumer services from the business perspective and illustrate its structural leverage points. It describes the main actors, roles and the vital value exchanges needed to support the shared purpose, and analyses the main dynamics of the development and growth of such ecosystem.

This paper is structured as follows: Section 2 presents the background of business ecosystems and value networks. Followed by Section 3, that describes the identified actors, roles and the primary value created for each of them and briefly discusses the ecosystem's dynamics. Section 4 concludes this paper with a summary and outlook.

2 Business Ecosystems as Value Networks

A business ecosystem refers to "an economic community supported by a foundation of interacting organizations and individuals" [8], that uses common standards and collectively provides goods and services to their customers [12]. Including customers, providers, competitors, institutions, and other stakeholders, which are integrated into a massive interconnected network, i.e., value network, business ecosystems create value through a process of cooperation and competition [6],[13]. The literature on business ecosystems suggests that the following factors are crucial for a successful ecosystem [6], [10], [13]. First, how value is created to attract and retain ecosystem's participants and provide growth potential, and second, how value is shared in the ecosystem as a whole.

Aiming to answer these questions for our business ecosystem for complex consumer services, we engage the widely-recognized Value Network Analysis (VNA) by [1]. Accordingly, a value network generates value through dynamic and complex exchanges between its actors and can be mapped as a flow diagram showing services, revenue streams, and knowledge flows, as well as dynamics visible through the value network perspective.

In this work, we utilized the VNA method to identify the overall pattern of exchanges and value creation within the ecosystem for complex consumer services. Thereby, we concentrated on the primary actors and their interactions considered essential for the business ecosystem to be established. The next section summarizes our initial findings.

3   Outlining an Ecosystem for Complex Consumer Services

Following, we describe and briefly discuss our findings beginning with the formulation of the shared purpose as establishing of a *consumer-oriented business ecosystem that enables complex consumer services in a decentralized, peer-to-peer manner.*

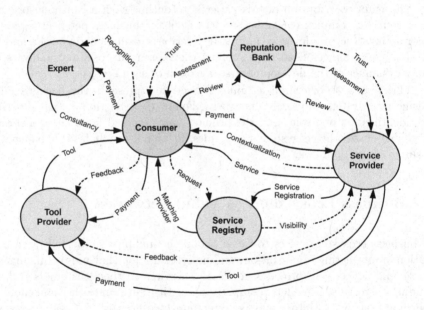

Figure 1: Mapping an ecosystem for complex consumer services.

3.1   Actors and Value Created

There are (at least) six roles for the actors of a consumer-oriented ecosystem for complex consumer services: *Consumer, Service Provider, Tool Provider, Expert, Service Registry and Reputation Bank.* Actors can be individuals, companies, institutions, associations, networks as well as autonomous agents (e.g., software agents and machines).

Whereas consumer and service provider are considered as the shaper roles, others are seen as enablers. They support the value creation within the ecosystem and contribute to its ability to provide comprehensive services, hence build the foundation for its health and vitality. Given the shared purpose, the ecosystem's value creation needs to be organized around the transaction process of complex consumer services. As to [2], the transaction process divides in information (formulating demand), negotiation (matching and ordering), settlement (realizing the transaction regarding payment and delivery), and after-sales (reviews).

Table 1: Roles and expected values.

Role	Description	Expected Value
Consumer	Requesting a complex consumer service.	To satisfy a particular need defined through a transaction of a complex consumer service in a reliable and trustful manner.
Service Provider	Offering services in one particular domain or many domains.	To earn revenue per service sold (*payment*), increase *visibility*, and the level of customization utilizing contextual information (*contextualization*).
Tool Provider	Providing tools to support the transaction process (information, negotiation, settlement and after-sales activities).	To earn revenue by guaranteeing availability only to paying users (*payment*), and to leverage the user's *feedback* for improvement and development of tools.
Expert	Offering noted knowledge and expertise to support consumers making informed decisions.	To earn revenue through *consultancy* and increase own image through consumer's *recognition* of providing consultancy as the value added service.
Service Registry	Matching requests and registered services and resolving information required for the transaction process.	To acquire knowledge about prevailing offerings (*service registrations*) and current demand for services represented through consumer's *requests*.
Reputation Bank	Assessing ecosystem's actors regarding their reliability, solvency and worthiness.	To capture *reviews* about current transactions needed for qualified *assessments* and establishing an adequate level of *trust* among actors considered essential for peer-to-peer networks [3].

Table 1 summarizes aforementioned roles briefly describing their core function and motivation, i.e., expected value from the participation in the ecosystem. Identified roles can overlap as a consumer can act as, e.g., a service provider, expert or tool provider, and be taken concurrently, as they do not exclude each other. Figure 1 illustrates the overall pattern of exchanges between these roles.

The nodes represent actors performing a role and the arrows the vital inter-actions indicating the 'value exchanges' between roles. Solid lines represent the 'tangible' exchanges such as payment or service and the dotted ones 'intangibles' like feedback or trust.

3.2 Ecosystem Dynamics

This section briefly discusses the dynamics considered relevant to ecosystem's development and growth. Following [11], the basic dynamics can be illustrated by a causal loop diagram, as shown in Figure 2.

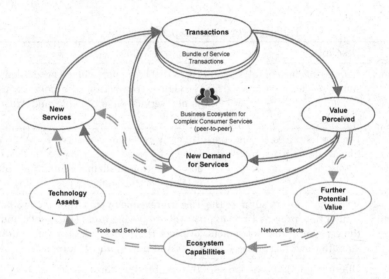

Figure 2: Dynamics of a business ecosystem for complex consumer services.

The transactions (a bundle of single service transactions in one enclosing transaction) constitute the basis for the 'value perceived' as the overall value created through value exchanges (cf. Table 1). Value perceived can generate additional value effects relevant for the ecosystem's operational level represented through solid line loops. Namely, to initiate the new 'demand for services' increasing the ecosystem's traffic and volume, that in turn may attract new consumer and service providers to join the ecosystem and thus, initiate new transactions. That can work in both directions, as either the availability of services can increase the demand, and higher demand may attract more provider and open up opportunities for the creation of entirely 'new services'.

Moreover, value perceived may generate 'further potential value' relevant to the strategic level of the ecosystem as illustrated by dotted lines. Reinforcing the operational loop can cause positive network externalities, i.e., network effects, increasing the value of services depending on the number of other consumers using it. Network effects may also open up the potential for the development of the ecosystem's foundations, i.e., technology assets like infrastructure and tools, as well as improve the quality of its services in general. Hence, build ecosystem's capabilities to adapt to evolving dynamics and provide for its health and vitality. Effects above may also manifest simultaneously, have a different impact on various stages of the ecosystem's life cycle, or even reinforce each other in a negative way; but due to the brevity of this paper, considered as part of the future work.

4 Conclusion and Future Work

This paper outlined a consumer-oriented business system for complex consumer services. First, we identified the primary roles and the overall value exchange pattern that must be supported by an underlying technical infrastructure while establishing such a business ecosystem. Afterward, we illustrated structural leverage points and discussed value dynamics considered important for development and growth. Thereby we concentrated on roles critical for the value creation organized around the transaction process, as well as, on the positive reinforcement loops neglecting other effects that may manifest over the time and balance the favourable ecosystem's dynamics. In our future work, we will focus on two areas that require additional analysis; the further roles and how they realize value from value exchanges, and the ecosystem's capabilities to create, extend and leverage value and provide comprehensive services to all ecosystem's participants.

References

1. Allee, V.: Value network analysis and value conversion of tangible and intangible assets. Journal of intellectual capital 9(1), 5–24 (2008)
2. Bakos, Y.: The emerging role of electronic marketplaces on the Internet. Communications of the ACM (1998), http://dl.acm.org/citation.cfm?id=280330
3. Einav, L., Farronato, C., Levin, J.: Peer-to-peer markets. Tech. rep., National Bureau of Economic Research (2015)
4. El Sawy, O.A., Pereira, F.: Business modelling in the dynamic digital space: An ecosystem approach. Springer (2013)
5. Hitz, M., Radonjic-Simic, M., Reichwald, J., Pfisterer, D.: Generic UIs for Requesting Complex Products Within Distributed Market Spaces in the Internet of Everything, pp. 29–44. Springer International Publishing, Cham (2016), http://dx.doi.org/10.1007/978-3-319-45507-5_3
6. Iansiti, M., Levien, R.: The keystone advantage: what the new dynamics of business ecosystems mean for strategy, innovation, and sustainability. Harvard Business Press (2004)
7. Lusch, R.F., Nambisan, S.: Service innovation: A service-dominant logic perspective. Mis Quarterly 39(1), 155–175 (2015)
8. Moore, J.: Predators and prey: a new ecology of competition. Harvard Business Review 71(3), 75–86 (1993)
9. Pfisterer, D., Radonjic-Simic, M., Reichwald, J.: Business model design and architecture for the internet of everything. Journal of Sensor and Actuator Networks 5(2), 7 (2016)

10. Rong, K., Hu, G., Lin, Y., Shi, Y., Guo, L.: Understanding business ecosystem using a 6c framework in internet-of-things-based sectors. International Journal of Production Economics 159, 41–55 (2015)
11. Sterman, J.D.: Business dynamics: systems thinking and modeling for a complex world. Irwin/McGraw-Hill Boston (2000)
12. Teece, D.J.: Business Ecosystem, pp. 1–4. Palgrave Macmillan UK, London (2016), http://dx.doi.org/10.1007/978-1-349-94848-2_724-1
13. Tian, C., Ray, B.K., Lee, J., Cao, R., Ding, W.: Beam: A framework for business ecosystem analysis and modeling. IBM Systems Journal 47(1), 101–114 (2008)

Customer Satisfaction

Approaches for sustaining cultural resources by adapting diversified context of customers in tourism: Comparison between Japanese and Slovenian cases

Hisashi Masuda[1], Dejan Krizaj[2], Hideyuki Sakamoto[3], and Kotaro Nakamura[4]

[1] Japan Advanced Institute of Science and Technology, Japan
masuda@jaist.ac.jp
[2] University of Primorska, Slovenia
[3] Kanazawa College of Art, Japan
[4] e-craft, Japan

Abstract. Amid changing economic situation rapidly, how to sustain local/cultural resources and distribute their value to many customers is crucial in a number of business communities. In tourism industry, although there are a lot of activities for such struggles, a small number of the global comparison studies are a problem for exploring and adopting the more effective ways worldwide. In this paper, we examine two Japanese cases and one Slovenian case doing well of sustaining and balancing cultural resources in terms of adapting the differences of customers' context in tourism. In the first case from Japanese tourism spa community "Awazu-onsen", the key point is a loose relationship between the traditional local hotels and the modern hotel chain. The second case from Kanazawa Creative Tourism in Japan is a NPO supported by the local art universities for connecting the local artists and the local tourism. The third case from the Ana Desetnica International Street Theatre Festival in Slovenia offers not only each street artistic performances simply, but also the unique city Ljubljana as a big theater for attracting many tourists who have a wide variety of touristic preferences. There are three approaches for attracting current customers with sustaining their local values, those are installing a new resources, making a new matching system and reintrepretation of the existing resources. In the future research, it is important to collect related cases by analyzing those countries' situations, issues, purposes, and the ways and results by more extensive surveys for understanding and making significant theories.

Keywords: Resource, sustainability, expansion, community, tourism

1 Introduction

1.1 Background

Matured industry is leading us to service economy as well as globalization while developing Information and Communication Technology (ICT) all over

© Springer International Publishing AG 2017
Y. Hara and D. Karagiannis (Eds.): ICServ 2017, LNCS 10371, pp. 55–63, 2017.
DOI: 10.1007/978-3-319-61240-9_6

the world. "Equally, as the digital divide narrows, service have enabled less-developed countries to participate on a leveller playing field in business and trade"[1]. In services sector, there are high potential of a lot of participants who have differential cultural background in the future.

In tourism industry, there are also influences of matured industry. Generally, high standardized businesses' entering, such as hotel chain, hypermarket and so on, into provincial cities can deteriorate the local, cultural unique values. In Japan, there are many related controversies in each province city.

Therefore, especially in local tourism community, some strategies for juggling sustain the unique core values and distributing them into many tourists competing with standardized big businesses are crucial in this current economic situation. For addressing such strategies, we have to consider what our core values are and what parts we are able to change flexibly without deteriorating the core values.

But, to generalize the best practice for sustaining local core values and distributing them widely is difficult. Because there are vast amounts of factors that affect the decision-making, such as differences of target customers, changing customers' needs, new technologies trend like social media and so on.

Meanwhile, there are a wide variety cases of tourism activities, some can achieve success, and the others cannot. First of all, to discuss what kind of tourism approaches can do well in terms of sustaining and distributing their values and the others cannot do well. And then, considering how to generalize these activities is important for adapting this matured global, service economy.

1.2   Research Question and Purpose

In this paper, we analyze promising tourism approaches that are juggling between sustaining local/cultural values and attracting many tourists. In tourism, characteristics of the activities as a community would have a key role in handling the issue. What kinds of the strategies in terms of a community are there? And are there meaning differences between countries based on the strategies?

The research purpose is to increase the possibility of utilizing insights based on abundant tourism cases all over the world. And also we can explore new theoretical approaches based on the generalized theory validated with data.

1.3   Approach

In this paper, we analyze tourism cases in terms of a community activity worldwide. The specific study targets are Japanese and Slovenian cases. For both countries, tourism industry plays a key role to their countries' economic activities. Thus, they have a wide variety of tourism cases. In addition, there are several tourism cases of a similar size in terms of community. We selected specific tourism cases from them that are the Japanese spa tourism community "Owazu-onsen", the Japanese tourism activity with artists "Kanazawa Creative Tourism" and the Slovenian Street Theatre Festival organized by "Ana Monró Theatre."

As the results from the cases, there are three approaches for attracting current customers with sustaining their local values. Those approaches are installing a new resources, making a new matching system and reintrepretation of the existing resources. In terms of countries differences, Japanese communities have a number of own tourism resources to make new values by only reclassification for now. But on the other hand, Slovenia is relatively a small country. They need to reinterpret a part of their own tourism resources for attracting new tourists. We believe different techniques are required depended on that kind of ways of how to utilize tourism resources.

There are some patterns in tourism communities for adapting changes of economic trend and their situations. It is important in tourism to collect information like those countries' situations, the ways to develop and distribute their values and the effects by this type of survey. Generalizing that kind of cases, we can share valuable trial and error in tourism activities.

In the following sections, we will give the detailed. Section 2 shows related works in terms of context and fidelity vs. convenience. Section 3 describes the results. And Section 4 is for discussion, then we will conclude in section 5.

2 Related Works

In this section, we show a concept of context and adapting diversified context in this paper. The former comes from Anthropology by Hall[2] and Context Aware Computing by Dey[3], the latter does from a fidelity and convenience concept by Maney[4].

From Anthropology, Hall explained context as a function of communication in terms of High Context communications(HC) and Low Context ones(LC) with figure 1. He says "a universal feature of information systems is that meaning is made up of: the communication, the background and preprogrammed responses of the recipient, and the situation", "Therefore, what the receiver actually perceives is important in understanding the nature of context" and "Most of the information must be in the transmitted message in order to make up for what is missing in the context."

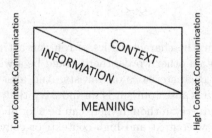

Fig. 1. Context as a function of communication by Hall

On the other hand, from an ICT perspective in Context Aware Computing, Dey says "Context is any information that can be used to characterize the situation of an entity. An entity is a person, place, or object that is considered relevant to the interaction between a user and an application, including the user and applications themselves."

In terms of diversified context in businesses, Maney proposed one perspective consisted of two dimensions: fidelity and convenience (Figure.2). Fidelity is the total experience of something like theaters experiences, rock concerts and so on. On the other hand, convenience is how easy or hard it is to get what you want. The examples of easy convenience are home theaters, iTunes, Amazon.com and so on. He explains that "Contrary to what many businesses want to believe, achieving both high fidelity and high convenience seems to be impossible." It means there is trade-off consumers were making between fidelity and convenience.

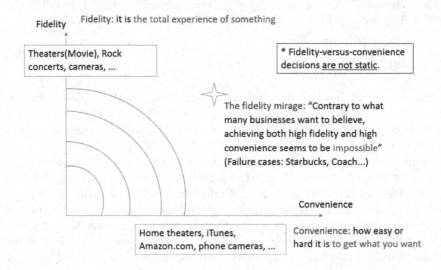

Fig. 2. Fidelity vs. convenience by Maney

In matured tourism, the characteristics of tourism activities become higher context ones than ever. In other words, there would be a wide variety of fidelity patterns depended on characteristics of tourists. And also we have to consider them as a community because tourism is an industry that has a lot of players. However, in tourism industry, although there can be a lot of activities considering the balance between low-context and high-context, or convenience and fidelity, a small number of the global comparison studies in terms of this direction is a problem for exploring and adopting the more effective ways worldwide in this global economy.

3   Case Results

We analyze tourism cases as a community activity in terms of low-high context or covenience-fidelity perspective. In Slovenia and Japan, tourism industry plays a key role to their countries' economic activities. And there are several tourism cases of a similar size of community in both countries. We, therefore, selected Japanese and Slovenian cases doing well of sustaining and distributing their cultural resources. The cases we selected are: Japanese spa tourism community "Awazu-onsen", a NPO "Kanazawa Creative Tourism" in Japan and Ana Desetnica International Street Theatre Festival by "Ana Monró Theatre" in Slovenia.

3.1   Japanese spa tourism community "Awazu-onsen"

Japan has a lot of spa tourism communities. The histories many have are old, and the Awazu-onsen community has their history for 1300 years. This is one of the longest traditional tourism communities in Japan. Meanwhile typically, the communities have hard time for their operations. Because young generation in Japan is familiar with the customs of modern hotel services. There is a gap between providing the value by the traditional hotels and the needs that young people have. In this Awazu-onsen case, despite the tradition powerful brand, it was same situation. However, a hotel chain happened to enter into this community since 2004 by acquiring a local facility that was bankrupted. There is no strong relationship between the tradition hotels and the hotel chain. But the chain could attract tourists using the local Awazu-onsen brand and serve their convenient service with low price.

The brand has been developed by the traditional hotels for long periods. The services are a classic type of Japanese luxury hotel. Generally the quality of hospitality, spa and cuisine is high and they require relatively high price. But installing modern facilities and business systems are very slow. We can say it seems to require to customers something like fidelity. On the other hand, the hotel chain happen to enter into this area. It has generated a loose cooperation generate. The hotel chain had modernized hotel systems and low-price strategy. It could attract casual tourists like family, business persons in the business trip and so on.

The figure 3 represents the structure of Awazu-onsen community in terms of the convenience-fidelity concept. There is no explicit cooperative relationship between the traditional tourism community and the new hotel chain. But the hotel chain is using the high brand value in Awazu-onsen for attracting their casual users. And then a part of casual users become heavy users of this Awazu-onsen community. However, by reason that the business the traditional community operates is still hard, supports by the local governments are very important for the traditional tourism community. The relationship with these three groups are working effectively in this area.

A Japanese hot spring community: "Awazu Onsen" since about 700

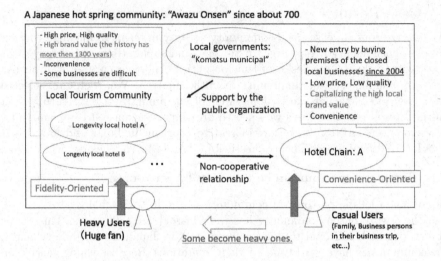

Fig. 3. A structure of Awazu-onsen community

3.2 NPO "Kanazawa Creative Tourism" for art tourism in Japan

Recently there are many tourism cases that they try to utilize artistic resources into tourism all over the world. In Japan, Kanazawa city has an old history and a wide variety of cultural aspects such as cuisine, craftwork/artwork and so on. A NPO called Kanazawa Creative Tourism is organizing a platform between local artists and the local tourism. The body is operated mainly by a member of local art school and so on. Although local arts and crafts graduates have a wide variety of niche, generally the niche business is difficult to grow as a stable work. Therefore, the body is playing a key role to sustain the arts/crafts communities.

The figure 4 represents the structure of the platform made by Kanazawa Creative tourism. The NPO arranges various kinds of local tourism products easily available like tour of inspection to craft studio, seminar, talk event, and so on. The target customers of the NPO are relatively casual users who have interests in creative activities. On the other hand, the artists have varied niche values. Typically to explore customers is difficult if the value is niche. It means the NPO is setting the opportunities to connect between artist and casual users. Kanazawa city aims to be a cultural city in Japan. Therefore this relationship of Kanazawa Creative Tourism, Artists/craftspeople community and several public organizations has potential to sustain and distribute the cultural value through tourism.

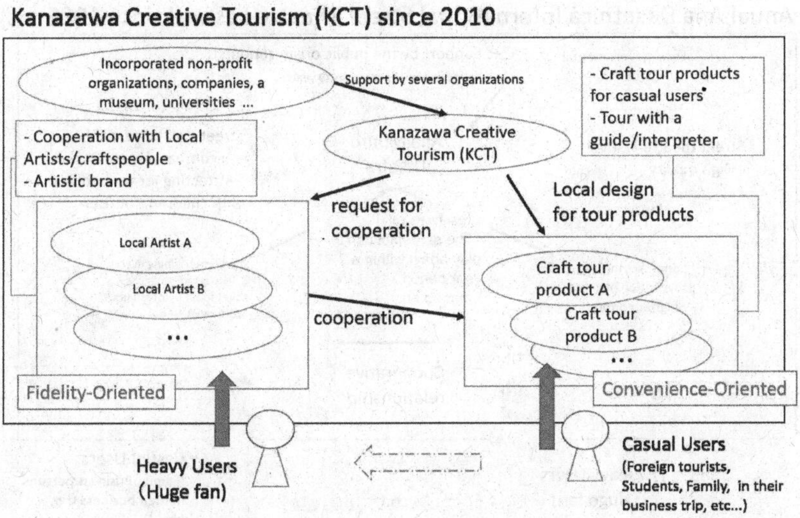

Fig. 4. A structure of a NPO Kanazawa Creative Tourism(KCT)

3.3   Ana Desetnica International Street Theatre Festival by "Ana Monró Theatre" in Slovenia

In Ljubljana, Slovenia, there is Annual Ana Desetnica International Street Theatre Festival. This festival has started since 1996. Ljubljana is a small size city. It means we can walk around the city easily. The size of the city is suitable for transforming the city into the street theatre during the festival. The director of this festival says this festival is not only for tourists but also for local citizens. In Europe, many people are working out of home country. This festival is also working as a social gathering opportunity for family in Ljubljana.

The figure 5 represents the structure of the Ana Desetnica International Street Theatre Festival. This festival has been started since 1996. The point of this festival is to connect between artistic performers and the city itself. It is difficult to attract a lot of casual users by Just only professional performances. The festival offers those performance conveniently through the city. It plays a role of theater during the festival. Then, tourists in the festival can get an easy access to those performances. This is an opportunity for connecting between artist and casual tourists. And Ana Monró Theatre has some rule for selecting the performers, for example, to restrict same performance within a 3 year period and so on, in order to giving new experiences to repeated tourists. Ljubljana is a small city. There are limited resources for utilizing the tourism. Thus, they changed the function of existing resources.

Anual Ana Desetnica International Street Theatre Festival since 1996

Fig. 5. A structure of Ana Desetnica International Street Theatre Festival

4 Discussion

These tourism cases have activities for how to sustain/extend their core values and also how to distribute them to casual and heavy tourists/customers. In terms of the fidelity-convenience concept, there cases have a part of developing values that is pursuing fidelity and a part of distributing values that is pursuing convenience as a structure/system of their communities. There are three approaches in this study for attracting casual users/customers with sustaining local core values. Those are installing a new resources, making a new matching system and reinterpretation of the existing resources. The common point of them is to separate between a part of developing values and distributing them widely. In other words, not only to have value developers, but also to have separated value distributors are needed for this kind of activities. Combination of each component can play a key role in sustaining and improving tourism communities.

In terms of comparison between Japanese and Slovenian cases, Japanese cases can adapt the current economic situation by installing a new function into the community or making a new matching system. This is because Japan is a relatively big country and there are a wide variety of available resources. On the other hand, the street festival case in Slovenia shows they had to seek new interpretations to existing resources. Slovenia is a relatively small country and surrounded by competitors in tourism industry in Europe. It may lead them to go into this direction. For sustaining/developing and distributing core values in tourism, if there are differences about available resources, the adequate strategy can be also affected with the difference. We do think that there are some patterns or combinations related to the strategy and constrained conditions for achieving this direction.

5 Conclusion

Generally in businesses, juggling making advanced values and also attracting casual users/customers at once is very difficult. In this paper, we studied that the treatments for the difficulty in selected Japanese and Slovenian tourism cases were to divide the part of sustaining/developing values and distributing values to casual tourists/customers as combined activities in one tourism community. And there are three approaches: installing a new resources, making a new matching system and reinterpretation of the existing resources for attracting casual users/customers with sustaining core values.

There are vast kinds of tourism activities all over the world. Because our survey is only a few of them, it is difficult to generalize our results in the wider sense. But we do think the promising patterns for this direction are finite. We consider that making theories related to this concept is important for extracting the essences of a lot of actual trial-and-error cases in tourism for increasing the productivity.

In the future research, it is important to collect cases for sustaining/developing tourism values and distributing them to casual tourists/customers by analyzing those countries' situations, issues, purposes, and the ways and results by more extensive surveys for understanding and making significant theories.

Acknowledgement

This work was contributed by Hiroki Fujimaru's master's thesis and supported by JSPS KAKENHI Grant Number 15H05396.

References

1. UNCTAD (2014) UNCTAD Findings on Services, Development and Trade. http://unctad.org/en/pages/PublicationWebflyer.aspx?publicationid=549 [Accessed: 28-Feb-2017]
2. Edward Twitchell Hall (1976) Beyond culture. Anchor Press
3. Anid K. Dey (2001) Understanding and Using Context. Personal Ubiquitous Computing. 5 (1). pp 4-7
4. Kevin Maney (2009) Trade-off: Why some things catch on, and others don't. Broadway Books, New York
5. Frankie Thompson (2014) Why Theatre Belongs on the Street: Takeaways from Ana Desetnica Street Theatre Festival in Ljubljana. Must Love Festivals http://mustlovefestivals.com/2014/07/30/theatre-festival-in-ljubljana/ [Accessed: 28-Feb-2017]
6. Peter Parkorr (2014) Spotlight on Ljubljana: The Highlights of Ana Desetnica Street Theatre Festival. Travel unmasked http://travelunmasked.com/peterparkorr/2014/ana-desetnica-photos-street-theatre-festival-ljubljana/ [Accessed: 28-Feb-2017]

An Economic Lab Experiment for the Best Offer and Approval in Face-to-Face Service Interaction Situation

Kenju Akai[1], Keiko Aoki[2], Kenta Onoshiro[3]

[1] Shimane University, 89-1, Enyacho, Izumo, Shimane, 6938501, Japan
[2] Yokohama National University, 79-5, Tokiwadai, Hodogayaku, Yokohama, 2408501, Japan
[3] Osaka University, 6-1, Mihogaoka, Ibaraki, Osaka, 5670047, Japan
akai@med.shimane-u.ac.jp
k-aoki@ynu.ac.jp
fge006ok@gmail.com

Abstract. This article investigates what types of social distance affect the best offer from an employee and its approval from a customer in general service situation. We conduct the deception game (Gneezy, 2005) and investigate the effects of the social distance (face-to-face vs. anonymous interaction) in a laboratory experimental economics method. We observed increases in the rate at which employees made best offers and the rates at which customers accepted offers when face-to-face interactions were conducted. But a statistically significant difference was not observed. Also, the level of trust in others reported by the subject playing the role of the employee had a statistically significant positive effect in cases in which the employee made a best offer. It was also observed that, regardless of whether the interaction was conducted face to face or anonymously, if the subject playing the role of the customer exhibited a low level of tolerance for falsehood, he or she was less likely to accept offers.

Keywords: Economic experiment, Deception game, Trust, Service management

1   Introduction

The exchange between employees and customers is the minimum level of behavior necessary to create a typical service. In many cases, a service occurs when an offer from a company through an employee is accepted by a customer. For instance, a variety of everyday cases qualify as a service, such as the offer of a special menu and its acceptance by a customer in a restaurant, or the offer of informative documents about a type of medical care and the subsequent consent of the patient. As services are intangible, simultaneous, diverse, and perishable, the fact that a customer does not fully understand the value of the service that he or she receives creates a dilemma. It is exceptionally difficult for a customer to discern whether a service offered by an employee represents his or her best interest, or whether it prioritizes the employee's profits. Thus, in the offer and acceptance of services by an employee and customer respectively, information is held asymmetrically. This asymmetry of information may create an incentive for the employee to offer a service that is beneficial to itself but not necessarily in the customer's best interests. In modern society, frequent reports of instances in which

© Springer International Publishing AG 2017

Y. Hara and D. Karagiannis (Eds.): ICServ 2017, LNCS 10371, pp. 64–74, 2017.
DOI: 10.1007/978-3-319-61240-9_7

first-class hotels or expensive restaurants have deceived their customers about the quality of the food they serve provide a classic example of a case in which employees have taken advantage of a customer's trust and offered services that prioritize their own profits. This is a form of fraud. Due to the asymmetry of information between the employee and the customer, services always involve this problem of deception. In this research, we focus on possible incentives for employees to deceive customers about the quality of their services, and perform economic experiments that investigate the influence of social distance between the customer and the employee.

In a demonstration experiment using Australian wine, Lacey et al. (2011) received responses indicating that, when ordering wine, customers depended as much on the offer of a service, in this case a recommendation from an employee, as they did on the taste of the wine or information such as where the wine was produced. This result implies that, in response to the uncertain nature of the wine, a recommendation from the employee had a strong effect on the customer's likelihood to order the wine.

As research on services often does not involve the mediation of specific goods, in this research we have used a deception game per Gneezy (2005), a type of experiment in which goods are not mediated. In the original study, a sender chooses to send either a true or a deceptive message containing receiver's payoffs in the two options that detect actual payoffs between two subjects. Gneezy discovered that higher stakes achieved by lying induce a higher fraction of lying. This result implies that the employee has an economic incentive to deceive when the customers do not know the true value. This game formation is a principle of the real service situation so that we focus on this game.

We compare the distribution of the honest behavior (the employee's best offer from to customer in the aspect of customer's profit) and the customer's approval under the social distance (anonymity vs. face-to-face interaction situation). The social distance is represented by the degree of anonymity between senders and receivers. According to Roth (1995), face-to-face communication, one of the central issues in social interaction, encourages cooperative behavior in public goods games (Isaac and Walker, 1988; Brosig et al., 2003; Bochet et al., 2006) and prisoner's dilemma games (Frohlich and Oppenheimer, 1998; Bohnet and Frey, 1999b). It also increases offers in dictator games (Bohnet and Frey, 1999a, 1999b; Burnham, 2003; Charness and Gneezy, 2008).

In the trust game, Scharlemann et al. (2001) showed that a facial expression elicits corporation under non-verbal communication environment. Holm and Kawagoe (2010) employed a bluffing game in which subjects played cards to deceive their counterparts. They discovered that lifting anonymity between players reduces lying. No study has evaluated the effects of social distance by using the deception game. However, we can refer to Sutter (2009), who found that groups are less likely to lie than individuals. This result implies that lifting anonymity among the senders reduces lying.

On the basis of the arguments above, we suggest a hypothesis: lifting anonymity increases the honest behavior. Since reducing social distance encourages an emphasis on others, lifting anonymity increases senders' beliefs for earning approves from the receivers, or it makes them less willing to let receivers down. On the other hand, the effect of increased cooperative behavior suggests the hypothesis: lifting anonymity enhances approval.

Also, the socio-economic background has various demographic components, such as age, gender, or income. To investigate the effects of these various components,

Gächter et al. (2004) found students to be less trusting than non-students in the trust game. In the deception game, only the difference of gender has been considered as an effect of subject type. Dreber and Johannesson (2010) found that men are more likely to lie than women in situations with small stakes, while Childs (2012) found no difference between genders in situations with large stakes.

The remainder of the paper is organized as follows. Section 2 presents the experimental design and procedures. Section 3 analyzes the results. Section 5 discusses and Section 6 summarizes the conclusions.

2   Experimental design and procedures

2.1   Design

We replicate the deception game (Gneezy, 2005). The subjects were allocated to separate rooms, designated as Rooms A and B. Subjects in Room A are randomly matched with subjects in Room B. Subjects in Room A plays the role of senders (employees), and subjects in Room B plays the role of receivers (customers).

Only senders are informed about the monetary payoffs for the two different options, A and B, as follows:

Option A: 1500 yen to you and 500 yen to the other student
Option B: 500 yen to you and 1500 yen to the other student

Receivers know only that there were two options, A and B, but do not know the context. Then, the senders send receivers one of the two messages below:

Message 1: Option A will earn you more money than Option B.
Message 2: Option B will earn you more money than Option A.

Message 1 is the best offer from the employee to the customer. If the receiver chooses Option A (B) as the response to Message 1 (2), he or she approves the offer from the customer. Receivers receive the messages and choose one of the two options. Receivers know nothing but the amount of money they will earn at the end of the experiment. Therefore, receivers cannot judge whether the sender has told a lie.

2.2   Procedures

We conducted the laboratory experiments at Osaka University. No one participated in more than one session. The anonymity treatments proceeded in the following steps:

1. Subjects gathered in one room before the experiment. The experimenter read a consent form aloud in front of the subjects. The subjects were then divided by a lottery into two rooms, A (senders) and B (receivers) as in Figure 1.
2. Senders and receivers were given separate instructions and read them silently and independently. Senders were given two cards with Messages 1 and 2. Receivers were given two cards describing Options A and B.

3. Senders inserted one card (Message 1 or 2) into an envelope. The experimenter delivered the envelope to the paired receiver in the other room. The receiver read the message and inserted a card (Option A or B) into the envelope. Then, everyone answered a short questionnaire about their expectations.

In the face-to-face treatment, the third step were customized. Each pair moved to a common space and stood face to face across a table separated by a partition to prevent receivers from seeing senders' decisions as they were being made as in Figure 2. Senders inserted one of the two cards (Message 1 or 2) into an envelope and then personally handed it to their paired receiver. Verbal communication was prohibited during this procedure. After returning to their original rooms, receivers read the message and inserted one of two cards (Option A or B) into the envelope, which the experimenter then delivered.

After this procedure, we investigate the effects of four types of variables self-reported in the questionnaire. The first type includes demographic variable, such as gender, age, and income. This is also used for evaluating differences in socio-economic backgrounds between students and non-students. The second type is a psychometric scale such as General Social Survey (GSS) scales and trust scales used in many previous studies. The third type, employed only in the face-to-face treatment, includes information about acquaintance levels, subjects' impressions of their partners, and paired gender effects. These variables can be used to check social distance in each pair. The definitions of the variables we employed in this paper are summarized in Table 1.

Fig. 1. Subjects in Room A

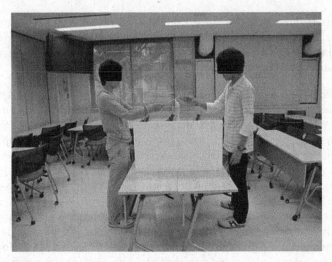

Fig. 2. Face-to-face interaction

Table 1. Quesionnairs

GSS	Normalized sum of de-meaned normalized and resigned GSS fair, GSS help, and GSS trust	
	GSS fair: "Do you think most people would try to take advantage of you if they got a chance, or would they try to be fair?"	1: Would take advantage of you; 2: would try to be fair; 1.5: depends; −: no answer/don't know
	GSS help: "Would you say that most of the time people try to be helpful, or that they are mostly just looking out for themselves?"	1: Try to be helpful; 2: just look out for themselves; 1.5: depends; −: no answer/don't know
	GSS trust: "Generally speaking, would you say that most people can be trusted or that you can't be too careful in dealing with people?"	1: Most people can be trusted; 2: can't be too careful; 1.5: depends; −: no answer/don't know
TrustBehave	Normalized and resigned sum of normalized Door unlocked, lend money, and lend possessions	
	Door unlocked: "How often do you leave your door unlocked?"	1: Very often; 2: often; 3: sometimes; 4: rarely; 5: never
	Lend money: "How often do you lend money to friends?"	1: More than once a week; 2: once a week; 3: once a month; 4: once a year or less
	Lend possessions: "How often do you lend personal possessions to friends?"	1: More than once a week; 2: once a week; 3: once a month; 4: once a year or less
TrustStranger	You can't count on strangers anymore	1: More or less disagree ; 0: More or less agree

TrustWorthi-ness	I am trustworthy	1: Disagree strongly; 2: Disagree somewhat; 3: Disagree slightly; 4: Agree slightly; 5: Agree somewhat; 6: Agree strongly
Re-pair	Do you want to be paired with the same person to share money even if he/she tells a lie?	1: Yes; 0: No
Re-pair2	Do you want to be paired with the same person after receiving the message?	1: Yes; 0: No
S_Known*	Relation to Role B	1: I have never seen him/her before; 2: I have seen but never talked to him/her; 3: I just exchange greetings with him/her; 4: I talk with him/her sometimes; 5: I often talk with him/her; he/she is a good friend of mine
S_Impression*	How do you feel about Role B?	1: Not good at all; 2: Not very good; 3: Neither good nor bad; 4: Good; 5: Very good
R_Known*	Relation to Role A	1: I have never seen him/her before; 2: I have seen but never talked to him/her; 3: I just exchange greetings with him/her; 4: I talk with him/her sometimes; 5: I often talk with him/her; he/she is a good friend of mine
R_Impression*	How do you feel about Role A (B)?	1: Not good at all; 2: Not very good; 3: Neither good nor bad; 4: Good; 5: Very good
Pair_MM*	Sender/receiver pairings	1: Male with male; 0: Others

Notes:* these variables are employed in the face-to-face interaction only.

3   Results

We conducted a total of 10 sessions with 200 students. The sessions lasted for 40–60 minutes. Each session consisted of 4–26 subjects, and they earned an average of approximately 1,500 JPY. Females were 38% of students. The average age was 20.1 years for students.

Figure 3 shows the proportion of offers from the employee's side that were beneficial to the customer ("best offers") and the ratio of approvals, i.e. ratio of customers who accepted what they were offered. These ratios are organized by whether the experiment involved face-to-face or anonymous interactions. In the results of the experiment, the ratio of best offers was 0.62 for face-to-face and 0.51 for anonymous interactions, so employees were more likely to make a best offer in face-to-face interactions. However, the results of Fisher's exact test did not exhibit statistical significance ($p = 0.17$). The rate of customer acceptance was 0.71 for face-to-face and 0.64 for anonymous interactions, again showing a higher ratio for face-to-face interactions. However, as before, the results of Fisher's exact test did not exhibit statistical significance ($p = 0.42$).In the interactions between students, a statistically significant difference based on whether an interaction was performed face to face or anonymously was not observed.

Next, we focus on the social attributes of the subjects, which are factors separate from the purposefully controlled environment in which the interactions took place. Here, in addition to basic data such as gender, household, and age, we used answers to the GSS and questions related to psychological factors such as trust in others, reliability of behavior, and self-reliance as representative variables for social capital, which was itself used as a representative variable for social distance. Furthermore, for experiments conducted as face-to-face interactions, we included partner impressions and levels of familiarity between partners as variables. Also, in measuring customer acceptance, we introduced a variable representing tolerance for the pair's falsehood.

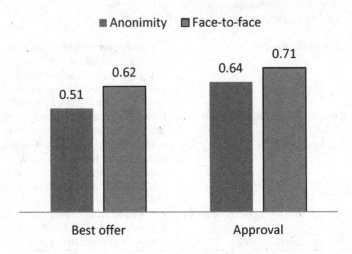

Fig. 3. Proportions of best offer and approval

With these as explanatory variables, and with the likelihood that an employee would make a best offer and the likelihood that a customer would agree to an offer as response variables, we performed a logit analysis. Tables 2 and 3 show the results. Concerning the likelihood of a best offer being made by an employee, in the anonymous interaction there were no statistically significant variables. In the face-to-face interaction, the only variable showing significance was TrustStrangers, with a p-value of 10%. This indicates that, in face-to-face interactions, the degree to which an employee trusted others corresponded to the rate at which they would submit a best offer. That is, in face-to-face interactions, a subject's trust in others had a strong effect. On the other hand, other variables, such as the impression a partner made (S_impression), did not show this effect. This indicates that the psychology of the party making the offer is the source of this effect.

Next, with regards to whether the customer accepted an offer or not, in the anonymous interaction, rather than trust scales, we found that Re-pair (tolerance for falsehood) had a negative effect with a p-value of 5%. The degree to which a person asserted that they would not tolerate someone lying to them corresponded to the likelihood that they would not agree to an offer. This tendency also appeared in face-to-face interactions as a significant factor with a p-value of 1%. The customer's tolerance for falsehood had a very strong effect on whether he or she would accept an offer. This appears to represent the extent to which a customer will be vigilant of, be conscious of the risks associated with, and be tolerant of a fraudulent offer from an employee in a real situation. Furthermore, in the face-to-face interactions, age showed a negative effect with a p-value of 5%. We found that how old a subject was corresponded to how readily they would refuse offers from an employee. As our subjects were undergraduate and graduate students, the range of possible ages was not large, but we still found that older subjects were less likely to accept offers. On the other hand, levels of trust, partner impressions (R_Impression), and degree of partner familiarity (R_Known) had no effects.

Table 2. Logit regressoin for lying

	Anonymous interaction	Face-to-face interaction
Female	0.40 (0.51)	0.13 (0.53)
Household	-0.14 (0.18)	-0.02 (0.13)
Age	0.04 (0.09)	-0.09 (0.12)
GSS	-0.07 (0.24)	-0.04 (0.22)
TrustBehave	-0.24 (0.25)	-0.26 (0.21)
TrustStranger	0.01 (0.54)	0.75* (0.41)
Trsutworthiness	-0.08 (0.19)	0.09 (0.15)
S_Known		-0.27 (0.21)
S_Impression		0.37 (0.26)
Men&Men		0.17 (0.53)
Constant	-0.35 (2.07)	0.52 (2.84)
Psedo R2	0.03	0.05
# of Obs.	70	129

Notes: Standard errors are in parentheses. *, **, and *** indicate significance at the 10%, 5%, and 1% levels, respectively.

Table 3. Logit regression for approval

	Anonymous interaction	Face-to-face interaction
Female	0.43 (0.60)	-0.42 (0.65)
Household	0.00 (0.17)	0.13 (0.15)
Age	-0.04 (0.13)	-0.31** (0.14)
GSS	0.08 (0.32)	-0.09 (0.27)
TrustBehave	-0.31 (0.29)	0.10 (0.28)
TrustStranger	-0.19 (0.61)	-0.53 (0.47)
Trsutworthiness	0.04 (0.26)	0.31 (0.19)
Repair	-1.14** (0.57)	-1.84*** (0.48)
R_Known		0.68* (0.35)
R_Impression		0.02 (0.30)
Men&Men		-0.62 (0.68)
Constant	1.78 (3.14)	6.22** (3.14)
Psedo R2	0.09	0.18
# of Obs.	68	129

Notes: Standard errors are in parentheses. *, **, and *** indicate significance at the 10%, 5%, and 1% levels, respectively.

4   Discussion

The fraction of lies in our observation is consistent with original study of Gneezy (2005), who found that larger stakes for students in the anonymity condition induced a higher fraction of lying. Fractions of trust were more than 0.6 for both treatments, which is consistent with the original study of Gneezy (2005), who found more than 60% of receivers trust messages. Lifting anonymity reduces the frequency of lying and non-approval but it does not have significant effects. This observation was consistent with Holm and Kawagoe (2010), who found that the face-to-face treatment reduces the fraction of lying. Our result implies a possibility that face-to-face communication closes social distance and enhances altruistic behavior. To see more robust statistical result as shown in Holm and Kawagoe (2010), it is needed to gather more data from subjects with various socio-economic background.

The logit analysis indicates what the most important measures of trust are. More than how well the subjects playing the employees knew the customers, or what sort of impression they made, the internal, psychological factor of how trusting they were of others generally had the most powerful effect. This indicates that they were not thinking of how their partner would respond to a fraudulent offer, but rather pondering larger questions about whether they could trust other people. According to these results, which indicate that trust in others has a strong effect on offers of service, it will be difficult to get employees to make best offers to customers simply by relying on their independence and human nature. Our research implies that employees must be educated in the best way to make an offer, and, more importantly, in the human and the mental aspects of offering services.

On the other hand, whether an offer was accepted or not was strongly reliant on the customer's tolerance for falsehood, regardless of whether customer acceptance occurred in face-to-face or anonymous interaction. This implies that customers always viewed offers with suspicion. The degree to which customers would not tolerate being lied to corresponded to how unlikely they were to agree to an offer. This implies a dislike of being deceived. In this experiment, subjects playing the role of customers did not know how benefits were distributed between themselves and the employee, and so made decisions based solely on messages received from the employee about what would benefit them. As such, whether they accepted an offer or not was a simple expression of whether they were willing to believe the employee. People who hated being lied to did not want to agree to the employee's offer. It appears that, more than the actual message from the employee, they disliked the possibility of trusting the employee and then being betrayed, and made decisions that opposed the employee as a result.

A customer's choice to accept a service was strongly affected by their own tolerance for falsehood. Conversely, this implies there are some people who will continue to frequent expensive restaurants or first-class hotels that lie about the food they serve. If customers are tolerant of falsehood, they will believe and agree to whatever the employee offers them. However, from the employee's perspective, regardless of whether they take pains to make best offers, they may offend their customers if their offer is not believed. In the long run, they may damage their customers' trust. By demonstrating that the customer is not being lied to, they can make clear that they are offering a genuine service. For example, in a restaurant, this would be accomplished by having things like an open kitchen or a broadcast showing the activity in the kitchen, therefore ensuring that the food preparation process is transparent. Due to this problem of trust, systems and methods by which to reassure the customer become issues of importance.

5 Conclusions

In this experiment, we observed increases in the rate at which employees made best offers and the rates at which customers accepted offers when face-to-face interviews were conducted. As a statistically significant difference was not observed, the next topic of investigation will be to collect data from a broader sample set. Also, the level of trust in others reported by the subject playing the role of the employee had a statistically significant positive effect in cases in which the employee made a best offer. It was also observed that, regardless of whether the interaction was conducted face to face or anonymously, if the subject playing the role of the customer exhibited a low level of tolerance for falsehood, he or she was less likely to accept offers. Our research indicates that, in service interactions between employees and customers, the importance of trusting relationships is unambiguous. Trust in others and tolerance for falsehood have clear effects on such interactions.

However, as our sample was composed of students, it lacked variation in terms of social attributes, and each of the variables that we used to measure social distance also lacked variation. In future experiments, it will be important to include even more variables related to social capital such as feelings of trust, isolation, and loneliness, and also to assemble a sample with a broader range of age brackets. We expect our next topic to include an experiment asking whether having a person lie to a customer, apologize, and be forgiven will build a trusting relationship. Based on such an experiment, it may be possible to understand how long-term relationships of trust that occur in service interactions are established. In this sense, the results of this experiment have shed new light on how trust is established between employees and customers in the offering and consumption of services.

Acknowledgments. This work was supported by JSPS KAKENHI Grant-in-Aid for Young Scientists. We also wish to acknowledge the helpful comments of the participants in the 2014 Japan Servicelogy conference in Hakodate. Further, we thank Yoko Terada, Shizuru Yamagiwa, Katsuyuki Aoki for their assistance in conducting the experiment.

References

1. Bochet, O., Page, T., & Putterman, L. (2006). Communication and punishment in voluntary contribution experiments. *Journal of Economic Behavior & Organization, 60*(1), 11-26.
2. Bohnet, I., & Frey, B. S. (1999a). Social distance and other-regarding behavior in dictator games: Comment. *American Economic Review, 89*(1), 335-340.

3. Bohnet, I., & Frey, B. S. (1999b). The sound of silence in prisoner's dilemma and dictator games. *Journal of Economic Behavior & Organization, 38*(1), 43-57.
4. Brosig, J., Weimann, J., & Ockenfels, A. (2003). The effect of communication media on cooperation. *German Economic Review, 4*(2), 217-241.
5. Burnham, T. (2003). Engineering altruism: a theoretical and experimental investigation of anonymity and gift giving. *Journal of Economic Behavior & Organization, 50*(1), 133-144.
6. Charness, G., & Gneezy, U. (2008). What's in a name? Anonymity and social distance in dictator and ultimatum games. *Journal of Economic Behavior & Organization, 68*(1), 29-35.
7. Childs, J. (2012). Gender differences in lying. *Economics Letters, 114*(2), 147-149.
8. Dreber, A., & Johannesson, M. (2008). Gender differences in deception. *Economics Letters, 99*(1), 197-199.
9. Frohlich, N., & Oppenheimer, J. (1998). Some consequences of e-mail vs. face-to-face communication in experiment. *Journal of Economic Behavior & Organization, 35*(3), 389-403.
10. Gneezy, U. (2005). Deception: The role of consequences. *American Economic Review, 95*(1), 384-394.
11. Gächter, S., Herrmann, B., & Thöni, C. (2004). Trust, voluntary cooperation, and socioeconomic background: survey and experimental evidence. *Journal of Economic Behavior & Organization, 55*(4), 505-531.
12. Holm, H. J., & Kawagoe, T. (2010). Face-to-Face Lying–an experimental study in Sweden and Japan. *Journal of Economic Psychology, 31*(3), 310-321.
13. Isaac, R. M., & Walker, J. M. (1988). Communication and free-riding behavior - The voluntary contribution mechanism. *Economic Inquiry, 26*(4), 585-608.
14. Lacey, S., Bruwer, J., & Li, E. (2009). The role of perceived risk in wine purchase decisions in restaurants. *International Journal of Wine Business Research, 21*(2), 99-117.
15. Roth, A. (1995). Bargaining Experiments. *Handbook of Experimental Economics*, ed. by J. Kagel and A. Roth. Princeton, NJ: Princeton University Press, pp.253-348.
16. Scharlemann, J. P. W., Eckel, C. C., Kacelnik, A., & Wilson, R. K. (2001). The value of a smile: Game theory with a human face. *Journal of Economic Psychology, 22*(5), 617–640.
17. Sutter, M. (2009). Deception through telling the truth?! experimental evidence from individuals and teams. *The Economic Journal, 119*(534), 47-60.

Development of a Three-Stage Public Observation Service System Model with Logics for Observation/Assessment

Satoko Tsuru[1*] and Maki Kariyazaki[2]

[1] The University of Tokyo, 7-3-1 Hongo, Bunkyo-ku, Tokyo, 113-8656 JAPAN
tsuru@tqm.t.u-tokyo.ac.jp
[2] The University of Tokyo, 7-3-1 Hongo, Bunkyo-ku, Tokyo, 113-8656 JAPAN
kariyazaki@tqm.t.u-tokyo.ac.jp

Abstract. We considered appropriate frameworks and functions for the public observation service system and created a 3-stage model for it with logics for observation to ensure the quality of required functions by reducing unintended omission and unevenness due to human characteristics. The study method and tool were used for all children belonging to an elementary school in X district. The public observation support service system based on the 3-stage model with a logic for observation, may facilitate the logical and efficient identification of problems, management of cause analysis results, and reasonable promotion of liaison among those involved in personalized support. This system to support the observation of children's growth and development provides a basis for creating a value of co-creation. This study provided a basis for maximizing the value of co-creation in public services, aiming to nurture human resources for the future.

Keywords: public service, observation service, system framework, problem solving, three-stage logic for observation

1   Introduction

When residents recognize their own need for support, they seek public/private support resources, and adopt actions to access them. However, if their abilities to: 1) recognize, 2) demand, 3) seek, 4) and obtain necessary support are insufficient, their conditions may deteriorate, and become serious, resulting in the development of social problems. In order to address this, it is necessary for local governments to provide 'observation services', through which they previously assess communities, households, and residents with an increased risk of such situations, and prevent it from further increasing while observing changes in negative factors.

Traditionally, in both urban and rural areas of Japan, systems that enable residents to participate, perform activities, and lead their daily lives in their communities had been established by the mechanism of 'mutual help and assistance'. However, with economic development, interpersonal relationships in households and communities have become poor, consequently weakening such a mechanism, and interfering with

© Springer International Publishing AG 2017
Y. Hara and D. Karagiannis (Eds.): ICServ 2017, LNCS 10371, pp. 75–87, 2017.
DOI: 10.1007/978-3-319-61240-9_8

the identification of residents requiring help and provision of support for them throughout Japan. This has brought unexpected results, such as 'lonely death', abuse, and crimes.

Under these circumstances, observation services provided by local governments may be crucial. Such services should aim to predict and prevent safety and other risks by observing the statuses of residents and communities. They should also be provided while sufficiently considering issues, such as the population and area of each community, service users and the diversity of their problems, and the cost performance of using public resources. Their provision as public services is difficult, unless systems to provide them with fairness, logicality, and efficiency are established.

2   Purpose

This study aims to consider appropriate frameworks and functions for the public observation service system; and create a 3-stage model for it with logics for observation to ensure the quality of such functions by reducing unintended omission and unevenness due to human characteristics.

We investigate a problem to be resolved for public service from the viewpoint of service science.

3   Target setting and procedure

A research project was performed, involving elementary school children as community residents whose abilities to: 1) recognize, 2) demand, 3) seek, 4) and obtain necessary support are insufficient, and appropriate systems to observe their growth and development were considered through collaboration with a local government (the Section of Educational Affairs and Board of Education), a medical association, and the Department of Pediatrics of a university hospital located in a district of the Tokyo Metropolitan area. The study procedure was implemented in 5 steps:

Step 1: conducting a status survey on elementary school children's growth, and identifying related challenges from a medical viewpoint (short stature);

Step 2: conducting a status survey on activities to support elementary school children's growth and development, and identifying related challenges;

Step 3: designing a framework for the observation support system;

Step 4: designing a 3-stage model with logics for observation to be used in public and private spaces; and

Step 5: using it as a system to support the observation of elementary school children's growth and development

We obtained agreement for this study from the board of education and medical association of District X, Pediatrics Laboratory in the Jikei University School of Medicine and Tsuru Laboratory in the University of Tokyo. District X has about 50 public elementary schools, and the living standard of this district is considered approximately the same as the national standard. The ethics committee of the Jikei University School of Medicine approved the study, and children's health data were anonymized. We are continuing this study from 2014.

4   Design and Development

4.1. A status survey on elementary school children's growth, and identifying related challenges from a medical viewpoint (short stature)

Health problems in children should be identified and treated promptly so that the condition does not hinder their development. In elementary school, school nurses are responsible for health management among the children. Growth disorder is an important health problem that should be detected by school nurses. Cotterill et al. show that body measurement made by them would be sufficiently reliable for screening of growth disorder [1]. The two symptoms of this are short stature and growth failure. Short stature is defined as a height value that is 2 standard deviations (SD) below the mean for age. In contrast, growth failure is difficult to define [2], and hence, various studies have defined it differently. For example, Jonathan [3] defined it as growth deceleration (falling across major percentiles on the growth curve). Growth disorder has many different causes [4], and therefore, it is not only a symptom of another disease, but also an environmental condition [5,6,7,8,9]. Furthermore, growth disorder may cause another problem. For example, younger and shorter children tend to be bullied in the classroom [10]. Hence, a focus on the height of the children may facilitate the detection and prevention of various health and social problems.

However, each school has only one school nurse. The nurse's skills have to spread over several tasks that have to be done each day: treating children's injuries, investigating school hygiene, providing health guidance, and ensuring the children's mental health care. At present, they are unable to always detect children's health problems such as growth disorder because of a lack of knowledge, intuition, and time.
In addition to early detection, early treatment is also important [11,12]. However, information available to the school nurse is not sufficient; accordingly, players involved in the children's health care such as their homes, schools, and hospitals have to share information. Cooperation between school nurses and these players will enable the analysis of the problems children have and the provision of appropriate treatment [13].
Growth disorder is an important problem in child health. School nurses are responsible for child health management in elementary schools; although this task is important, it is also difficult. We aimed to develop a support system for school nurses performing this task [14]. First, we focused on the screening process for growth disorders, and developed a method to identify these conditions regardless of the differences of in their ability, by using height data of approximately 400 students from the fourth to sixth grades in elementary school. Second, we evaluated the

process of examining the condition in each child after screening. Finally, we developed a supporting tool that school nurses can use, in practice. This system could help school nurses in managing children health.

The information required to analyze the problem is dispersed among various players, so cooperation of the players is required. In this study, we developed a method where school nurses gather information about children, analyze it, and determine the appropriate intervention.

First, we designed the following narrowing process so that school nurses can analyze problems efficiently and effectively.

- Primary narrowing: They gather information such as medical history and allergies from medical checkups.
- Secondary narrowing: They ask homeroom teachers questions not only about health but also about lifestyle, home environment, and friendship.
- Tertiary narrowing: They ask people at home detailed questions to obtain information that could not be obtained in the previous phases.

4.2. A status survey on activities to support elementary school children's growth and development, and identifying related challenges

Elementary school days are the most important period of children's growth process. Delays in the identification of growth-related problems may lead to the occurrence of intellectual, mental, or physical impairments. As children's self-care abilities are limited, it is necessary to mainly manage their health in their households, but the management capacity varies among households. Therefore, educational institutions play an important role in identifying growth-related problems in the early stages. In Japanese elementary schools, health examinations for all students are conducted 3 times annually, and data, such as somatometric values, necessary for screening are stored as records. In recent years, approximately 80% of all public schools throughout Japan have adopted the school affairs support system to manage information necessary to operate schools, including health-related data such as somatometric records. This facilitates the comprehensive management of all data regarding school activities, such as student lists, class attendance-related information, learning achievements, and events, in a single system. Using the system, it is possible to manage the results of health examinations at school, mainly somatometric records, as electronic data.

We examined the statuses of use of the school affairs support system and related data entry in a district of the Tokyo Metropolitan area. The system was initially adopted in all public elementary and junior high schools in FY 2011. However, the rate of entering health examination results, such as heights and weights, varied among schools, showing a mean of approximately 60%. Problematic issues, such as the situation in which the Board of Education had adopted a similar system, but they were unable to manage the status of data entry, were also revealed.

Furthermore, analytical support systems with algorithms to identify problems, represented by growth disorder, underweight, and obesity, incorporated were unavailable, necessitating the school nurse at each school to perform this procedure manually, without sufficient quality. Thus, although a data management system was available, data entry was arbitrary, and the use of entered data was difficult. We noted this as an operational problem, and recognized the necessity of making data entry obligatory and offering data analysis support systems.

4.3. Design of a framework for the observation support system

This system consists of core, support, and management systems (Fig.1). Core system is processes associated directly with health management service from problem detection to daily observation. There are processes of problem detection, cause analysis, improvement activity, and daily observation in Core system. Support system including necessities for the core system such as human resources, tools, information technology and so on. Management system is a section for overall grasp and management. Core system is observation service support system.

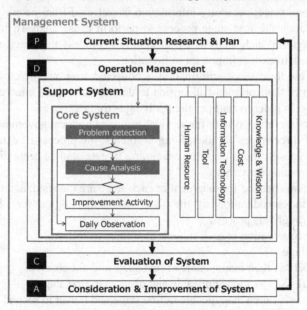

Fig. 1. Framework of the Public observation services System

Public observation services provided by the core system are expected to address the following challenges: 1) covering the entire population and area of each community; 2) considering the diversity of problems faced by targets; 3) using public resources efficiently; and 4) ensuring the appropriates of activities in both public and private spaces. Thus, the system should be designed with the following functions: 1) screening to process extensive data, and identify problems within a short time; 2) navigating to efficiently collect information needed to clarify the cause of each problem; 3) selecting optimal intervention methods and observers to resolve each challenge; and 4) promoting liaison with observers.

4.4 Design of a three-stage model with logics for observation to be used in public and private spaces

In the observation system for services provided by local governments, observation targets are extracted through three-stages. Each stage is designed with a combination of functions related to 'data and information used' and 'narrowing down' (Fig.2).

In the first stage, targets with an increased risk are identified using data representing the statuses of communities and residents of the district. The reasonable management of extensive data and persons to extract problematic cases is an important viewpoint for this process. At this point, it is necessary to: 1) incorporate a reasonable logic to process extensive data within a short time; and 2) establish a system to provide support in accordance with each target's condition.

In the second stage, necessary information is collected from people around targets extracted through the first stage process to perform cause analysis. It is possible to efficiently perform such analysis by designing a process that navigates observers' thought process to extract important information.

Lastly, in the third stage, information is collected from people close to targets in consideration of their problems identified to determine optimal intervention methods and observers, in order to start problem-solving activities.

Thus, the observation system for services provided by local governments is a model consisting of three-stages: 1) identifying problems: the process of extracting targets, 2) analyzing causes: the process of examining targets, and 3) promoting liaison and starting intervention for targets.

Standard items needed for judgment in each stage are clarified, and their values are determined in consideration of the local situation. Logics for observation are developed through this process.

The logic for observation in each stage is expressed as follows:

a)First stage

If $X1<a1$ then inapplicable in first stage and not observe

If $a1<X1<b1$ then applicable and observe in first stage

If $b1<X1$ then inapplicable in first stage and transit to second stage

b)Second stage

If $X2<a2$ then inapplicable in second stage and transit to first stage

If $a2<X2<b2$ then applicable and observe in second stage

If $b2<X2$ then inapplicable in second stage and transit to third stage

c)Third stage

If $X3<a3$ then inapplicable in third stage and transit to second stage

If $a3<X3<b3$ then applicable and observe in third stage

If $b3<X3$ then choice of applicable intervention and provision it

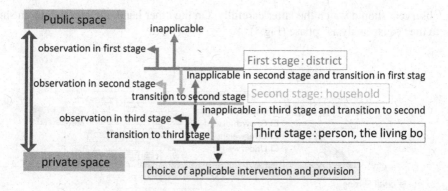

Fig. 2. A model consisting of three-stages

4.5. Use of the model as a system to support the observation of elementary school children's growth and development

We used the system model to elementary school, designed detail.

Core system has processes of problem detection, cause analysis, improvement activity, and daily observation for healthy child growth management. We took advantage of body measurement data from school health examinations to detect "growth problems" efficiently. The methodology for judging the presence or absence of abnormality was developed using indexes of height and weight.

"Growth problem" refers to not only defects that have already occurred but also every matter in need of some action considering both present and future. Therefore, "action" requires regional support such as improvement of lifestyle or living environment.

Next, a "cause" has to be specified in order to solve any problems. This includes not only direct but also indirect factors. We should clarify the relationship between a "growth problem" and its "cause" and decide what kind of intervention is needed. Therefore, we developed follows.

- visualization of process flowchart
- development of problem detecting Logic
- development of a support tool
- design of database structure for cause analysis

The state of children's growth is classified into "normally," "observation," and "cause analysis" through a combination of physical findings based on height and weight. The children classified into "normally" and "observation" transfer to the phase of observation. However, the management levels of the two are different. The observers should watch the latter carefully. On the other hand, the other children shift to the "cause analysis" phase (Fig.3).

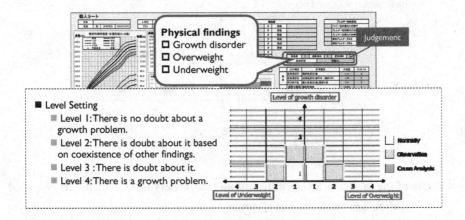

Fig. 3. Comprehensive Judgement

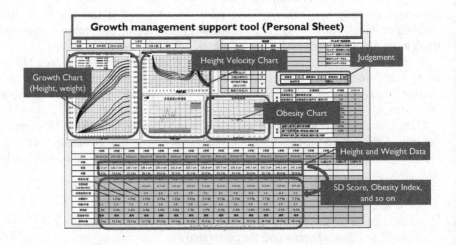

Fig. 4. The personal data sheet in support tool for growth management

We developed a support tool that can utilize the body measurement data efficiently and effectively and extract information necessary to analyze the growth problem [15]. This support is mainly for early detection, since the tool can calculate the SD score and obesity index and plot the growth curves of all children based on the data input into the school job support system. It can thereby diagnose growth problems automatically, using the previously mentioned rule. Height and weight data and the growth chart for each child are output in a single sheet. When a child is suspected to have a growth disorder, the tool outputs a danger signal. Aside from the personal data sheet, this tool has functions to visualize the distribution of all school data and to search optional children in a collective data sheet (Fig.4).

As shown below, the processes of analyzing causes for children identified as those with problems are classified into 3 stages: 1) the process can be performed only by school nurses or other persons in charge of health management; 2) the process includes interviews with homeroom teachers to collect information related to the children; and 3) the process requires access to the children's households to collect further information.

Through these processes, optimal intervention methods to clarify the causes and improve the situation are determined. Such interventions address: lifestyle-related factors by improving diets, exercise habits, and sleep; environmental factors by improving school and home environments; and disorder-related factors by promoting consultation in medical institutions. When it is difficult to clarify the causes, the children are classified into: those requiring consultation in medical institutions; those requiring course observation; and those without problems, based on their physical findings (Fig.5).

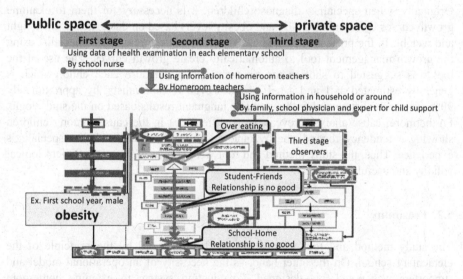

Fig. 5. Process of three stages in an elementary school children

5.   Trial use of the study method

The study method and tool were used for all children belonging to an elementary school in X district. Their logical validity and usefulness were examined as follows:

The use of the tool we developed to identify problems made the creation of personal sheets and diagnosis for nearly 650 children within approximately 2 hours (approximately 10 seconds per person) feasible. It was confirmed that automatic diagnosis provided by the tool facilitates screening within such a short time frame. Based on their diagnostic results, less than 10% of children were shifted to the cause analysis unit.

Cause analyses were performed for the target children. Excluding those for whom data entry was clearly erroneous and those with whom interviews were not possible due to moving out of the district, 29 were managed through the second stage process. During this process, an interview with the homeroom teacher of each child was conducted, and the relevant cause analysis was completed. In all cases, in which the necessity of the third stage process and the causes of problems were clarified, actions to be adopted for improvement were advised.

Based on these results, interviews with the principle of the elementary school and medical association in the district were also conducted to examine the feasibility of the study system.

5.1. Logical validity and usefulness of the study method/tool

Originally, when specialists diagnose children, it is necessary for them to examine growth curves by calculating SDs and obesity levels based on data, such as the height and weight. In the present pilot study, diagnosis was performed by a specialist using the growth management tool to automatically create growth curves. The use of the tool was suggested to shorten the time needed to diagnose each child, which is generally estimated at 1 and a half minutes even for specialists, by approximately 90%. The specialist agreed with automatic judgment results based on the study logic. Furthermore, cause analyses revealed sex differences in the causes among children showing a tendency toward obesity, and this was consistent with the specialist's experience. Thus, the study method and tool were shown to have a sufficient logical validity and usefulness.

5.2. Feasibility

The study method and tool were also regarded as useful by the principle of the elementary school. On the other hand, as the necessity of an operational model and supporters was noted, we designed a navigation system to examine homeroom teachers' thought process, and collect information. The chairman of the Committee of Pediatrics of the local medical association also favorably evaluated the study method/tool, and recommended their use on a community-wide basis. By sharing data obtained using this growth management support tool with school doctors, it may also be possible to obtain support from doctors. The Section of Educational Affairs of X district made health examination data entry obligatory for elementary schools, and ensured a budget for past data entry. These outcomes also support the feasibility of the study method.

6   Discussion

6.1. Advantages of this system as a service system

Interactions between teachers as professionals and students are important to strengthen the value of co-creation in education services. In the case of children, it is necessary to provide education services while supporting their growth and development. This system to support the observation of children's growth and development provides a basis for creating a value of co-creation.

The system has 3 advantages: 1) logically and efficiently identifying children with health problems; 2) logically and efficiently supporting teachers who analyze the causes of such problems from the perspectives of daily life, diseases, and environments; and 3) providing players in charge of problem-solving intervention with information regarding corresponding children's developmental histories and the results of analysis. Advantage 1) reduces human errors related to judgment by shortening the time needed for screening and processing, with multiple logics for medical and epidemiological judgment; 2) reduces the energy and time needed for thoughts, as the system is designed to guide thoughts toward the clarification of causes through a process based on medical interviews; and 3) facilitates the efficient and effective use of the obtained information.

6.2. Remaining issues of the proposed system

The system may improve the quality of education services by: identifying problems related to children's growth and development; logically and efficiently supporting the process of analyzing the causes; creating time for players involved with education services; and reducing the energy needed for thoughts. It is also suggested to provide children without such problems with an enhanced value of co-creation. On the other hand, as a future perspective, it is necessary to design appropriate intervention for those with growth- and development-related problems, and develop functions to sup-port the efficient and effective implementation of such intervention. These approaches will facilitate the realization of a PDCA cycle that covers all children.

6.3. Challenging points and/or contribution of this study as service research

The present study provided a basis for maximizing the value of co-creation in public services, aiming to nurture human resources for the future. It also provided useful findings on the development of methodologies to ensure logicality necessary for the classification service users, as well as those for the efficient typification of individual cases.

6.4. Problem to be resolved for public service from the viewpoint of service science

As the majority of public services are provided by local governments, their quality depends on such governments' organizational abilities, and consequently varies among districts. Therefore, it is necessary to improve the quality of public services by visualizing them and organizing them as logics, while streamlining the process of providing them.

7   Conclusion

The public observation support service system based on the 3-stage model with a logic for observation, may facilitate the logical and efficient identification of problems, management of cause analysis results, and reasonable promotion of liaison among those involved in personalized support. As a future perspective, the system will be further used for elementary school children while developing such systems for other community residents.

Ackowledgement

We deeply thank for collaboration of this project members and these organizations, Dr. Takanori Motoki, Dr. Masako Fujiwara, Prof. Hiroyuki Ida, Dr.Hitoshi Mio, Mr. Yuichi Shiozawa, Mr. Kazunari Ishiai, Mr. Yusuke Suzuki, Mr. Katsuhiko Kubo and Mr. Akito Kuwajima.

Part of this work was supported by Research Institute of Science and Technology for Society (RISTEX) : Creating a Safe and Secure Living Environment in the Changing Public and Private Spheres. ID 16816144 "Research and Development of Public-Private Connected Caring Model Respond to Multiple Help-Longing in Urban Environment " Susumu Shimazono   Director, Institute of Grief Care, Sophia University and Satoko Tsuru as co-reseacher, University of Tokyo.

References

1. Cotterill, A., Majrowski, W., Hearn, S., Jenkins, S. and Savage, M., "Assessment of the reliability of school nurse height measurements in an inner-city population. (The Hackney Growth Initiative)", Child Care Health Dev, Vol.19, No.3, pp.159-165(1993)
2. Stalman, S., Hellinga, I., van Dommelen, P., Hennekam, R., Saari, A., Sankilampi, U., Dunkel, L., Wit, J., Kamp, G. and Plötz, F., "Application of the Dutch, Finnish and British Screening Guidelines in a Cohort of Children with Growth Failure", Horm Res Paediatr. (2015)
3. Jonathan, E. ·T., "Growth/development", In a Page: Signs & Symptoms, editated by In Scott, K. and Smith, E. G., Lippincott Williams & Wilkins, Pennsylvania, p.24(2004)

4. Rogol, A. and Hayden, G., "Etiologies and Early Diagnosis of Short Stature and Growth Failure in Children and Adolescents", The Journal of Pediatrics, Vol.164, No.5, pp.S1-S14(2014)
5. Mukaida, K., Kusunoki, T., Morimoto, T., Yasumi, T., Nishikomori, R., Heike, T., Fujii, T. and Nakahata, T., "The Effect of Past Food Avoidance Due to Allergic Symptoms on the Growth of Children at School Age", Allergology International, Vol.59, No.4, pp.369-374(2010)
6. Lee, E., Park, M., Ahn, H. and Lee, S., "Differences in Dietary Intakes between Normal and Short Stature Korean Children Visiting a Growth Clinic", Clin Nutr Res., Vol.1, No.1, pp.23-29 (2012)
7. Castaño, L., Restrepo, A., Rueda, J., Aguirre, C. and López, L., "The effects of socioeconomic status and short stature on overweight, obesity and the risk of metabolic complications in adults", Colomb Med (Cali), Vol.44, No.3, pp.146-154(2013)
8. Naruse, Y., Tada, H., Izawa, M. and Hamashima, T., "Siblings that exhibited significant growth failure as the example of inadequate dietary restrictions from mother" (Japanese), Pharma Medica, Vol.31, No.6, p.167(2013)
9. Wattchow, N., Lee, H. and Brock, P., "Psychosocial short stature with psychosis: a case report", Australas Psychiatry, Vol.23, No.1, pp.63-65 (2013)
10. Naiki, Y., Horikawa, R., Tanaka, T., and Child Health and Development Network, "Assessment of Psychosocial Status among Short-stature Children with and without Growth Hormone Therapy and Their Parents" (Japanese), Clinical Pediatric Endocrinology, Vol.22, No.2, pp.25-32(2013)
11. Darendeliler, F., Lindberg, A. and Wilton, P., "Response to growth hormone treatment in isolated growth hormone deficiency versus multiple pituitary hormone deficiency", Horm Res Paediatr, Vol.76, No.1, pp.42-46 (2011)
12. Antoniazzi, F., Cavarzere, P. and Gaudino, R., "Growth hormone and early treatment", Minerva Endocrinol, Vol.40, No.2, pp.129-143 (2015)
13. Procter, S., Brooks, F., Wilson, P., Crouchman, C. and Kendall, S., "A case study of asthma care in school age children using nurse-coordinated multidisciplinary collaborative practices", J Multidiscip Healthc, Vol.8, No.8, pp.181-188 (2015)
14. Kariyazaki Maki, Tsuru Satoko, Motoki Takanori and Fujiwara Masako: Development of Early Detection and Problem Analysis Methods for Growth Disorders among Elementary School Students -The Methods based on Height Data- , Total Quality Science Vol.2, No.2 91-104 (2016)
15. Kariyazaki Maki, Tsuru Satoko, Motoki Takanori and Fujiwara Masako: Development of Growth Management Support Tool and Structure of Information Gathering for Child Health, Total Quality Science (accepted) (2017)

Service Innovation and Marketing

An Analysis of the Cognitive Processes Related to "Service Awareness" of Cabin Attendants

Ryo Fukushima[1*], Koji Tachioka[1], Tatsunori Hara[1], Jun Ota[1],

Yuki Tsuzaka[2], and Narito Arimitsu[2]

[1]The University of Tokyo, Tokyo, Japan
[2]ANA Strategic Research Institute Co., Ltd, Tokyo, Japan
fukushima@race.u-tokyo.ac.jp

Abstract. The purpose of the present study is to develop a way by which junior cabin attendants (CAs) can get the customer service skills dependent on experience as soon as possible. To achieve this, it is effective to analyze the service skills of skilled CAs. We argue that one customer service skill that varies widely among CAs, depending on variation in work experience, is "service awareness." The term "service awareness" is defined as a related series of cognitive skills that includes "the CA perceives a passenger's needs before that passenger verbalizes them and finds ways to satisfy those needs." This research will examine the cognition processes of the CAs as they perform customer service. Cognition in this context refers to things the CAs noticed as well as their feelings and thoughts while providing service. We record CAs' customer service behavior and conducted retrospective interviews referring to the footage. After that, we analyze the interviews based on the grounded theory approach to get to know the relationship between cognition and conducted customer service. As a result, we gained an understanding that the cognitive process of "inferring a passenger's persona and investigating services to fulfill it" is crucial.

Keywords. Cognitive Process, Service Process Model, Qualitative Research, Grounded Theory Approach

1 Background

The airline industry has recently been experiencing a general increase in the number of air passengers worldwide and continued strong growth is anticipated. Along with efforts to enhance its international network, All Nippon Airways (ANA), the leading Japanese airline, is hiring increasing numbers of cabin attendants (CAs), which decreases the average length of CA tenure. It is necessary for junior CAs to acquire effective service skills to improve the quality of customer service. We argue that one customer service skill that varies widely among CAs, depending on variation in work experience, is "service awareness." The term "service awareness" is defined as a related

© Springer International Publishing AG 2017
Y. Hara and D. Karagiannis (Eds.): ICServ 2017, LNCS 10371, pp. 91–100, 2017.
DOI: 10.1007/978-3-319-61240-9_9

series of cognitive skills that includes "the CA perceives a passenger's needs before that passenger verbalizes them and finds ways to satisfy those needs."

The purpose of the present study is to develop a way by which junior CAs can understand and obtain the concept of service awareness in the context of their work. As Shuman et al. stated that "process skills" such as communication and teamwork can be taught by active and cooperative learning [1], it must be also possible to teach service awareness to junior CAs. To achieve this, it is effective to analyze the service skills of skilled CAs. This paper initially describes relevant studies and past research findings of the authors regarding service awareness of cabin attendants (CAs). Thereafter, it discusses the approaches used in this research and describes the measurement experiment and interview results conducted to investigate "service awareness" displayed by CAs when performing their duties toward their customers. Finally, it describes the CA customer service process model.

2   Relevant Studies

2.1   Research measuring the behaviors and identifying the customer service skills of employees

Due to the lack of appropriate methods to evaluate employee skills in the food service industry, Kurata et al. proposed a skill evaluation system that utilizes employee behavioral measurement and visualization systems [2]. The system is composed of a Pedestrian Dead-Reckoning (PDR) terminal that performs differential positioning and a sensor-data fusion system that calibrates, initializes tracking, and improves accuracy. It also includes a performance index to help determine issues in the workplace that require improvement based on the results of motion tracking using a visualization tool, determine the behaviors that require improvement, and evaluate the effectiveness of those efforts using POS data. In addition, based on the results of improvement activities, it examines the acquisition of customer service skills using an employee's precision and recall as measured by order acquisitions, and makes proposals regarding employees' skill improvement processes based on the following four employee categories: Lack of goal awareness type, working at full capacity type, precise type, and veteran type.

2.2   Past findings and tasks of this research

The authors conducted analyses of customer service skills of cabin attendants (CAs). Besides conducting behavioral measurements of CAs using the method described in 2.1 with the cooperation of the Service, Sensing, Assimilation, and Modeling Research Group of the Human Informatics Research Institute in the National Institute of Advanced Industrial Science and Technology (AIST), The authors analyzed customer service skills of CAs by making behavioral observations and developed a CA customer service process model that considers "service awareness" [3]. Behavioral observations, visual confirmation of task contents, positioning and details of customer service behavior, and recording onto a paper medium revealed the reasons for and details of the communications between CAs and passengers. From this, differences were noticed between junior CAs and skilled CAs, such as the time they spent serving drinks and the frequency of cabin inspection.

Based on the above, Tachioka et al. considered passive and active behavioral decision-making strategies [4], which they combined with the knowledge gained from behavioral measurements and observations to develop the CA customer service process model indicated in Figure 1. While this model shows the characteristics of the CA customer service, of which "service awareness" is a part, the knowledge they gained from behavioral observations is fragmented. There is no clarity on the cognition processes involved while carrying out the service (i.e., why a specific service was carried out).

Fig. 1. CA-customer service process model including both passive and active behavior decision-making strategy[3]

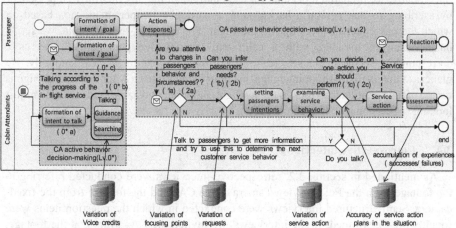

3   Research Methods

3.1   Cognition, the focus of this research

From the background given above, this research will examine the cognition processes of the CAs as they perform customer service. Cognition in this context refers to things the CAs noticed as well as their feelings and thoughts while providing service.

3.2   Recording customer service behavior

We draw out the cognitive processes in the CAs through a retrospective interview regarding their customer service behavior after serving the passengers. However, the CAs may find it difficult to recall their customer service behavior and conditions. To resolve this problem, Kitajima et al. conducted interviews based on footage from a field-of-view camera worn by the subjects and investigated how the decline of cognitive functions in the elderly is tied to their behavior on the premises of a railway station [5]. Similarly, in this research, CAs wore a field-of-view camera, and retrospective interviews were conducted referring to the first-person footage recorded.

3.3   Persona and scenario

In recording the customer service behavior of CAs within this research, experiment cooperators played the role of passengers on the aircraft. Subsequently, the experiments were conducted in a cabin mockup, an on-the-ground training facility resembling a cabin. Recreating this service environment was to draw out the cognitive aspects of the CAs during the service. We also attempted making passenger roles realistic. Specifically, we prepared a persona for each individual playing the role of a passenger by ascribing to that person a background, a particular temperament, etc., based on which the passenger behaves during the flight. For example, as a persona, we set "a businessman in his 40s, with a calm and conservative personality," and as a corresponding scenario, we set "(during boarding) he gets to his seat smoothly. He glances at the in-flight-shopping magazine after being seated. (After the seatbelt sign is turned off) he continues to look at the in-flight-shopping magazine, and states, 'I'm just looking' when engaged in a conversation."

3.4   Retrospective interviews

As mentioned in section 3.2, retrospective interviews were conducted referring to the footage from the field-of-view camera of the CAs and the footage from the fixed-camera. Semi-structured interviews were conducted in which the question items were roughly pre-determined. In the interviews, we invited the CAs to look at the footage, recollect what they could while they served customers, and to speak freely so that their cognition processes come into full play. When the CAs were speaking, the footage was paused and we asked them four questions regarding ① Things they noticed; ② What led them to notice such things; ③ Things that came to their mind while observing passenger behavior; and ④ Reasons for performing/not performing a particular service.

3.5   Interview analysis based on the grounded theory approach

By conducting retrospective interviews, we obtained speech data that pertain to cognitive processes while the CAs carried out their service. From this data, we analyzed the cognitive characteristics of each CA. We utilized the grounded theory approach (henceforth, GTA). GTA is a methodology by which roles played by characters in a particular situation and their interactions and the resulting multiple processes of change are expressed as a theory[6]. GTA, characterized by its ability to derive theories from phenomena, is considered most suitable for this research.

GTA procedure comprises (1) – (4) below: (1) segregate interview data into text fragments; (2) understand the characteristics of the text fragment data; (3) categorize text fragments; (4) understand the relationship between the categories; and (5) write out new findings from the relationship between categories.

In (1), we gained an understanding of the contents of the interview data. Subsequently, we fragmented the data based on their meaning. When segregating the text fragment data, sentences with different implications were separated based on their meaning. For example, in this experiment, we obtained a text fragment data: "I thought about the fact that he was wearing a mask while walking, and when I gave him the blanket, I think at that moment, I was thinking of what should I say next."

In (2), we gained an understanding of the characteristics of the text fragment data. We extracted contents from the text fragment data, which we called properties and dimensions. "Properties" refer to the perspectives of looking at the data and the sections into which they are divided. As a specific example of properties, we have "things one remembered while walking." "Dimensions" refer to the characteristics of the data from the perspective of the property created. The dimension corresponding to the prior-mentioned property would be, "he was wearing a mask."

Having indicated as many properties and dimensions as possible against the text fragments, we created a label that simply represents a given text fragment. If we were to label a specific example, it would be "reflecting on what to say while walking."

In (3), all text fragment data are compared and categorized. As an example of a text fragment similar to a specific example of a text fragment, we have the label, "troubled by serving a passenger with a stomachache." By combining, we have the category, "thoughts about the service to be performed."

In (4), we separated categories into paradigms, which are "situations/conditions," "behaviors," and "conclusion." By separating them into such paradigms, we were able to understand under what "situations/conditions" "behaviors" were executed and what "conclusions" were achieved because of the links between categories.

In (5), we wrote out the links between categories that we identified in (4). In so doing, we clarified the specific roles played by properties and dimensions.

4   Experiment to extract cognitive processes

4.1   Experiment outline and setting

In this research, we conducted an experiment to extract information about the cognitive processes involved when CAs served their customers. The experiment in this study can be divided into two parts: recording the customer service process and retrospective interviews to understand the cognitive processes at play. To record the customer service process, we used a cabin mockup owned by ANA and targeted 25 minutes of in-flight service to passengers on the left side of the rear cabin. Experiment participants, as indicated in Table 1, were 11-20 passengers in the cabin (different on the different dates of the experiment), one CA (junior/skilled) each to provide service, and one CA to assist with the experiment. We used the HX-A1H camera from Panasonic Inc. for the field-of-view, two omnidirectional cameras, and the THETA from Ricoh Inc. as the fixed camera. Retrospective interviews were conducted 40 minutes after serving the passengers in a separate room, using footage from the field-of-view and fixed cameras as a reference. Interviews lasted approximately 35-45 minutes.

Table 1. Outline of personnel for customer service process recording

Date	September 27	December 8	December 12
CA experiment cooperators	Junior: 1 person, Skilled：1 person (Each time with one CA experiment assistant)		
Passengers（with scenario）	20persons (8 persons)	11 persons (9 persons)	13 persons (10 persons)

4.2   Results of the customer service process recording experiment and considerations

In the customer service process recording experiment, reviewing during the interview was done with the help of the field-of-view and fixed cameras. Reviewing is possible only if three requirements are met: (1) using field-of-view camera, CA interaction should be clear and comprehensive with regard to the content of the conversation; (2) using the omnidirectional cameras, it must be possible to distinguish the service the CAs are providing for the passengers; and (3) all passengers should be visible to have a broad understanding of what they are doing. The footage obtained fulfilled these three requirements and was sufficient to conduct the interviews.

4.3   Results of the retrospective interviews and its considerations

In the September experiment, we conducted a questionnaire survey asking the CAs whether they were aware of the scenario prior to the retrospective interview. This influenced the remarks made during the interview to act as a verification of the CAs' customer service and the scenario. We were unable to obtain enough information on what their original thoughts were while serving the passengers. Based on this reflection, in the December experiment, we did not provide any information to CAs prior to the interviews. As a result, we were able to obtain information focused on the actual cognitive processes during the December experiment.

5   Result of the interview analysis using GTA and its considerations

5.1   The result of the interview analysis

The interview result of each CA was analyzed using GTA. The categorized results are as indicated in Table 2

Table 2. The result of categorization

Category	September 27		December 8		December 12	
	Junior	Skilled	Junior	Skilled	Junior	Skilled
Regarding service and operation	3	0	8	13	6	10
Regarding service intent	0	1	5	8	11	7
Regarding service performed	0	0	1	0	7	1
Understanding cabin conditions	0	0	0	0	1	0
Actual service performed	11	12	10	8	10	20
Anticipating passenger needs	1	9	5	6	3	9
Understanding passenger condition	12	9	8	13	11	18
Inferring passenger condition	0	3	2	4	3	7
Collecting information to grasp passenger condition	0	0	3	4	1	9
Other	34	63	10	8	13	1
Regular tasks undertaken	5	10	0	10	3	0
Inferring passenger action	0	0	3	4	0	0
Not talking to passengers while providing service so as to avoid disturbing other passengers	0	0	2	0	0	0
Giving priority to operation	0	0	3	0	0	0
Things unnoticed	7	6	0	0	0	0
Insignificant things	0	5	0	0	0	0
Impression on passengers	3	1	0	0	0	0
Things one was unaware of	2	0	0	0	0	0

Following the categorization, we developed a graphic display for each CA of the categories for each passenger. Figure 2 indicates a graphic display of categories for the passengers who played the role of a couple. In Figure 2, the blue squares represent the paradigm "situation/condition," and the orange squares represent the paradigm "behaviors."

Next, we wrote down the relationship between the categories as indicated in Figure 2. Below is the written version of the category graphic displays for each junior and senior CA (written as 《categories》 and "properties").

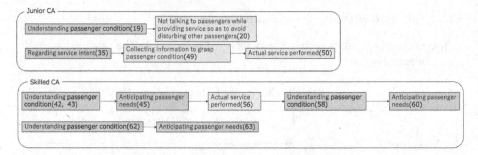

Fig. 2. Graphic display of categories related to the couple.

Junior CA
The Junior CA "noticed" the passengers looking at the Otaru travel guide prior to preparing for departure and 《grasped the condition》 of the couple. Nonetheless, she perceived the passengers who looked like they had a stomachache or were sick "to prioritize them for larger concern" and chose 《not to speak to them so as to be considerate to other passengers》. Regarding the couple, who were her "target passengers," she listed out the tourist-related information as "things she hoped to tell them." However, her concerns about delaying other services was "a reason not to talk to them," and the "service she performed" was not a time to engage them in such action. She saw drinks collection as "the ideal time to speak to them." After 《considering intended service》, she "performed the action" of checking the guidebook from the side, during "the period" when she was walking the aisle, as a way to 《gather information to understand passenger conditions》. She had a high "level of understanding" about what the passengers were looking at. Having "seen" the word Otaru, "she talked about things" such as destinations and sightseeing with passengers as 《service performed》. The "passengers' response" was regarding their destination.

Skilled CA
In terms of 《grasping passengers' conditions》 the skilled CA listed boarding as "the appropriate time" and mentioned looking at the guidebook as one of the "things she noticed" the couple doing. Regarding the "condition of the passengers," she felt that they were very close. On observing this condition, "the thing she thought of" was that it would be best to leave the two to their own, indicating that she was 《inferring passengers needs》. While thinking about these things, she greets them 《service performed》 and "the content of the greeting" was to ask if they were going on a trip. "The impression from the passenger's response" was not very enthusiastic, thus indicating under "things she thought of" that she might be interrupting them, thereby signaling that she was 《inferring passengers needs》.

5.2   Considerations for interview analysis

We conducted an analysis similar to the above for each passenger. The following differences can be seen in the cognitive processes of junior CAs and skilled CAs:
(1) No difference was observed in the things they noticed about passenger conditions.
(2) Junior CAs move on to perform a service directly after understanding the situation.
(3) Skilled CAs infer passenger needs before performing a service.
(4) Skilled CAs understand passenger conditions and often anticipate behaviors.

With regard to (1), this research introduced a scenario that determines passenger behavior and therefore not much difference was found in the scenario witnessed by each CA.

With regard to (2), we clarified that junior CAs would engage right away in some sort of approach toward the said passengers after understanding their conditions.

On the contrary, as stated in (3) and (4), skilled CAs examine passengers before approaching them. During this examination, they gain an understanding of the passenger's character (anticipation of passenger behavior and condition) and consider what service behavior might be desired (inferring needs) by such an individual.

From the above, we consider that the differences between skilled CAs and junior CAs lie in the cognitive processes that precede their service behavior. Such cognitive processes indicate an insight into the passenger's character and an ability to foresee what he/she would like/dislike.

This research hypothesized "service awareness" skills as being the source of excellent customer service. With regard to such "service awareness," we consider that a deep insight into the possible behavior of passengers and their internal state become essential cognitive skills that need to be a part of customer service requirement.

6   Conclusion

This research recorded customer service processes in a cabin mock up, and drew out the cognition process of CAs during customer service using retrospective interviews while referring to such recordings. Furthermore, by analyzing and examining the interview data using GTA, we analyzed the cognitive processes required for excellent customer service skills. As a result, we gained an understanding that the cognitive process of "inferring a passenger's persona and investigating services to fulfill it" is crucial.

In future, we will engage in the development of training methods to help junior CAs acquire these cognitive processes without having to depend on the length of service to gain this knowledge.

Reference

1. Larry J. Shuman., et al. "The ABET "Professional Skills" — Can They Be Taught? Can They Be Assessed?", The research journal for engineering education, Volume 94, Issue 1, pp41-55, 2005
2. Kurata T., et al. "Estimating skills of waiting staff of a restaurant based on behavior sensing and POS data analysis: A case study in a Japanese cuisine restaurant", Proceedings of the 5th International Conference on Applied Human Factors and Ergonomics (AHFE2014), pp.4287-4299, 2014
3. Tachioka K., et al. "Behavioral Measurements of Cabin Attendants Together with Observations and an Analysis of Their Tasks by Using Service Process Model", Proceedings of the 4nd International Conference on Serviceology, pp 271-277, 2016.
4. Omori T, Yokoyama A. "Model-Based Analysis of the Behavior Decision-Making Process Based on Intention Inference in Cooperation Problems", Journal of the Institute of Electronics, Information and Communication Engineers. 92(11), pp 734-742, 2009. (in Japanese)
5. Kitajima M. "Usability of Guide Signs at Railway Stations for Elderly Passengers-Focusing on Planning, Attention, and Working Memory", The Japanese journal of ergonomics 44(3), pp 131-143 ,2008.
6. Saiki Y, "Grounded Theory Aproach-analysis workbook", Japanese Nursing Association Press,2014

Automating Motivation: A Workplace Analysis of Service Technicians and the Motivational Impact of Automated Assistance

Katja Gutsche[1], Jennifer Griffith[2]

[1] Furtwangen University, Furtwangen, Germany,
[2] University of New Hampshire, Durham, NH, USA

Katja.gutsche@hs-furtwangen.de
jennifer.griffith@unh.edu

Abstract. Like every industrial sector, the service sector will likely experience a digital transformation. The blending of technology with the service sector will have an enormous effect on business processes and the service staff. Despite expected changes and the relevance of well-performing service staff, research on the effects of smart service devices on the worker motivation and service excellence is missing. This paper outlines research-in-progress whose aim is to outline the consequences on worker motivation caused by an increase of assistance through smart service devices. Our starting point is the analysis of the current workplace of maintenance technicians. Further work will test causal relationships between automated assistance and motivation as a function of work design.

Keywords: Service operation, Human-centered service processes, Smart service devices, Workplace analysis, Services in Industry 4.0

1 Introduction

Services in Industry 4.0 are not just about technology. Operation of technical services is personnel-intensive. Maintenance of high-investive (production) facilities demands skilled workers. Due to mostly not repetitive working situations thus far, the degree of freedom at work is comparatively high. However, changes are expected as more digital devices, such as wearables or head-mounted displays, guide service technicians through their tasks. This infusion of technology may impact employee motivation and, as a result, influence performance. To analyze this potential cause-effect loop it is critical to

© Springer International Publishing AG 2017
Y. Hara and D. Karagiannis (Eds.): ICServ 2017, LNCS 10371, pp. 101–108, 2017.
DOI: 10.1007/978-3-319-61240-9_10

evaluate the state of the current workplace of service technicians and what elements of work design are motivating to employees.

2 Workplace analysis

2.1 The Work Design Questionnaire (WDQ)

The WDQ [18] is a well-established measure that draws from the broader work design literature [17] to create a comprehensive taxonomy of the key characteristics of work. The development of the WDQ follows decades of evidence that employee motivation and satisfaction is driven, at least in part, by work design [11-12]. In short, positions designed to address employee motivational needs, such as autonomy, purpose, and mastery [12], tend to result in more motivated, more satisfied, and more committed employees [14]. In this study, the WDQ was distributed to measure the current work characteristics of service technicians. While such employees have enjoyed high levels of autonomy and mastery in the past, the introduction of technology aids may decrease the amount of discretion that employees have to troubleshoot and problem solve.

2.2 Motivation

The modern field of motivation is largely driven by the work of Deci and Ryan [5-6]. In short, Deci and Ryan proposed Self-Determination Theory (SDT), which focuses on individuals' motivational inclinations. What drives behavior has largely been categorized into two dimensions – intrinsic motivation and extrinsic motivation. Intrinsic motivators are those that come with within the person, such as interest, mastery, purpose, and altruism. Extrinsic motivators, on the other hand, are those that come from external sources, such as praise and rewards. SDT has widely been applied to the workplace [7], and research in this area has noted some robust findings. Perhaps most pertinent to service technicians, employees in jobs that are cognitively taxing (i.e. those that require creative or complex problem solving) respond more favorably to intrinsic motivators [2]. In fact, the use of extrinsic motivators, such as bonuses, has been found to decrease performance on cognitively challenging tasks [2, 8-9]. However, when tasks are repetitive and require little cognition, traditional rewards, such as bonuses and pay raises, appear to work well to motivate employees. The job of a service technicians is a unique blend of cognitive tasks and manual work. As such, the motivators of service technicians may also show unique patterns that do not clearly align with past SDT findings.

2.3 Service technicians

Service technicians are mandatory to assure a long, useful life of manufacturing equipment, buildings, and infrastructure facilities; all instruments are highly capital-intensive and must be productive over a longer period of time (> 5 years) to result in a positive return on investment (ROI). Service technicians are understood to be part of a service department or as an external service partner who is called regularly for preventive measurements or irregularly in case of equipment failures. Irrespective of the service case, smooth communication between service technician and production employee (customer) is always needed to assure good service performance. Therefore, soft skills are needed for successful service fulfillment in addition to technical knowledge and methodological know-how [16]. In addition, service technicians must have manual skills as most of their work is difficult to replace by robots or automated tools. Even if the degree of automation in service processes is comparatively low thus far, the idea of increasing work efficiency through the use of Internet of Things (IoT), data analytics, and proactive service measurements becomes more relevant.

Current surveys by the German Engineering association show another challenge within the workplace of service technicians. There is a disadvantageous demographic trend. In 2015 60 percent of the service technicians were 45 years and older, and the number of staff for maintenance is decreasing [21] despite production equipment increasing in number and complexity. The status quo is a well- experienced workforce used to "analog" service processes during their working years. As such, change processes are expected to face a higher level of resistance. The generational shift in the workforce from older, experienced technicians to younger, more digital-oriented technicians must to be considered. These circumstances speak to the urgency of defining a human-centered service strategy that takes the abilities and operational constraints within service operation into account within Industry 4.0.

To sum up, the workplace of a service technician in Industry 4.0 is a socio-technical system of increasing complexity. Industry 4.0 being a success is a function of well-established technology, process management, and adapted workplace design. [10] (Fig. 1). Smart services ask the service technician for creative, improvising actions based on experience, logic, and intuition [1]. However, as process assistance and automation increases, the intensity of interaction with the manufacturing equipment, buildings, and infrastructure facilities decreases. This hinders technicians' ability to build experience and intuition and leads to difficulties in the diagnosis of machine breakdowns [13]. In addition, it is expected that the service tasks will continue increasing in complexity within an Industry 4.0 manufacturing setting.

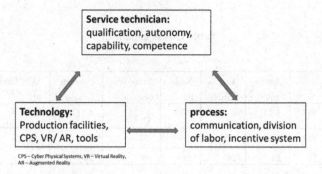

Fig. 1. Workplace of a service technician (according to [13])

The study outlined in this paper focused on issues of task complexity, feedback, information processing and motivation in service technicians workplace nowadays. These aspects were chosen as they are expected to be strongly influenced by upcoming changes in service operation due to smart service devices [1, 13, 15].

3 Study

3.1 Method

This study consists of an online survey sampling service technicians in Germany. The survey was available for completion between 1.6.2016 and 31.8.2016. The authors asked service managers in different industries to promote the survey to their technicians. In total, 90 service technicians (2 female, 88 male) for maintenance from 8 different industries took part. The average age of the respondents was 44,6 years. The survey included an abbreviated version of the German WDQ by Stegmann [20], items measuring motivation orientation (e.g., intrinsic, extrinsic) adapted from Deci and Ryan's [5] General Causality Orientations Scale, and demographic variables.

3.2 Results

To answer the research questions associated with the work environment of service technicians, basic descriptive and inferential statistical analyses were reviewed.

Research Question 1: What influences whether workers say that their **Task Complexity** is rather high or low?

• ANOVAs comparing self-reported job complexity among respondents produced significant differences in autonomy, task variety, task identification, information processing, problem solving, skill diversity, and specialization (See Table 1). Interestingly, there are no differences in terms of the use of technology in jobs with high v. low complexity.

Table 1. Task complexity

Com-plexity		Auton-omy	Task Variety	Task ID	Info Pro-cessing	Problem Solving	Skill Diver-sity	Special-ization
High	M*	3.79	4.45	3.02	4.42	4.11	4.35	4.05
	SD	.65	.46	.91	.52	.52	.58	.54
	N	28	28	28	28	28	28	28

Low	M*	3.04	4.29	2.92	4.15	3.87	4.07	3.90
	SD	.85	.66	.88	.64	.67	.72	.58
	N	15	15	15	15	15	15	15

* all means are out of 5

- Compared to those who report low complexity in their work, service technicians in positions that are more complex self-report greater autonomy ($F(1, 41) = 9.12$, $p<.01$), greater task variety ($F(1, 41) = 4.94$, $p<.05$), greater task identification ($F(1, 41) = 16.06$, $p<.01$), more information processing ($F(1, 41)=21.03$, $p<.01$), higher amounts of problem solving ($F(1, 41)$, $=15.17$, $p<.01$), greater skill diversity ($F(1, 41) =17.93$, $p<.01$), and greater specialization ($F(1, 41) = 5.87$, $p<.05$).

Research Question 2: Is **Feedback** related to job complexity and/or motivation?

Bivariate correlations between feedback and job complexity were not significant. However, the means for feedback are also relatively low ($M= 3.07$, $SD =.83$) considering the type of work completed by service technicians, which suggests service technicians don't currently get a lot of feedback from others.

- Feedback was, however, correlated with some aspects of motivation, including job fulfillment ($r = .21$, $p<.05$) and feeling that their effort is being rewarded ($r=.44$, $p<.01$). Feedback also appears to be important for people who are motivated to contribute to their team's success ($r=.33$, $p<.01$).

Research Question 3: Are **Information Processing** and job complexity and/or motivation related?

- Information processing was positively related to complexity ($r=.49$, $p<.01$). As might be expected, as one's tasks becomes more complex, more information processing is required.
- In terms of motivation, information processing was also related to increased self-efficacy ($r=.21$, $p<.05$) and skill development ($r=.25$, $p<.05$). Information processing was also associated with being motivated by contributing to the organization ($r=.31$, $p<.01$) and one's team ($r=.33$, $p<.01$) and being accountable to one's boss ($r=.30$, $p<.01$).

Research Question 4: Is the **variety of equipment** used already a workplace challenge?

- As noted above, there were no meaningful differences in the use of technology between high and low complexity jobs, suggesting that both types of environments require roughly equivalent amounts and types of technology use. Respondents from all environments reported a relatively high amount of technology in the workplace currently ($M=3.75$, $SD=.79$), so it's likely that service technicians are comfortable with technology already. However, it's also important to consider that the proposed future devices may be different than what are currently in use, so this metric may not provide much useful information- just that service technicians are comfortable with current technology and are probably tech savvy. However, these findings do suggest that the *use* of tech won't be a hurdle; it's the reasoning and *purpose* for the tech that may cause issues in the future.

Research Question 5: What **motivates** service technicians?

- Service technicians show a high level of intrinsic motivation. Autonomy is of high importance whereas public recognition or any kind of rewards show low motivational impact. Service technicians are highly motivated by defining their own work process and the responsibility they have towards colleagues and organization. However, there are differences in motivational power through responsibility towards team, organization, coworkers or supervisors. (Fig. 2) The high motivational impact of autonomy is remarkable and will have to be considered very carefully within a desired change process in service processes addressing an increase in assistance. Positive impulses will give the indicated high desire to develop new skills, which might ease the introduction of new technical devices.

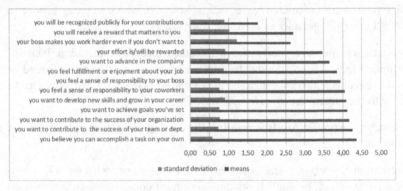

Fig. 2. Service technician's motivation (N=90)

4   Summary and outlook

To sum up the results of the survey, the workplace of service technicians, especially focusing on maintenance technicians, can be described through:

1. Low level of standardized tasks, (Task variety $M = 4.33$, $SD = .67$; Skill diversity $M = 3.91$, $SD = .73$)
2. (Temporary) uncontrolled/ not-mastered with a high percentage of improvisational action, (Autonomy $M = 3.54$, $SD = .72$)
3. Allowing the technician to work very self-dependent work with a high freedom of decision making,
4. Especially within failure elimination tasks low amount of repetitive work (uniqueness), (Task variety $M = 4.33$)
5. (Partially) ad-hoc decisions and actions needed, (Problem Solving $M = 3.74$, $SD = .71$, Info Processing $M = 4.09$, $SD = .66$)

6. Partially "lone fighter", which gives less opportunities to exchange thoughts with colleagues, (Interaction $M = 2.85$, $SD = 1.07$)

In addition, the survey showed that service technicians regularly have to deal with time pressure (time pressure M = 3.81, SD = 0.82). It is assumed that this is most likely caused by high numbers of unplanned work (e.g. failure elimination) at which customers expect fast repair to keep downtime of their assets as low as possible.

On the whole, the workplace characteristics of service technicians suggest that they are responsible for a wide range of unstandardized tasks and often work independently. Employees working within the parameters of this sort of work design typically respond to intrinsic motivators that allow employees to increase mastery and purpose within their field. This expectation is confirmed when motivators of service technicians, specifically those associated with autonomy, are examined.

These results are essential for the ongoing research. This will focus on empirical studies looking for answers to the following questions:

- How likely is a service technician to accept an electronic device leading him/her through the task, as he/she is used to high level of autonomy?
- How does an increase of assistance affect the motivation level of service technicians?
- Do service technicians feel a loss of control/ reduction of self-determination at work when technology-aided assistance is introduced to the work setting?
- Can we see a loss in situation awareness [4, 19] of service technicians as there is a shift Industry 4.0 and an increasing use of smart service devices?
- Does introducing technological aids create a dependence on assistance, causing the maintenance staff to stop thinking on its own [3]?
- Will the introduction of technology aids into daily work result in skill decay, reducing knowledge retention and application?
- As organizations transition to using more electronic devices to guide employees, how can organizations harness lessons from change management by taking individual characteristics (age, sex, experience etc.) into account?

References

1. Acatech (2015). Smart Maintenance für Smart Factories - Mit intelligenter Instandhaltung die Industrie 4.0 vorantreiben, Berlin
2. Ariely, D., Gneezy, U., Loewenstein, G., & Mazar, N. (2009). Large stakes and big mistakes. The Review of Economic Studies, 76(2), 451-469.
3. Badke-Schaub, P. & Hofinger, G. & Lauche, K. (2011). Human Factors: Psychologie sicheren Handelns in Risikobranchen, Springer
4. Bainbridge, L. (1983). Ironies of automation. In Automatica 19, 6, 775-779

5. Deci, E. L. & Ryan, R. M. (1985). The general causality orientations scale: Self-determination in personality. Journal of Research in Personality, 19, 109-134.
6. Gagné, M. (2014). The Oxford handbook of work engagement, motivation and self-determination theory. Oxford University Press
7. Gagné, M. & Deci, E. L. (2005). Self-determination theory and work motivation. Journal of Organizational Behavior, 26(4), 331-362.
8. Glucksberg, S. (1962). The influence of strength of drive on functional fixedness and perceptual recognition. Journal of Experimental Psychology, 63(1), 36-41.
9. Glucksberg, S. (1964). Problem solving: Response competition and the influence of drive. Psychological Reports, 15(3), 939-942.
10. Gutsche, K. (2013). Proactive Maintenance – what about the maintainer?, In Rao, R. BKN: 26th International Congress on Condition Monitoring and Diagnostics Engineering Management, 81-86
11. Hackman, J. R., & Lawler, E. E. (1971). Employee reactions to job characteristics. Journal of Applied Psychology, 55(3), 259- 286.
12. Hackman, J. R., & Oldham, G. R. (1976). Motivation through the design of work: Test of a theory. Organizational Behavior and Human Performance, 16(2), 250-279.
13. Hirsch-Kreinsen, H. & ten Hompel, M. (2015): Digitalisierung industrieller Arbeit - Entwicklungsperspektiven und Gestaltungsansätze. In Vogel-Heuser et al., Handbuch Industrie 4.0., Springer NachschlageWissen, p. 1-20
14. Humphrey, S. E., Nahrgang, J. D., & Morgeson, F. P. (2007). Integrating motivational, social, and contextual work design features: A meta-analytic summary and theoretical extension of the work design literature. Journal of Applied Psychology, 92, 1332-1356.
15. Kaber, D. & Hendsley, M. (2004). The effects of level of automation and adaptive automation on human performance, situation awareness and workload in a dynamic control task. Theoretical Issues in Ergonomics Sciences, 5 (2), 113-153
16. Lay, G., Nippa, M. (2005). Management produktbegleitender Dienstleistungen. Springer
17. Morgeson, F. P., & Campion, M. A. (2003). Work design. In W. C. Borman, D. R. Ilgen, & R. J. Klimoski (Eds.), Handbook of psychology: Industrial and organizational psychology (Vol. 12, pp. 423-452). Hoboken, NJ: John Wiley & Sons.
18. Morgeson, F. P., & Humphrey, S. E. (2006). The Work Design Questionnaire (WDQ): Developing and validating a comprehensive measure for assessing job design and the nature of work. Journal of Applied Psychology, 91, 1321-1339.
19. Nof, S.Y. (2009). Handbook of Automation, Springer
20. Stegmann, S. et al. (2010). Der Work Design Questionnaire - Vorstellung und erste Validierung einer deutschen Version. Zeitschrift für Arbeits- u. Organisationspsychologie, 54, 1 – 28
21. VDI (2015). Betriebsingenieure – eine Männerdomäne vor dem Generationenwechsel. CITplus 7+8/2015, S. 21

Stiction-Free Learning Method for Service Design Beginner

Atsunobu Kimura[1*], Koki Kusano[1*], Ryo Ymamashita[1], Yurika Katagiri[1*]

1 NTT Service Evolution Laboratories, Japan

* Tel: +81 46 859 2702, E-mail: kimura.atsunobu@lab.ntt.co.jp

Abstract. For people to become adapt in the methodology of Service Design, it is important that they achieve small but initial success which will encourage them to take the initiative in solving problems, before they learn skills and knowledge. However, books and instruction courses on Service Design focus on the learning of skills and knowledge, so beginners hesitate to apply Service Design freely. We propose 3 heuristic requirements for beginners to apply Service Design in practice and introduce the Stiction-free learning method in book-form. We evaluate the method and the results showed the effectiveness of our easy book-form, trouble check-sheet and verbalized implicit knowledge.

Keywords: Service Design beginner, Stiction-free method, easy book-form, trouble check-sheet, verbalized implicit knowledge, Service Design, design thinking, UX design

1   INTRODUCTION

In recent years, companies have begun to consider the experience they provide to users rather than mere functionality. Service providers are paying attention to methodologies like Design Thinking [1-5], UX Design [6, 7] to provide attractive user experiences. Not only service providers but also social enterprises are tackling the user centered approach, for example Participatory Design [8] and Future Centre [9], to create value or form consensus with users. These methodologies are similar but each philosophy calls them by different names. In the broadest sense, they are called Service Design [10-12], which is an activity to iteratively create solutions to human needs and wants.

In the past, Service Design activities were mainly pursued by experts who applied to own particular skills. Recently, Service Design has attracted rising attention as a methodology that can identify the basic knowledge and skills needed by service providers. However, beginners who lack the basic knowledge and skills hesitate to apply Service Design in their tasks. Our initial goal is to acquaint the beginner with the necessity of Service Design and to appreciate its effectiveness; this should be achieved before they undertake the classic acquisition of basic knowledge and skills. Our hope is that the beginner can execute Service Design dialogues and interactions with experts. This paper raises 3 requirements for beginners that would like to enter the world of Service Design; we introduce the Stiction-free learning method in book form.

© Springer International Publishing AG 2017   109
Y. Hara and D. Karagiannis (Eds.): ICServ 2017, LNCS 10371, pp. 109–120, 2017.
DOI: 10.1007/978-3-319-61240-9_11

2   Hesitation of beginners

2.1   Problems from interviews

The difficulties organizations face in deploying Service Design are summarized in our previous work [13]. For companies wanting to utilize Service Design, there are three key difficulties. One is the inability to create high-quality ideas, inability to execute the created ideas, scant understanding of Service Design activities. The first one includes 'Lack of skills & Knowledge on human-centered service idea creation'. This is one of the most critical difficulties faced by the beginner.

To identify the key problems, we conducted interviews on how to get basic knowledge and skills. Interview targets were experts in Service Design (career in excess of 5 years), experienced persons with a few years of Service Design, and beginners in Service Design in our company; all had experience to plan or develop services. The results of the interviews are detailed below.

2.2   Starting is hard

The concept of Service Design is too abstract for beginners to understand easily. They are not convinced that it is effective. Some said 'Listening carefully to the user's comments is just commonsense and I've already listened' and others said 'Best practices are excuses after the service launch'. The beginners are busy with their own mission and 'can't spare the time to learn a new concept'. They 'feel bothered by being forced to learn something not to directly relate to their mission' because coworkers in the same room are focused on the same mission'. The first step is for the beginner to realize that Service Design is effective. This requires books, training or something else. Books are not well received; 'Shrink back when seeing fat book', 'feel impossible to keep the reading schedule.' Training is even more of a direct interruption of their mission, 'no time to participate in classes'.

In sum, it is critical that beginners be introduced to Service Design in the most effective manner possible.

2.3   Not leading to actual task

After the beginner makes sense of the concept of Service Design and wants to apply it, movement is hindered by the difficulty of applying the basic knowledge. The following comment shows this; 'it is hard to understand how to use Service Design in my own mission.' In addition, some want to acquire the whole image of Service Design as in 'I want to know how to create a business project book of service development' 'How is Service Design related to system requirements?'

To summarize, it is important to show how knowledge and skills can be applied to actual tasks.

2.4   Process hard to understand

Can beginner practice initiatively upon receiving tools that lead to actual task? Experts made the following comment; 'This kind of book is appropriate for experienced people, but it is difficult for beginner to apply as the background knowledge is missing.' This means knowledge and skills are not verbalized in the Service Design field. International standard ISO9241-210 [14] about human centered design, double-diamond [15] by the Design Council of the UK and design-thinking [4] by Stanford Univ. and d.school of the US show the basic philosophy and rough processes for knowledge acquisition. However, the beginner needs a lot of implicit knowledge and skill in implementing the rough process.

To summarize, existing material provides a distillation of the knowledge of experts but to help the beginner make the first step, different approaches are needed that do not use specialized words or jargon.

2.5   Related works

As described before, many methodologies have been proposed that are related to Service Design as referred to above, along with concrete methods for implementing those methodologies [16-21]. Best practices with regard to utilizing those methodologies and methods have been reported and their effectiveness has been examined. In the educational field, d.school [4] in Stanford Univ. and System Design Management Dept. [22] in Keio Univ. provide formal educational courses to learn and practice Design methodologies and methods.

Examples in the business field include IBM Design Thinking [23] by IBM and Design Sprint [24] by Google Ventures, but to create high quality output they assume that the user is already experienced in Service Design. For example, IBM positioned 'Design' as one of its corporate strategy, and has invested more than $100 million (and hiring over 1000 UX designers) in an effort to recast its corporate culture as design-friendly [25]. Each company created confidentially its own training program intended for use by company staff so that general requirements are not clear.

3   Proposed Method

Based on the above problems, this study tackles a learning method that encourages the beginner to take the first step in learning Service Design. Of course our study was conducted in accordance with Service Design principles, so booklet prototypes were initially examined by target users and then enhanced.

3.1   Passion is sustainable

Issues that can degrade one's enthusiasm include 'takes too long to read or try', 'not directly related to one's job', 'failure to understand effectiveness of Service Design'. We constructed a booklet prototype to overcome those issues.

   a) beginner can access material (physical booklet or digital data) whenever desired

b) appearance does not deter use on the job (Figure 1)

c) thin (only 83 pages) to encourage perusal

d) short work modules within 10 pages and taking less than 60 min. each

e) concentrates on typical trouble in service development

f) explain short summery of Service Design's trend, case studies and effectiveness

g) explanation of each work module including purpose, effect and procedure (Figure 2)

h) explanation of each step in each work module is as short and simple as possible

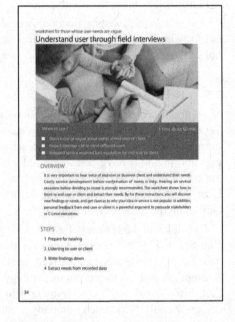

Fig.1. Cover of booklet   Fig.2. Explanation of each work module

3.2 Place leading to actual task

The issues of 'difficult to apply' and 'how to plan business project book of service development', 'relation to system requirements' were tackled by the four steps described below.

i) Service Design processes including business project and system requirement (Figure 3). The processes consist of 1 Goal Set (Set the project direction and obtain consensus of project members), 2 Target Set (Set opportunity area to tackle for the project), 3 Understand User (Understand target user and environment deeply and find needs), 4 Concept Creation (Create concept that will trigger empathy from user), 5 Concept Test (Test whether concept triggers empathy from user), 6 Business Plan (Plan business model to put the concept at the core), 7 System Plan (Plan system as an approach to realize business plan) and 8 System Dev (Develop the planned system).

j) Focusing on only typical trouble on service development for beginner's start, not general knowledge just like book. Trouble check-sheet is placed on first page (Figure 4). The check-sheet has 7 questions below, related for each process.

**Goal Set : Our project goal is vague!

**Target Set : Our idea is just ordinary!

**Understand User : Needs of our target users are vague!

**Concept Creation : We have not found convincing answer!

**Test Concept : Our idea is not tested by user!

**Business Plan : We are failing to draw in stakeholders!

**System Plan :We have little idea of whether our system is usable!

k) Beginner can use this booklet to tackle practical problems and realize its effectiveness

l) After completing a work module, last page of the module recommends the next few actions

Fig.3. Service Design Process

Fig.4. Trouble Check-Sheet

3.3   Process easy to understand

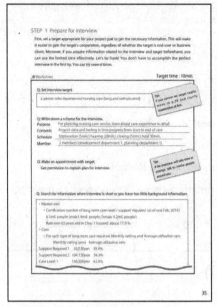

Fig.5. A page of work module

The issue 'difficult for beginner to utilize without background knowledge' was resolved by making the booklet prototype processes easy for the beginner to understand.

m)   detail processes for easy understanding by beginners, without jargon

n)   work modules consist of multiple steps in short segments (Figure 5), for example in STEP1: Prepare for interview in 'Understand User' process, there are how to determine target user, how to fix overview of interview, how to make appointment, how to research information beforehand and so on. Regular service design activities don't include such detailed descriptions.

o)   basically short explanation considering requirement 'Passion is sustained', with mindset and know-how added as tips (Figure 5)

4   Evaluation

4.1   Overview of evaluations

The booklet prototype was written to meet 3 requirements; 'Passion is sustained', 'leading to actual task' and 'ease to understand'.

Tests compared the booklet to formal books appropriate for beginners of Service Design. Candidates were books on Service Design as referred to above and business planning [26-29]. Idea Maker [29] is selected as a conventional method because it is nearest material to meet 3 requirements. Two experiments were conducted; a quantitative evaluation (by questionnaire) to examine first impression, qualitative evaluation (by interview) after use.

4.2   Experiment 1

After reading each material (proposed/traditional) for 4 min., each subject responded to a questionnaire. The subjects were 22 beginner of Service Design. Three subjects had a few years of experience in Service Design and 19 had no experience. Order effect was considered.

Before reading the material the questionnaire instructed each subject as follows 'please select the issue appropriate for your own job'. The following trouble-lists were provided;

i : Our project goal is vague!

ii : Our idea is just ordinary!

iii : Needs of our target users are vague!

iv : We have not found convincing answer!

v : Our idea is not tested by user!

vi: We are failing to draw in stakeholders!

vii: Little idea of whether our system is usable!

After selection, questionnaire said 'using this material, try to find a solution to the selected issue, and read it'. The 4 min. period commenced in which the subject was required to find and read about the issue.

After the test, the subjects provided a 7 step evaluation of 13 questionnaire items for 3 requirements.

Questionnaire group about 'Passion is sustained'

-This material made it easy for me to realize want I wanted to do

-This material is useful for me

-This material made my job fun

-I like to use this material

-I ready to use this material during my job

Questionnaire group about 'leading to actual task'

-I want to use this material for my job

-I can work efficiently with this material

-This material is effective for learning Service Design

-This material is effective for practicing Service Design

-This material resolved the service development issue I selected at first

Questionnaire group about 'ease to understand'

-This material is clear and easy to understand

-This material makes it easy to learn how to use Service Design

-This material made my next step clear

4.3   Results of experiment 1

Figure 6 to 8 show averages of subjects' the sum score of each questionnaire group, so that maximum sum score for each is 35 (5 items have score 7 in max on figure 6, 7) or 21 (3 items have score 7 in max on Figure 8). Results of Wilcoxon signed-rank tests were here. There is no significant difference on 'Passion is sustained' (p=0.12>.10). There is a significant difference on 'Leading to actual task' between Proposed method and traditional method (p=0.04<.05). There is a significant difference on 'ease to understand' between Proposed method and traditional method (p=0.002<.05).

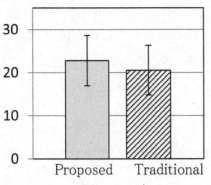

Fig.6. Passion is sustained

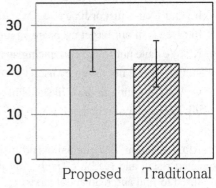

Fig.7. Lead to actual task

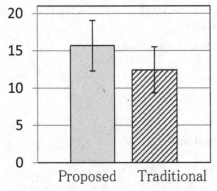

Fig.8. ease to understand

4.4   Experiment 2

First, the subject selected a trouble with service development from trouble-lists same as Experiment 1 based on their experience. They were instructed to undertake the work module that corresponded to the trouble within 30 min. Subjects were 6 people belonging to the service development. Five people persons had a few years of experience in Service Design while one person had no experience. Order effect was considered.

4.5 Results of Experiment 2

Interview results of 'Passion is sustained' about the traditional method are 'easy to understandable, but thick. Must read deeply', 'takes time to read', 'if many members join the same big project, traditional method can be useful, but not for one person's quick task'. On the other hand, those about the proposed method are 'simple, a few pages, can read quickly', 'take it in hand in my job', 'want to use it in my job right now', 'can be used within working time'.

Traditional method gave the impression to subjects that it would cost more than the proposed method. The proposed method was regarded as of use in the actual task. In addition to the interview responses, questionnaire item 'I can make time to use this during my job' in experiment 1 yielded a positive significant difference for the proposed method. It is supposed that easy book-form based on requirement c) thinness (83 pages) and requirement d) short work modules (within 60 min) were positives influences.

Interview results of 'Lead to actual task' about traditional method are 'appropriate for people like university students who start to learn Service Design from zero, and who are not facing actual job'. Then those about proposed method are 'good for business people who experience difficulty when tackling service development tasks', 'easy to use contents for person who have trouble with service development on the job', 'when someone experiences trouble with service development, I want to recommend this booklet.'

The traditional method is effective for students, while the proposed method is effective for business people. Questionnaire item 'This booklet is effective for learning Service Design' yielded a positive significant difference for traditional method and questionnaire item 'This booklet is effective for practice Service Design' yielded a positive significant difference for proposed method. In light of experiment 2 results, subjects seemed to feel that traditional method is effective for formal learning and proposed method is effective for on-the-job practice. In addition to the interview, questionnaire item 'This booklet resolved trouble with service development that I selected previously' in experiment 1 was a positive significant difference. It is supposed that requirement j) trouble check-sheet (Figure 4) was the dominant influence. During experiment 2, almost all subjects read the trouble check-sheet at first.

Interview results of 'Ease to understand' about the traditional method are 'good for expert in Service Design. Difficult for beginner', 'it is difficult for beginner to practice Service Design in their job. They need previous knowledge'. And those about the proposed method are 'this booklet is understandable without background knowledge on some level',

The traditional method requires background knowledge, unlike the proposed method. Questionnaire item 'It is easy to learn how to use Service Design' in experiment 1 is a positive significant difference for the proposed method. It is supposed that verbalized implicit knowledge based on requirement m) detailed processes was the prime influence.

5   Discussion

The proposed Stiction-free Service Design learning method decreases the beginner's hesitation and encourages the start of active learning and attempts to put it into practice. The beginner realizes the effectiveness of Service Design and is motivated to learn and implement it. The proposed method lets the beginner acquire the common language of Service Design making it easier to converse with and utilize outside Service Design experts. The software development field had the same structure as Service Design. Traditionally, only a few experts could practice in that field so that the company delegated software development to programmers exclusively, but nowadays big companies train their staff in IT literacy and the expert department exists to utilize outside experts.

We aim to provide a bridge from the era of Service Design by experts to the era of Service Design by everyone. Our research team intends to make Service Design knowledge and skills more explicitly verbalized and thus accessible to all beginners as a support environment, in which some problems are solved by themselves while others are assisted by experts. Our intent is for Service Design to become a kind of infrastructure to create value for users and stakeholders.

Stiction-free learning is just a first step of the aim. First target is company that has engineering culture and is weak for providing complete solutions to users' problems. The empirical maturity model for user studies was proposed in [30]. For the next step, we will study the relation between Stiction-free learning and organization maturity.

6   Conclusions

This paper described our study on Service Design beginners and proposed 3 requirements in assisting beginners in starting to learn and implement Service Design. From our research we developed the Stiction-free learning method and implemented it in booklet form. Our method was evaluated and the results showed the effectiveness of its easy book-form, trouble check-sheet and verbalized implicit knowledge.

We used this booklet to introduce Service Design to our group companies and conducted a workshop program related to this booklet after the experiments. Over 200 business people participated in the workshop and then used it in their job.

References

1. Kelley, T., Littman, J. (2001) The Art of Innovation: Lessons in Creativity from IDEO; America's Leading Design Firm, Crown Business, 1st edition
2. Brown, T. (2008) Design Thinking; Harvard Business Review, Vol. 86, No. 6, pp. 84-95

3. Brown,T. (2009) Change by Design: How Design Thinking Transforms Organizations and Inspires Innovation, HarperBusiness

4. d.school teaching team (2010) The Bootcamp Bootleg; Stanford, http://dschool.stanford.edu/use-our-methods/thebootcamp-bootleg

5. Saso K. (2013) Necessary reason of design thinking for 21th century business, CrossMedia Publishing Inc., in Japanese

6. Buley, L. (2013) The User Experience Team of One: A Research and Design Survival Guide; Rosenfeld Media, 1st edition

7. Quesenbery, W., Brooks, K. (2010) Storytelling for User Experience: Crafting Stories for Better Design, Rosenfeld Media, 1st edition

8. Schuler D., Namioka A. (1993) Participatory Design; Principles and Practices, CRC Press

9. Dvir, R., Schwartzberg, Y., Avni, H., Webb, C., and Lettice, F. (2006) The future center as an urban innovation engine, Journal of Knowledge Management, Vol. 10(5), pp.110-123

10. Mager, B. (2004) Service design; A review, Koln International School of Design

11. Zomerdijk, L.G., Voss, C.A. (2010) Service design for experience-centric services; Journal of Service Research, Vol. 13, No. 1, pp. 67-82

12. Stickdorn, M. Schneider, J. (2012) This is Service Design Thinking: Basics, Tools, Cases; Wiley,1 edition

13. Akasaka, F., Ohno, T., Yasuoka, M. (2015) Challenges to Deploy Service Design in Organizations: Analysis through "Scaling Up" Workshops; ICServ2015

14. ISO: ISO 9241-210 ergonomics of human-system interaction - part 210: Human-centred design for interactive systems. (2010) Directly by ISO

15. Design Council, Double diamond design process. (2006) Design Council

16. Kumar, V. (2012) 101 Design Methods: A Structured Approach for Driving Innovation in Your Organization; Wiley, 1 edition

17. Boeijen, A., Daalhuizen, J., Schoor, R., Zijlstra, J. (2014) Delft Design Guide: Design Strategies and Methods, BIS Publishers

18. Cooper, A., Reimann, R. and Cronin, D. (2007) About face 3: the essentials of interaction design, John Wiley & Sons,Inc

19. Yamazaki, K., Ueda, Y., Takahashi, K., Hayakawa, S., Go, K., Yanagida, K. (2012) Experience Vision: Vision Proposed type Design method to plan delightful experience staring user, Maruzen Publishing co., LTD, in Japanese

20. Tanahashi, K., (2008) What is next after making Persona? Web site construction by user centered design, SB Creative Corp. in Japanese

21. Tago, M., Tago, Y., Hashiguchi, H. (2014) Design Management, Nikkei Business Publications, Inc., in Japanese

22. Maeno, R., Yasui, T., Shirasaka, S., Tomita, Ishibashi, K., Iwata, T., Yagita, H. (2014) Change the world by System x Design Thinking ? Keio SDM 'How to make innovation happen', Nikkei Business Publications, Inc., in Japanese

23. IBM Design Thinking, http://www.ibm.com/design/thinking/

24. Knapp, J., Zeratsky, J., Kowitz, B. (2016) Sprint: How to Solve Big Problems and Test New Ideas in Just Five Days; Simon & Schuster, http://www.gv.com/sprint/

25. 10 Design Thinking Principles for Innovative Organizations, (2016) http://blog.btrax.com/en/2016/08/19/10-design-thinking-principles-for-innovative-organizations/

26. Aulet, B. (2013) Disciplined Entrepreneurship: 24 Steps to a Successful Startup,Wiley; 1st Edition

27. Osterwalder, A., Pigneur, Y. (2010) Business Model Generation: A Handbook for Visionaries, Game Changers, and Challengers, Wiley; 1st Edition

28. Osterwalder, A., Pigneur, Y.,Bernarda, G. (2014) Value Proposition Design: How to Create Products and Services Customers Want, Wiley; 1st Edition

29. Yamaguchi, T., (2015) Idea Maker: textbook and workbook to create innovative idea and design business model, TOYO KEIZAI INC. in Japanese

30. Nielsen, L., Madsen, S., Jensen, I., Hautopp, H., Mulvad, L. (2014) International user studies: How companies collect and present data about users on international markets, IT University of Copenhagen

A Proposal of a Visualization Method for Service Ideas Using Paper Card Based-Fieldwork

Kazutoshi Sakaguchi[1], Nobuyuki Kobayashi[2], Aki Nakamoto[3] and Seiko Shirasaka[4]

[1] Fujitsu Design Limited, Kanagawa, Japan
kazu-sakaguchi@jp.fujitsu.com
[2] KATO WORKS CO., LTD., Tokyo, Japan
n-kobayashi@kato-works.co.jp
[3] The System Design and Management Research Institute of Graduate School of System Design and Management, Keio University, Kanagawa, Japan
a.nakamoto.sdm@gmail.com
[4] Graduate School of System Design and Management, Keio University, Kanagawa, Japan
shirasaka@sdm.keio.ac.jp

Abstract. This study proposes a visualization method for service ideas by considering the usage context based on various stakeholders' experiences gained in tabletop fieldwork. The proposed method is characterized by "idea generation through making combinations" as well as "experience-sharing based on tabletop fieldwork". We applied the proposed method to two workshops, and confirmed that a total of 118 people successfully visualized their ideas in a short time using the proposed method. This study details the procedure of visualization, and shows that the proposed method assists in developing master plans and future visions.

Keywords: Context; Service idea; Fieldwork; Card; UX

1   Introduction

Generating service ideas requires target user selection, and consideration of the flow of their experience. Designers need to grasp the users' needs, and usage context in order to create concrete ideas, for which journey map visualizing the flow of experience in time series may be used. Service ideas thereby become concrete at every touch point, and interaction is designed for each scene and scenario. However, this procedure takes lengthy time for an elaborate survey and visualization, which is not suitable for idea generation by a large number of people in a short time.

This study proposes a visualization method for service ideas by considering the usage context based on various stakeholders' experiences gained in tabletop fieldwork. The proposed method is characterized by "idea generation through making combinations" as well as "experience-sharing based on tabletop fieldwork", and the functions are elaborated in this paper. The method enables, in a short time, a dialogue among multiple stakeholders and idea generation through their tabletop experience. Moreover, it is an interface providing information related to the service to be designed, and visualizes the system structure of the generated ideas. This study applied the proposed method to two

© Springer International Publishing AG 2017
Y. Hara and D. Karagiannis (Eds.): ICServ 2017, LNCS 10371, pp. 121–134, 2017.
DOI: 10.1007/978-3-319-61240-9_12

workshops, and confirmed that a total of 118 people successfully visualized their ideas in a short time using the proposed method. This study details the procedure of visualization, and shows that the proposed method assists in developing master plans and future visions.

2   Current Challenges in Generating Service Ideas

Due to the difficulty in predicting future in the environment with high uncertainty, it is effective to take human centered-approach, and steps of defining vision and mission based on the "To-Be" envisaged in the dialogue with stakeholders, followed by incorporating the defined vision and mission into concrete actions and plans in order to develop an overall plan including master plans and mid-to-long term plans. This study, however, identified following challenges in generating service ideas in collaboration with stakeholders, and summarized them as follows:

1. Service designers are unable to have the stakeholders conduct an activity in a short time to understand the context for idea generation:
   Utilizing the process of design thinking is useful to generate ideas from user perspectives. Service designers, however, are unlikely to have enough time for getting the participants to conduct activities to understand the context, including fieldwork, and generate ideas using the gained insights.
2. Service designers are unable to quickly induce a dialogue among multiple stakeholders with an aim to develop a vision:
   Ideally, service designers should be able to induce a dialogue among various stakeholders, and anyone should easily generate service ideas based on the vision. There are, however, no methods and procedures that allow service designers to use.
3. Service designers are unable to get stakeholders without their fieldwork experience to generate service ideas:
   Use experience (UX) is defined as "people's perception and response to the actual or expected usage of products, systems, and services" [3]. UX design needs to make the situation and the scenario of the service, including those before and after the service is offered, concrete by using persona, fieldwork site, tools, and defined interaction. Since the experience gained in the field using five senses often generates insights for UX design, stakeholders without their fieldwork experience may find it difficult to elaborate UX.
4. Service designers do not have interfaces providing the stakeholders with information related to the service to design:
   Effective input of survey results to the stakeholders is necessary in service design. However, the input is currently insufficient with the participants possibly generating existing ideas as they lack professional knowledge or relevant knowledge, and uses only the information they are aware of.
5. Service designers are unable to visualize the system structure of the generated ideas:
   Description of lifecycle in time series shows the overall view, allowing service designers to confirm the boundary, and grasp the context with a bird's-eye view. However, the designers find it difficult to clarify the relationship between the system as

a whole, and the elements because many ideas are fragmented in the stage of idea generation.

3   Literature Review

Based on the current challenges in generating service ideas, which were discussed in Section 2, Section 3 describes previous studies on visualization methods relevant to this study.

Context Diagram

Context diagram is a method used to analyze stakeholder needs and show the system boundary, as well as to clarify the described system. Used for describing concepts of "As-Is" and "To-Be" for customers [4], context diagram needs to be written in simple language, and viewed by all the stakeholders related to the project. Stakeholders are thereby capable of understanding the system structure and boundary in the context diagram [5]. Context diagram can be created in a relatively short time depending on the experience, and thus is suitable for work by multiple people. Visualizing UX, however, is hard with context diagram since the users using this method are unable to read between the lines, which differs from a scenario.

Customer Journey Map

Originally having been developed as a visualization method in user research, customer journey map shows the experience, emotion and phycology of users in time series. This method is used for the three motivations of "Articulating Insights", "Communicating insights", and "Keeping empathy" [6]. In recent years, as a visualization method in UX design, it helps clarifying the core value by designing "As-Is" and "To-Be" respectively [7]. Customer journey map also enables design in a short time as well as work by multiple people. However, combination with other methods is necessary for making the service ideas concrete at every touch point.

Service Blue Print.

Service blue print chronologically grasps the process of provision and usage of service, in relation to the functional elements consisting the service. It then describes the whole process in a flow chart format. This method separately describes observable elements regarding customers, and unobservable process regarding systems and operators [6][8]. Design in this way takes considerable time for considering the system structure based on the customer needs and results of business analysis.

4   The Relation between Previous Studies, and Current Challenges in Generating Service Ideas

Table 1 shows the respective characteristics of the three visualization methods (discussed in Section 3) in terms of current challenges in generating service ideas (discussed in Section 2). On one hand, Context diagram fails to visualize visions and UX easily though ensuring description in a short time and visualization of the whole system. On the other hand, Customer journey map and Service blue print take a long time to consider UX while giving a good understanding on UX. We therefore assume that currently there are no visualization methods providing the following functions at the same time:

1. Ensure that service designers have the stakeholders conduct an activity in a short time to understand the context for idea generation;
2. Ensure that service designers quickly induce a dialogue among multiple stakeholders;
3. Ensure that service designers get stakeholders without their fieldwork experience to generate service ideas;
4. Ensure that service designers have interfaces providing the stakeholders with information related to the service to be designed;
5. Ensure that service designers visualize the system structure of the generated ideas.
   This study developed a new visualization method with these functions, and evaluated the results of two workshops to which we applied the proposed method.

5   Proposed Visualization Method

To address the five challenges detailed in Section 2, this study developed a visualization method for service ideas, in which participants in idea generation make combinations while discussing with the use of pictures in paper card format. This method prepares the context of the system to be designed as elements, and have the participants generate ideas through making combinations, and thereby design systems with constraints in a short time. The visualization method is shown below by steps.

1. Survey the surrounding environment of the service to be designed
2. Make paper cards of the survey results
3. Brainstorm using the cards
4. Evaluate the generated ideas
5. Analyze the relationship of ideas

1. Survey the surrounding environment of the service to be designed.
Service designers first collect relevant information through fieldwork including observation and interview with a focus on how the site is used. In addition, they select based on tabletop research relevant keywords from visions, and mid-to-long term plans of local governments. The collected information is grouped into three categories

of "ISSUE (points to be discussed for the future)", "PLACE (places of daily life)", and "RESOURCE (technology, human resources, natural resources, and asset)", and listed subsequently.

2. Make paper cards of the survey results.
Service designers prepare paper cards by using the information collected in Step 1. Examples of the cards are shown in Figure 1. Designers make the cards by putting the pictures taken during the fieldwork, as well as pictures related to the keywords. The keywords are also written on each card in a way as simple as possible.

Table 1. The Relation between Previous Studies, and Current Challenges in Generating Service Ideas

Current Challenges	Context Diagram	Customer Journey Map	Service Blue Print	Function the proposed method provides
1)	○ Can be created in a short time.	Δ Takes slightly longer time to consider customer emotion.	× Takes time to consider the process of systems.	Can be created in a short time.
2)	× Suitable for describing elements, but not for visions.	Δ Hard to reflect various opinions though ensuing to design a "To-Be" journey based on "As-Is".	Δ Hard to reflect various opinions though ensuing to design a "To-Be" service based on "As-Is".	Induce a dialogue among stakeholders.
3)	× Multiple descriptions are necessary for each phase of the lifecycle.	○ Capable of visualizing user experience including before and after the usage.	○ Capable of visualizing service including before and after the usage.	Generate ideas based on the experience of tabletop fieldwork.
4)	Δ No professional knowledge is necessary with only elements being described.	× Stakeholders participating in the idea generation may not be able to express their emotion with the image in	× Professional knowledge on system structure of operation may be necessary.	An interface providing information related to service to be designed.

				mind due to lack of actual experience.
5)	○ Can visualize system architecture, by being used with a use-case description and FFBD.	× Focused on user experience.	○ Can visualize a service system by separately describing observables and unobservables.	Visualize the system structure of the generated ideas.

3. Brainstorm using the cards

An idea is a new combination of existing elements [9]. The participants in idea generation thus combines three of the aforementioned cards and jot down "what kind of future you would realize or what kind of problem you would solve, what kind of resource you would use, and where you would do that". Figure 2 and Figure 3 shows a workshop this study conducted, and examples of the output.

Fig. 1. Example of prepared cards

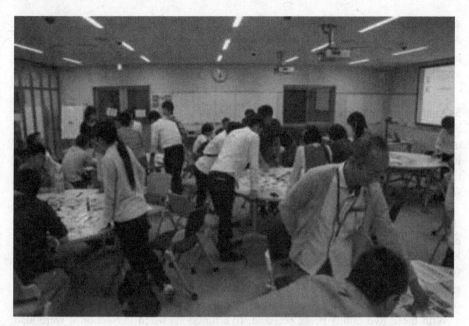

Fig. 2. Workshop

Fig. 3. Examples of workshop output

4. Evaluate the generated ideas

After each group chooses and presents one of the ideas they generated, all the participants make a vote in the end. Thereby the degree of sympathy to the generated ideas is assessed.

5. Analyze the relationship of ideas

Service designers and the participants consider the relationship of the cards which generated the ideas, and confirms the potential needs. Using an affinity diagram to group ideas visualizes tendency and framework that have not been noticed [10]. Users' potential needs may be fragmentarily visualized when some ideas have been generated for innovative activities and experience.

Based on the steps above, the method proposed in this study thereby ensures "Idea generation through making combinations" [9] as well as "Experience-sharing based on tabletop fieldwork" [11]. "Idea generation through making combinations" is realized by forced association measure through making combination of cards in card-based brainstorming. "Experience-sharing based on tabletop fieldwork" is realized with the cards of survey results, which are created with pictures taken in the actual fieldwork.

With these two points being realized, five functions listed in Section 4 were also realized as follows.

For realizing the function "Ensure that service designers have the stakeholders conduct an activity in a short time to understand the context for idea generation", "Idea generation through making combinations" supports brainstorming in a short time, and forced association measure makes ideation easy. Moreover, tabletop fieldwork takes less time than actual fieldwork. As a result, an activity to understand the context for idea generation is shortened.

For realizing the function "Ensure that service designers quickly induce a dialogue among multiple stakeholders", "Experience-sharing based on tabletop fieldwork" enables the participants to gain the same experience as actual one by viewing pictures. As a result, multiple stakeholders can have a dialogue through this experience.

For realizing the function "Ensure that service designers get stakeholders without their fieldwork experience to generate service ideas", "Idea generation through making combinations" motivates participants to join a dialogue for their own sake using the "experience gained in the field by using five senses" which is recorded on the cards. As a result, participants can generate ideas based on their "experience."

For realizing the function "Ensure that service designers have interfaces providing the stakeholders with information related to the service to design", "Experience-sharing based on tabletop fieldwork" leads to UX-based idea generation. The created cards therefore turn into interfaces providing the stakeholders with context information.

For realizing the function "Ensure that service designers visualize the system structure of the generated ideas", "Idea generation through making combinations" describes the ideas generated through combination as s system, and the existing elements as subsystems. As a result, the system structure of the generated ideas is visualized.

Table 2. Workshop Schedule

Activity	Time (min.)
Lecture and demonstration	15
Work 1.1: Read cards	5
Work 1.2: Generate action ideas + Recapitulate the activity in the group	30
Work 1.3: Share the action ideas with other groups + Vote	15
Work 2.1: Generate action ideas + Recapitulate the activity in the group	30
Work 2.2: Share the action ideas with other groups + Vote	15
Wrap-up	10
Total	120

6. Results of Applying the Proposed Visualization Method

6.1 Results 1 : Workshop – Idea Generation for Campus Master Plan of a National University

In contrast to existing campus master plans, most of which focused on facility design, we intended to develop a campus master plan in a new, human-centered approach, and applied the proposed method for idea generation [12]. We organized a workshop to generate action ideas for the facilities in each of the three campuses. The schedule is shown in Table 2. 94 people (24 people from Campus A; 31 people from Campus B; 39 people from Campus C) participated in 30 minute-idea generation activities twice, using 743 cards prepared (89 ISSUE cards; 281 PLACE cards; 373 RESOURCE cards). They generated 288 ideas in the process shown in Figure 4. Each idea was created using more than three cards, and visualized elements required to realize the ideas. Table 3 shows examples of the generated ideas.

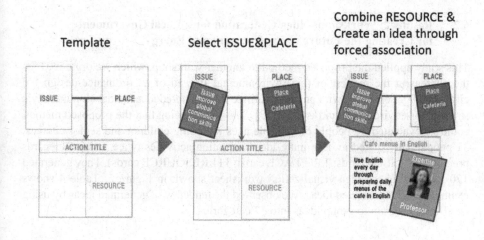

Fig. 4. Worksheet and process of visualizing an idea (1)

Table 3. Examples of Generated Ideas (1)

Title	Contents	ISSUE	PLACE	RESOURCE
Plan for fostering Monozukuri (manufacturing) Meisters ~ Learning history and spirits of Monozukuri	Hold seminars on Monozukuri taught by lecturers from various sectors of manufacturing industry, in order to foster "Meisters" equipped with the knowledge on history, and the spirits of Monozukuri.	Sense of Monozukuri	Monozukuri lab	Promote collaboration of industry, government and academia; Hold a seminar on intellectual property management
Business training in the local field ~ Learn about society at a university shop	Students of the university opens a shop in a local market; and learn about the society while interacting with the local community and experiencing actual business.	Communication with graduates	Local markets	Developing algorithm to save cost and time

6.2   Results 2: Workshop – Idea Generation for a Local Government for Creating the Future of Environment and Energy

This study applied the proposed method to another workshop, which we organized for the citizens at the request of the Environmental Bureau of an ordinance-designated city's local government, with an aim to utilize the generated ideas to develop the city's strategy for environment and energy [13]. The reason being that the proposed method could be evaluated by people of multiple ages including children and senior citizens. 31 people participated in 45 minute-idea generation activities twice, using 311 cards prepared (70 ISSUE cards; 130 PLACE cards; 111 RESOURCE cards). They generated 170 ideas using the idea-visualization worksheet shown in Figure 5. Table 4 shows examples of the generated ideas. We observed the tendency of generated ideas by using an affinity diagram to group ideas into 37 categories.

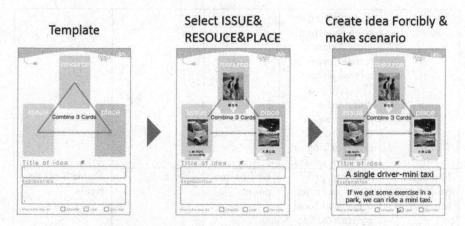

Fig. 5. Worksheet and process of visualizing an idea (2)

7   Discussion

Questionnaire results of Workshop 1 showed that the proposed method was evaluated positively by 69 people (17 people from Campus A; 20 people from Campus B; 32 people from Campus C), negatively by 5 people (3 people from Campus A; 1 person from Campus B; 1 person from Campus C), and neutrally by 20 people (4 people from Campus A; 10 people from Campus B; 6 people from Campus C), out of 94 people in total. The proposed method was perceived favorably by the participants with 69 out of 94 respondents making a positive evaluation.

Comments included "Easy to participate in the activity", "Easy to think concretely thanks for a large number of cards", "Helpful for coming up with problems and future image like a game", "Practical and enjoyable way for discussion", "Gradually enjoyed the activity though the rules were difficult to understand at the beginning" and "Easy to generate ideas". These comments suggest that the method was effective in terms of the Understanding and Utility. Nevertheless, negative comments included "More difficult than expected to jot down ideas in words", "How the ideas will be used to develop the campus master plan is not clear enough" and "Hard to deal with too many cards".

After analyzing user needs from the generated ideas, we made a road map for action items, in the order shown in Figure 6 for reflecting ideas to the vision. Action items shown in Table 5 were reflected in the mid-to-long term plan of the campus master plan [14]. Accordingly, we confirmed that the proposed method was useful in the process of developing master plans and future visions.

Table 4. Examples of Generated Ideas (2)

Title	Contents	ISSUE	PLACE	RESOURCE
Garbage is a mine of wealth!	Get connected with Asia by	More net-work with Asia	A major local shrine	Garbage

	picking up gar-bage together with Asian tourists visiting a local shrine. The city pro-vides infor-mation as an eco-oriented city working on garbage issues.			
Eco point program for tourists	The city pro-vides a service aiming at local revitalization, in which the tourists coming to a major an-nual festival can get a cou-pon at a local shop depending on the number of steps in walking	Utilize eco points	City hall	Major local fes-tivals

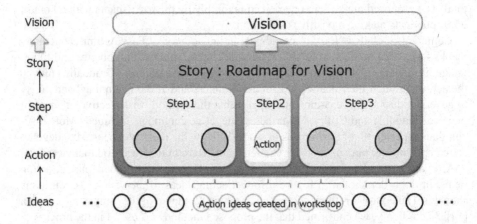

Fig. 6. Order of reflecting generated ideas to the vision

Workshop 2 received questionnaire responses from 24 out of 31 participants. Responses were given on a five-point ordinal scale. All the respondents evaluated this workshop using the proposed visualization method "Highly satisfying" or "Satisfying". Comments included "Enjoyed hearing various comments", "The more the participants can feel how these ideas will lead to the future actions of the city, the more future vision is likely to be improved as the output.", "Many positive comments, and groupwork with members in various positions expanded my imagination.", and "It was nice to learn the method." The comments were reflected to the mid-to-long term plan of the local government's environment and energy strategy. Accordingly, we confirmed that the proposed method is useful in the process of developing a future vision.

Table 5. Examples of Actions Reflecting the Generated Ideas

ACTION TITLE	ACTION	PLACE
International Cafe ~ Place for international exchange and learning	For international exchange and learning English, provide a cafe space where Japanese people can interact with international students and native speakers, and enjoy the food of various countries the international students came from.	Cafeteria
Healthy cafeteria on campus ~ Get together with local people	Open a cafeteria which gives opportunities for kids and their mothers in the area to come to the university, and enjoy healthy menus as well as health check-up developed utilizing the university's technology.	Lecture hall building; Cafeteria

8 Conclusions

This study proposed a visualization method for service ideas based on various stakeholders' experiences gained in tabletop fieldwork. We applied the method to two workshops and evaluated the results.

The paper cards are created based on the actual fieldwork results, which set the scope of the ideas to be generated. In other words, the cards also set scope of the system, which will actualize the idea.

With pictures put on the cards, even beginners can generate many ideas within a short time by combining the cards intuitively. Participants found using PLACE cards particularly similar to actual fieldwork. The cards made it easier for participants to generate ideas based on their own tabletop "experience." This study however is intended to propose a method enabling beginners to generate ideas in a short time, and thus we will evaluate the quality of generated ideas in the future study. Moreover, since a special application for card preparation is likely to useful and generally used by service designers, we will consider the development in the future study.

The results suggested that "Experience-sharing based on tabletop fieldwork" enables the participants on the occasion of their first meeting to reveal their experience and emotion relevant to the picked cards, and induces a natural dialogue through the sharing advances. The proposed method thereby ensured idea generation through their tabletop experience, which made not only problem solving but future-oriented ideation easier.

Elements constituting the generated idea are visualized with the idea being linked with three kinds of cards. The relationship among the cards, ideas and purpose are as follows. The cards are enablers of the ideas, and the ideas are enablers of the purpose [16]. An enabler utilizes the enabler above to realize the purpose.

Future research includes developing a software program for this method with a focus on the order of making cards, and idea traceability, and evaluating the quality of the output.

References

1. Sakaguchi Kazutoshi, Shirasaka Seiko (2016) Evaluation of visualized vision planning and its outcomes, Proceedings of the 4th International Conference on Serviceology, pp239-245.
2. Stanford University Institute of Design (2013) The Bootcamp Bootleg, http://dschool.stanford.edu/wp-content/uploads/2013/10/METHODCARDS-v3-slim.pdf
3. ISO 9241-210 (2010) Ergonomics of human- system interaction -- Part 210: Human- centred design for interactive systems
4. INCOSE (2015) Systems Engineering Handbook 4E
5. Alexander Kossiakoff, William N. Sweet, Samuel J. Seymour, Steven M. Biemer (2011) Systems Engineering Principles and Practice
6. Takeyama, Masanao (2012) Service design and its visualization techniques, The Hiyoshi review of the social sciences, No.23, pp.15- 35
7. Ando, Masaya (2016), Textbook of UX Deign, Maruzen Publishing
8. Shostack, L. (1982) How to design a service, European Journal of Marketing, 16 (1), pp. 49-63.
9. James Webb Young (2003) A Technique for Producing Ideas, McGraw-Hill Education
10. Graduate School of System Design and Management, Keio University (2013) Innovation Dialogue Tool: Guidebook on basic methods for the use in workshops,
11. http://www.mext.go.jp/component/a_menu/science/detail/__icsFiles/afield-file/2014/06/06/1347910_4.pdf
12. Kurose, Masaaki (2002) Developmental method at the early stage for generating an adequate interactive system concept, Media and Education, No.9, pp. 1-14.
13. Sakaguchi, Kazutoshi, Hirano, Takashi, Hashimoto, Hisashi, Sato, Yoshitaka, Harada, Hirokazu" Putting community design into practice: Campus master plan for Kyushu institute of technology" Fujitsu Scientific and Technical Journal, 2013
14. Community developed through energy creation ~ Workshop for creating the future of environment and energy of Fukuoka City ~, http://www.city.fukuoka.lg.jp/kankyou/saiene/index.html
15. Kyushu Institute of Technology, Facilities Division (2012) The Campus Master Plan for Kyushu Institute of Technology, http://jimu-www.jimu.kyutech.ac.jp/sisetsu/sisetsu_info/si-infor.htm
16. Fukuoka City (2014) Environment and Energy Strategy of Fukuoka City, http://www.city.fukuoka.lg.jp/kankyo/energie/hp/senryaku.html
17. Shirasaka, Seiko (2009) A Standard Approach To Find Out Multiple Viewpoints To Describe An Architecture Of Social Systems- Designing Better Payment Architecture To Solve Claim-Payment Failures Of Japan's Insurance Companies, INCOSE

Introduction to a Service Prototyping Tool Box

Abdul Rahman Abdel Razek[1], Christian van Husen[1], Saed Imran[1]

[1] Furtwangen University, Service Innovation, Robert-Gerwig-Platz 1, 78120 Furtwangen
aba,vahu,ima@hs-furtwangen.de

Abstract. Service prototyping is a relatively new discipline that requires s innovative ways for using current technologies, tools and approaches to offer rapid, accurate and cost-effective service prototyping solutions. These solutions should bear the capability to mitigate the risks connected with unforeseen problematic issues based on the service design specification, or aspects of it delivery. Thus, offering cost saving and effective service prototyping solutions with improved quality. One of key challenge in this quest relates to the selection of tools and established techniques that can provide fast iteration development process to service prototyping by enabling the integration of user comments and suggestions. For this reason, an innovative toolbox approach is taken for services prototyping where set of appropriate tools depending on the nature of service can be picked at different phases of service prototyping lifecycle. The paper presents the investigation conducted under the scientific project dimenSion, where initially service prototyping development matrix is created to support service provider to design and experience offered services as realistic as possible, thereby, laying the foundation to establish toolbox solution for service prototyping.

Keywords: Service Prototyping, Service Innovation, Service Design, Service Digitalization & Visualizations

1.1 Introduction

Service prototyping is a relatively new discipline that supports innovation, aiding designers in forming inventive concepts and ideas enabling the investigating and un-covering of related data about the target group. It also motivates communication, helping stakeholders to communicate the service idea throughout the organization enabling fast decision making. Correspondingly service prototyping permits early evaluation and testing, the evaluation can be done in various forms, including but not limited to usability testing and user feedback, surveys and interviews throughout the design process [1] [2]. The result of our qualitative survey [3] shown that there are three main reasons for which companies use service prototyping, first is to explore and find new ideas and solutions, largely for experimenting idea development or to find solutions, where quarter of the surveyed companies always used service proto-typing for the creation of a new service, the second reason is to get feedback from employees and customers, primarily to prove a concept, analyze feasibility, identify weaknesses, choosing alternatives, executing tests, and process scheduling to enable fast decision making , to which a third of the surveyed companies used service proto-types to evaluate their service or

© Springer International Publishing AG 2017
Y. Hara and D. Karagiannis (Eds.): ICServ 2017, LNCS 10371, pp. 135–143, 2017.
DOI: 10.1007/978-3-319-61240-9_13

service idea, the third main reason is the cooperation between stakeholders for information exchanges, and learning process for employee training, principally used to make decisions, build competences, generate knowledge, involve the stakeholders, and create documentation, where almost half of the surveyed companies always used service prototyping for communicating a service idea. Service prototyping requires innovative use of current technologies, procedures, methods and tools in service design into creating a fast, accurate and affordable service prototype [4] [5]. Researchers differ on the definitions of service prototyping, and the definition of prototyping vary in different design domains [6]. Blomkvist [7] defines prototyping as the use of prototypes to explore, evaluate, or communicate in design, and describes prototype as physical manifestation of actual delivered service.

We considered all aspects and definitions to create our own definition, in which service prototyping is considered as an early or incomplete version of the real service and is allows the simulation of service experience. Therefore, permits the creation, evaluation and communication of service ideas at the same time supports conception and its visualization while the development phase. Another challenging aspect of service prototyping is the confidentiality of service prototyping solutions, where companies don't want to share information due to strong organizational opposition for having an edge on other competitors [8].

2 Service Prototyping Matrix

The service prototyping development matrix as shown in figure 1 consists of four design dimensions, each has a corresponding level of fidelity and resolution.

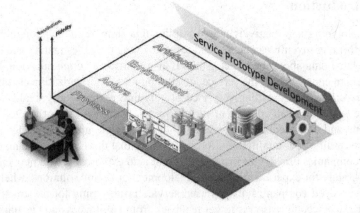

Fig. 1. Service Prototype Development Matrix

There is a direct correlation between the service prototyping development matrix and the service prototyping development key aspects in figure 2, which consists of the four key aspects: i) idea; ii) requirements; iii) design and iv) implementation, using a prototypical process of thinking where prototyping could be done at any time and as much as needed. Idea being the first key aspect, focuses on the idea-related activities like brainstorming, evaluation. In requirements aspect, the service prototyping requirements are gathered, separated, defragmented, and finally analyzed. In design aspect, the service concepts are created, developed and made ready for application. Lastly the implementation aspect where the service prototype concept is implemented before being introduced into the market.

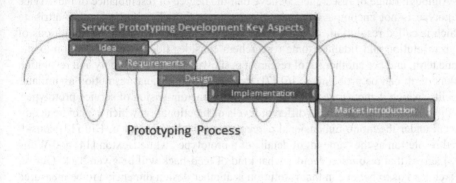

Fig. 2. Service Prototype Development Key Aspects

Research suggests that defining service prototyping and its design dimensions is a difficult process for designers [9] [10]. In this research, we have concluded that the best way to create the design dimensions of service prototyping is through describing the service prototype with four key dimensions, as show in Figure 1. Artefacts are the first dimension defined in the service prototyping matrix, artefacts are any physical objects, so as informational user interface like a homepage prototype and so as a tool or an object that helps in creating a prototype, the focus here is on how the objects will affect the service and its involvement. As the second design dimension is environment, where the setting of the service takes place, whether in an organization-al, industrial, or managerial setting or even in online or offline context, for example, customers contact oriented setting, where convince and comfort are key aspects for customers. The third design dimension of the matrix is actors, which are all the involved roles in service delivery, from internal like employees and external like customer. The fourth and final design dimension of the matrix is the process of service prototyping, in which all activities and interfaces in the process of service delivery like maintenance on customer's site or remote services.

2.1 Fidelity and Resolution in Service prototyping

The term fidelity refers to nearness to the final service design, Tullis [11] claims that the fidelity of a prototype is adjudicated by how it looks to the individual ob-serving it, and not by its similarity to the actual service. In other words, the degree to which the prototype accurately represents the appearance and interaction of the service is the determining factor in prototype fidelity, not the degree to which invisible attributes are precise [12]. Per Blomkvist [7] the degree of detail in a proto-type is the prototype's fidelity and can be thought of as how much of the final design the prototype represents. Fidelity is the level of improvement or degree of detail showed by a prototype while thoroughly assessing how the prototype resembles a finished service and how much of the information or interactivity it depicts [6]. To simplify we consider fidelity as the level of detail and functionality built into a prototype.

Although range of researchers believe that the degree of resemblance of the service prototype is not encompassed under the concept of fidelity but is another attribute which is called resolution. After careful research considerations on the definitions of both resolution and fidelity, some researchers consider fidelity and resolution as the same term, and per another set of researchers shown that having fidelity and resolution as one term can be problematic [6] [7]. Passera [1] argues that resolution assimilates fidelity, which demonstrated lack in representing the dimension of service prototypes, as the different attributes have different levels of functionality, which cannot be acquiescent under the mono-dimensional perception of fidelity. Houde & Hill [13] considered resolution as the "amount of detail" of a prototype" while Buxton [14] and Wong [15] agrees that resolution decides what kind of feed-back will be given back. Our research lead us to believe in that resolution is another design dimension to be measured other than fidelity, meaning that the resolution of a service prototype is defined by the degree of resemblance of the prototype and final design or final service.

Understanding the target group aids in defining the resolution and fidelity of a service prototype. The low resolution and fidelity of the prototypes are important not only for effectively sharing the insights of this abstract method with other designers and the client but also to communicate and persuade the audience [7] [12] [16].

Service Prototyping tools, procedures and methods also have a big impact on the creation and developing of service prototypes. Service prototyping tools can be identified with coherence with the service prototyping development matrix, which was also created within this research project, using the four design dimensions, actors, process, environment and artefacts, to position the prototypes in the matrix, with regards to both to fidelity and resolution. An upgrade of the matrix is currently under research and will be presented in the future work.

3   Service Prototyping Toolbox

The service prototyping tool box consists of procedures, methods, and tools. Procedures are the sequence of actions or directions to be followed in resolving an issue or accomplishing a task create, methods are a way of arranging or doing a service prototype, particularly with a methodical order of thought and action. Tools are any item that can be used to achieve an objective, especially if the item is not consumed in the process. The term item refers that it can be a physical, informational and data management item, or a simple online device. The snippet of the suggested toolbox for service prototyping is presented (See Fig. 3, 4 and 5). The creation of this proposed service prototyping's toolbox is guided by the questions:

- Which procedure, method or tool should be used?
- When to use it?
- How to use it?
- what is expected from it at the end?

Tool Box	Type	Description	Content
Service Blueprint	Tool	Delivered through different channels: creating service scenarios and customer trips that define how different customers will use a service	Strategy Development
Personas	Method	Fictive persons who present typical users of a target group. They highlight important characteristics of the target groups and help with design decisions in the development phase	Design Decision Making
Story Telling	Method	Supports the research of the service idea. Through the use of simple words, the narrator will illustrate the solution as if it were a story	Troubleshooting
Customer-Journey Scorecard	Tool	From touchpoints to journeys: Seeing the world as customers, episodes, end-to-end experiences, language, channels, duration, repetition	Customer Service
Cross Channel Views	Method	To map customer interaction for all phases of the lifecycle across all channels allows us to design a 'channel neutral' experience and then define specific channel requirements	Tables & Diagrams
Customer Journey Map	Tool	Visualization of the touch points of the user with the service	Diagrams
Hotspot view	Method	Identify areas with potential for the customer and the business-> Determine the intervention points from where we imagine a service concept or design a service	Tables
Voice-of-Customer Analysis	Method	Method, with which explicit and unspoken customer wishes are determined and transformed into quantified, structured and evaluated customer requirements	Ideas Brainstorming
Virtual Simulation	Tool	Service environment exploration	VR-Simulation
System Map	Procedure	Visual description of the service organization: the various actors, have their common connections and the flows of materials, energy, information and money through the system are included	Map & Images Connections
Offering Map	Tool	Describes what the service provides in words, pictures or graphs. Can be used during development, implementation or communication to the end user	Graphs, words, pictures
Context mapping	Method	Everyday experiences of the users with services / products, in order to adapt their future requirements	Diagrams
Lego Serious Play	Method	For example, generation of new business strategies - develop and optimize team collaboration or analyse crisis situations and work out solution concepts for this	Moderated, professional Lego block exercises
Video Prototyping	Method	Visualization of ideas and concepts	Video
Short Clips	Tool	Short visual representation of the service or part of the service	Short, compact video
Design Fiction	Method	Design Fiction uses report elements to present and explain possibilities for the design	Idea & Prototype in a video

Fig. 3. Snippet of the Tool Box with description & content

Tool Box	Category			Key Aspects				Effort			Fidelity			Resolution		
	Create	Evaluation	Commun-ication	1	2	3	4	Low	Medium	High	Low	Medium	High	Low	Medium	High
Service Blueprint	x	x	x			x		x				x		x	x	
Personas		x	x	x	x	x		x			x				x	x
Story Telling			x	x	x			x			x				x	
Customer-Journey Scorecard	x	x	x	x	x	x	x	x				x		x		
Cross Channel Views	x	x	x	x	x	x	x	x			x				x	
Customer Journey Map	x	x	x	x	x	x	x	x				x			x	
Hotspot view	x	x	x	x	x	x	x	x			x			x		
Voice-of-Customer Analysis	x	x	x	x	x	x	x	x				x			x	
Virtual Simulation	x	x	x			x	x			x			x			x
System Map		x	x	x	x	x	x	x				x				x
Offering Map		x	x	x	x	x	x	x			x			x		
Context mapping		x	x	x	x	x	x		x	x	x				x	x
Lego Serious Play	x		x	x	x	x		x			x			x		
Video Prototyping	x	x	x	x	x	x		x				x		x		
Short Clips	x	x	x	x	x	x		x				x				x
Design Fiction	x	x	x	x	x	x	x		x		x				x	
Wizard of Oz	x	x	x			x				x			x			x
Gamification	x		x	x	x	x	x			x		x	x			x
Workshop	x	x	x	x	x	x	x	x			x			x		
Moderation Workshop	x	x	x	x	x	x	x	x			x					x
Design Workshop	x	x	x			x		x			x			x		
Imagine Workshop	x	x	x	x					x		x	x			x	x
Understand Workshop	x	x	x	x	x	x	x	x	x			x				x
Experience Prototype	x	x	x			x	x			x			x			x

Fig. 4. Snippet of the Tool Box with Category, SPD Key Aspects, Effort, Fidelity & Resolution

When we asked companies about if these service prototyping tools, methods, and procedures are known in their respective companies, and if they are recognized within the organization, if they are being currently used by the company to create or enable the creation of a service prototype. Some of the tools that were relatively known and implemented are live prototyping and service sketching, while others like Mock-ups, paper prototyping, walkthrough simulations, and storyboard were moderately know and less implemented that the previous ones, on the other hand tools like roleplay, blueprinting, Wizard of Oz, and design fiction are unknown and not widely used in companies.

Tool Box	Rolle in SP Matrix			
	Actors	Artefacts	Process	Environment
Service Blueprint	x		x	
Personas	x			
Story Telling	x		x	x
Customer-Journey Scorecard	x	x	x	x
Cross Channel Views		x		
Customer Journey Map	x	x	x	x
Hotspot view		x		
Voice-of-Customer Analysis			x	
Virtual Simulation	x	x	x	x
System Map	x	x		x
Offering Map		x		
Context mapping		x		
Lego Serious Play	x	x	x	x
Video Prototyping	x	x	x	x
Short Clips	x	x	x	x
Design Fiction	x	x	x	x
Wizard of Oz		x		
Gamification	x	x	x	x
Workshop	x	x	x	x
Moderation Workshop	x			
Design Workshop	x			x
Imagine Workshop	x			x
Understand Workshop	x			
Experience Prototype	x	x	x	x

Fig. 5. Snippet of the Tool Box with Category, SPD Key Aspects, Effort, Fidelity & Resolution

4   Conclusion and Future Work

The paper concludes by presenting a service prototyping matrix along with the service prototyping development key aspect which may pave the way for service prototype developer to focus primarily on the service being offered rather unnecessarily getting under the burden of how in optimal way realize the service prototyping idea into an actual running service prototyping. The investigation also has presented in tabular format available list of possible tools, procedures to select from. This list is not exhausted and due to the space limited few snippets of are shown here.

The research is still in the ongoing process and the future work will emphasis on the overall improvement of the service prototype tool box and the service prototyping development matrix. The tool box will be applied on several case studies where different techniques including new technologies like Virtual Reality, Augmented Reality, and Mixed Reality will be used in either the service prototyping process or as a service prototype itself. We drive also to investigate the degree of fulfilment of the service prototyping requirements and expectations, whilst evaluating and assessing the service prototyping tool box. The aspect of effort will be revisited and explained in a broader concept. The representation of the service prototyping matrix will be reengineered to have the best dimensional representation possible.

5   Acknowledgment

This work is supported by the research project "dimenSion - Multidimensional Service Prototyping", funded (under grant number 02K14A160) by the Federal Ministry of Education and Research, Germany.

References

1. Passera S. (2011) When, how, why prototyping? A practical framework for service development.
2. Buchenau M., Suri J. F., (2000) Experience Prototyping, Brooklyn, New York ACM.
3. Sämann M., Abdel Razek A.R. , Imran S., van Husen C., Droll C. (2016) Innovation in Prototyping for Technical Product Service Systems. In Proceedings of 21st ICE IEEE.
4. Agarwal R., Selen W., Green R. (2015) The Handbook of Service Innovation, p.78-81.
5. Gallouj F., Weinstein O. (1997) Innovation in services. Research Policy, Elsevier, 26, (4-5), p.537-556.
6. Blomkvist J., Holmlid S. (2011) Existing Prototyping Perspectives: Considerations for service design
7. Blomkvist J. (2014) Representing Future Situations of Service: Prototyping in Service Design
8. Claude R. Martin Jr David A. Horne, (1993),"Services Innovation: Successful versus Unsuccessful Firms", International Journal of Service Industry Management, Vol. 4 Iss 1 p.49 – 65.
9. Schneider, K. (1996) 'Prototypes as Assets, not Toys: Why and How to Extract Knowledge from Prototypes'. Proceedings of the 18th international conference on Software engineering IEEE Computer Society, Berlin, Germany, pp. 522-531.
10. Lim, Y.-K., Stolterman, E. & Tenenberg, J. (2008) 'The Anatomy of Prototypes: Prototypes as Filters, Prototypes as Manifestations of Design Ideas'. ACM Transactions on Computer-Human Interaction, vol. 15, no. 2.
11. Tullis, T.S. (1990) High-fidelity prototyping throughout the design process. In Proceedings of the Human Factors Society 34th Annual Meeting (Santa Monica, CA, Human Factors Society), p. 266.

12. Rudd J., Stern K., Isensee S. (1996) Low vs. high-fidelity prototyping debate, Volume 3 Issue 1, p. 76-85

13. Houde, S. & Hill, C. (1997). 'What do Prototypes Prototype?', In Handbook of human computer interaction (2nd Ed.) M. Helander, P. Landauer, & P. Prabhu, Elsevier Science B. V., Amsterdam, pp 367-381.

14. Buxton, W. (2007). Sketching User Experiences: getting the design right and the right design. San Francisco, CA: Morgan Kaufmann.

15. Wong, Y. Y. (1992). Rough and Ready Prototypes: Lessons from Graphic Design. Posters and short talks of the 1992 SIGCHI on human factors in computing systems (pp. 83-84). Monterey, California: ACM.

16. McCrudy M. (2006) Breaking the Fidelity Barrier: An Examination of our Current Characterization of Prototypes and an Example of a Mixed-Fidelity Success, CHI 2006 Proceedings

Lab-Forming Fields and Field-Forming Labs

Takeshi Kurata, Ryosuke Ichikari, Ching-Tzun Chang, Masakatsu Kourogi,

Masaki Onishi, Takashi Okuma

AIST, 1-1-1 Umezono, Tsukuba, Ibaraki 305-8560, Japan
{t.kurata, r.ichikari, keishun-chou, m.kourogi, takashi-
okuma}@aist.go.jp, onishi@ni.aist.go.jp

Abstract. This paper presents the concept of Lab-Forming Fields (LFF) and Field-Forming Labs (FFL). LFF is to transform real service fields into lab-like places for bringing research methodologies in laboratories to real fields with IoT. FFL is to transform laboratories into real-field-like places for getting subjects' behavior and experimental results closer and closer to the ones which are supposed to be obtained in the real service fields with VR. In addition, this paper provides a summary table of previously conducted researches in AIST on LFF and FFL with geospatial computing.

Keywords: Lab-Forming Fields, Field-Forming Labs, Internet of Things, Geospatial IoT, MAR, Big data, Deep data, Comb data

1   Introduction

Industries and daily lives have been drastically changing by means of synergy of IoT (Internet of Things) and AI (Artificial Intelligence). One of the impacts that IoT gives us is that big data on what is happening in the real world can be gathered comprehensively. Especially positional and geospatial information has fundamental value in a variety of areas. As technologies for gathering and applying geospatial information, there are seamless positioning [1][2][3][4] and real-world modeling such as SLAM (Simultaneous Localization And Mapping) [5] and 3D modeling [6], MAR (Mixed and Augmented Reality), etc. We call them "geospatial computing", and we also call the interdiscipline between geospatial computing and IoT "G-IoT (geospatial IoT)".

Fig. 1 shows each technology and methodology such as G-IoT technology in association with each phase of service design loop [7] which consists of measurement, modeling, designing, and application. In such a way that we measure behaviors of customers and employees [8][9][10], measure service/living environments, and apply them for As-Is comprehension for QC circle activities [11][12][13], To-Be comparison for service operation planning [14], context-aware interface development for service operation support, etc., we can realize service-engineering based approaches for service improvement and innovation. By the coming of IoT and Industry 4.0 societies, those kinds of approaches, which we call "Hakatte Hakaru (Fig. 2)" in Japanese, are supposed to become more necessary and ordinary.

© Springer International Publishing AG 2017

Y. Hara and D. Karagiannis (Eds.): ICServ 2017, LNCS 10371, pp. 144–149, 2017.
DOI: 10.1007/978-3-319-61240-9_14

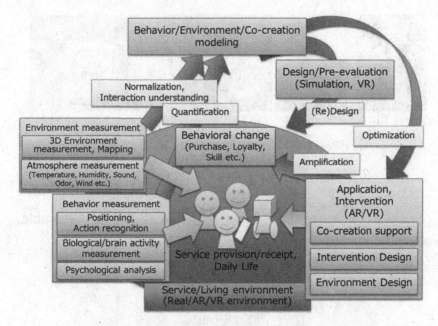

Fig. 1. Service design loop for supporting human-centered co-creation.

測って図る
Hakatte Hakaru

Measure	Plan
Weigh	Design
Survey	Attempt

Fig. 2. Hakatte Hakaru: service design loop for service improvement and innovation.

2 Lab-Forming Fields and Field-Forming Labs

There are two ways of realizing Hakatte Hakaru; Lab-Forming Fields (LFF) and Field-Forming Labs (FFL). For making these terms, we analogically utilized a term, "Terraforming", which means transforming some planet such as Mars from its current environment to another environment that is closer to Earth so that we can live on the planet. We illustrate how each technical field is exploited for LFF and FFL in Fig. 3.

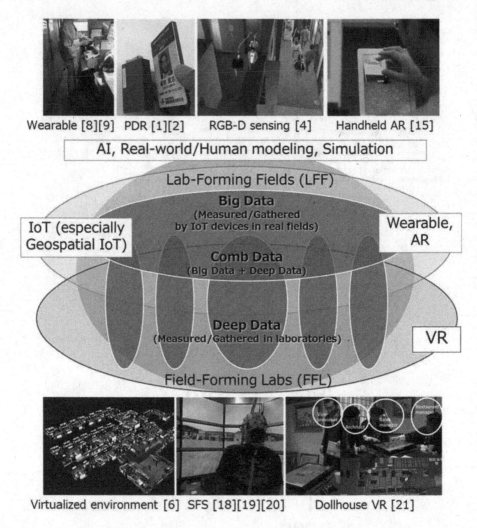

Fig. 3. Lab-Forming Fields (LLF) and Field-Forming Labs (FFL).

LFF is to transform real service fields into lab-like places for bringing methodologies in which hypothesis testing is repeatedly conducted by giving stimuli to service providers/customers and by observing the responses. Conventionally it was not practical to realize such methodologies in real service fields. However, they are finally getting practical by measuring service customers, employees, and service/living environments with IoT and wearable technologies including G-IoT for modeling and comprehending the real service fields, and then by intervening in there with information provision by means of AR [15][16] or other interfaces and with physical actuation by means of robotic interfaces.

On the other hand, FFL is to transform laboratories into real-field-like places for getting subjects' behavior and experimental results closer and closer to the ones which are supposed to be obtained in the real service fields. For that purpose, VR environments [17][18][19][20][21] are often developed and utilized. Such VR environments should provide repeatability of real service fields; however, the extent of repeatability depends on what we want to explore. Note that it is obvious that we can also utilize the advantages of VR environments in FFL; well-controlled environments and a variety of measurements such as gaze, biological, and brain activity measurements.

3 Research cases on LFF and FFL

Although it might be still difficult to conduct full-fledged research and development on LFF and FFT, there have already been many research cases in which the concept of LFF and FFL is partially introduced and implemented. In order to facilitate concrete discussion on LFF and FFL, we summarized previously conducted researches in AIST which are relevant to LFF and FFL with geospatial computing and G-IoT as shown in Tab. 1.

Tab. 1. Research cases with G-IoT in AIST on LFF and FFL.

	Study Case	Measurement	Modeling	Design/Pre-evaluation	Application/Intervention
Lab-Forming Fields (LFF)	Maintenance service (MAR-based support) [15][16]	User's position and orientation, Target objects, Machine condition	Machines, Road environments	N/A	Computer-supported work
	As-Is comprehension on employees' behavior in restaurants (CSQCC) [11][12][13]	Employees' trajectories, POS data, Real environments	Work indicators, Skills, 3D Indoor environments,	Kaizen plan by discussion with visualization	Improved service provision
	To-Be comparison on operation plans in warehouse picking [14]	Trajectories of employees and carts, WMS data, Shelves' layout	Picking work, Work indicators	Kaizen-plan comparison by simulation	(Improved operation)
Field-Forming Labs (FFL)	Ethnography in a hotel (CCE Lite) [17]	Trajectories of employees, Real environments, Interviews	Skills, 3D Indoor environments	N/A	N/A
	Marketing for product design in virtual stores (SFS) [19][20]	Trajectories/Gazes/Brain activities of subjects in VR, Real environments	Customer behavior, Indoor 3D environments	Product Design	(New product)
	Restaurant floor planning with multi-stakeholders (Dollhouse VR) [21]	N/A	3D Indoor environments, Human body	Floor planning in collaborative VR	(Improved floor plan)

4   Conclusion

In this paper, we introduced the concept of Lab-Forming Fields (LFF) and Field-Forming Labs (FFL). Based on LFF, we can obtain big data from real service fields on a daily basis. In addition, FFL can intensively give us deep data. To the best of our knowledge, the definition of deep data is not firm at this moment; however, deep data should contain heterogeneous types of data such as behavior, gaze, biological, and brain activity data, or high-quality data such as ground truth and reference data which are often created manually or interactively.

AI technologies are expected to help us combine big data with deep data for constructing models of real service fields consisting of customers, providers, and environments. As shown in Fig. 3, the combination of big data and deep data seems like a comb shape. That is the reason why we call it "Comb Data". Future works would include how to develop strategy for gathering comb data efficiently [10], and how to utilize it for better understanding the real service fields towards service improvement and innovation.

Acknowledgement

This research is partially supported by JST's Program on Open Innovation Platform with Enterprises, Research Institute and Academia (OPERA).

References

1. Masakatsu Kourogi and Takeshi Kurata, Personal Positioning Based on Walking Locomotion Analysis with Self-Contained Sensors and a Wearable Camera, Proc. ISMAR 2003, pp. 103-112, 2003.
2. Ryosuke Ichikari, Luis Carlos Manrique Ruiz, Masakatsu Kourogi, Tomoaki Kitagawa, Sota Yoshii, and Takeshi Kurata, Indoor Floor-Level Detection by Collectively Decomposing Factors of Atmospheric Pressure, Proc. IPIN 2015, 11pp, 2015.
3. Tomoya Ishikawa, Masakatsu Kourogi, and Takeshi Kurata, Economic and Synergistic Pedestrian Tracking System with Service Cooperation for Indoor Environments, Proc. International Journal of Organizational and Collective Intelligence, 2(1), pp.1-20, 2011.
4. Yuri Miyagi, Masaki Onishi, Chiemi Watanabe, Takayuki Itoh, Masahiro Takatsuka, Feature Extraction and Visualization for Symbolic People Flow Data, International Conference Information Visualisation (IV2016), 2016.
5. A.J. Davison, N. Kita, 3D simultaneous localisation and map-building using active vision for a robot moving on undulating terrain, Proc. CVPR 2001, 8 pages, 2001.
6. Tomoya Ishikawa, Kalaivani Thangamani, Masakatsu Kourogi, Andrew P. Gee, Walterio Mayol-Cuevas, Jungwoo Hyun, and Takeshi Kurata, Interactive 3-D Indoor Modeler for Virtualizing Service Fields, Virtual Reality, 17(2), pp.89-109, 2013.
7. Takenaka, T., Koshiba, H. and Motomura, Y., Development strategy of service engineering for retail and restaurant services, The Philosopher's Stone for Sustainability (Proceedings of the 4th CIRP International Conference on Industrial Product Service Systems), pp.121-124, 2012.

8. Ryuhei Tenmoku, Ryoko Ueoka, Koji Makita, Takeshi Shimmura, Masanori Takehara, Satoshi Tamura, Satoru Hayamizu and Takeshi Kurata, Service-Operation Estimation in a Japanese Restaurant Using Multi-Sensor and POS Data, Proceeding of APMS 2011 conference, Parallel 3-4: 1, 2011.

9. Koji Makita, Masakatsu Kourogi, Tomoya Ishikawa, Takashi Okuma, and Takeshi Krata, PDRplus: human behaviour sensing method for service field analysis, Proc. ICServ 2013, pp.19-22, 2013.

10. Karimu Kato, Takashi Okuma and Takeshi Kurata, Proposing an Interactive Label Attaching System for Supervised Service Operation Estimation", Proceedings of ICServ2016, pp.281-287, 2016.

11. Tomohiro Fukuhara, Ryuhei Tenmoku, Takashi Okuma, Ryoko Ueoka, Masanori Takehara, and Takeshi Kurata, Improving Service Processes based on Visualization of Human-behavior and POS data: a Case Study in a Japanese Restaurant, Proc. ICServ 2013, pp.1-8, 2013.

12. Tomohiro Fukuhara, Ryuhei Tenmoku, Ryoko Ueoka, Takashi Okuma, and Takeshi Kurata, Estimating skills of waiting staff of a restaurant based on behavior sensing and POS data analysis: A case study in a Japanese cuisine restaurant, Proc. AHFE2014, pp.4287-4299, 2014.

13. Takashi Okuma, Tomohiro Fukuhara, Ryosuke Ichikari, Ching-Tzun Chang, Manrique Carlos, Takeshi Shinmura, and Takeshi Kurata, Role of Servicing Activity Visualization in Quality Control Circle, Proc. ICServ 2015, 6pp., 2015.

14. Tatsuro Myokan, Mitsutaka Matsumoto, Takashi Okuma, Ryosuke Ichikari, Karimu Kato, Daichi Ota, and Takeshi Kurata, Pre-evaluation of Kaizen plan considering efficiency and employee satisfaction by simulation using data assimilation -Toward constructing Kaizen support framework-, Proc. ICServ 2016, 7 pages, 2016.

15. Koji Makita, Thomas Vincent, Soichi Ebisuno, Masakatsu Kourogi, Tomoya Ishikawa, Takashi Okuma, Minoru Yoshida, Laurence Nigay and Takeshi Kurata, Mixed Reality Navigation on a Tablet Computer for Supporting Machine Maintenance in Wide-area Indoor Environment, Proceedings of ICServ2014, pp.41-47, 2014.

16. Ching-Tzun Chang, Ryosuke Ichikari, Koji Makita, Takashi Okuma, and Takeshi Kurata, [POSTER] Road Maintenance MR System Using LRF and PDR, Proc. ISMAR 2015, pp.204-205, 2015.

17. Nakajima, M., Yamada, K. C., and Kitajima, M, Cognitive Chrono-Ethnography Lite, Work: A Journal of Prevention, Assessment and Rehabilitation (IEA 2012: 18th World congress on Ergonomics - Designing a sustainable future), Vol.41, pp.617- 622, 2012.

18. Jungwoo Hyun, Yoshiko Habuchi, Anjin PARK, Tomoya Ishikawa, Masakatsu Kourogi and Takeshi Kurata, Service-Field Simulator using MR Techniques: Behavior Comparison in Real and Virtual Environments, Proceedings on ICAT2010, pp.14-21, 2010.

19. Takashi Okuma and Takeshi Kurata, Service Field Simulator: Virtual environment display system for analyzing human behavior in service fields, Proceedings of ICServ2014, pp.55-60, 2014.

20. Yuji Takeda, Takashi Okuma, Motohiro Kimura, Takeshi Kurata, Takeshi Takenaka, and Sunao Iwaki, Electrophysiological measurement of interest during walking in a simulated environment, INTERNATIONAL JOURNAL OF PSYCHOPHYSIOLOGY, Vol.93, No.3, pp.363-370, 2014.

21. Hikaru Ibayashi, Yuta Sugiura, Daisuke Sakamoto, Natsuki Miyata, Mitsunori Tada, Takashi Okuma, Takeshi Kurata, Masaaki Mochimaru, and Takeo Igarashi, Dollhouse VR: a multi-view, multi-user collaborative design workspace with VR technology, In SIGGRAPH Asia 2015 Emerging Technologies (SA '15). ACM, Article 8 , 2 pages, 2015.

Service Design

A Modelling Method for Digital Service Design and Intellectual Property Management Towards Industry 4.0: CAxMan Case

Nesat Efendioglu, Robert Woitsch

BOC Asset Management GmbH, Operngasse 20B, 1040 Vienna, Austria

{firstname.lastname@boc-eu.com}

Abstract. The fourth industrial revolution, so-called Industry 4.0 is triggered by digitalization of manufacturing industries. According to global studies, Industry 4.0 will have significant positive impact in sense of revenue and cost reduction, but it will trigger also change and transformation of business, and the only actors, who can keep up with this transformation, and come up with innovative business models, can take advantages of this revolution. The value proposition proposed in those business models, nowadays are created collaboratively with using several intellectual properties, targeting characteristics of complex and relatively new market structures. We propose a model-driven approach and a corresponding toolkit, so-called "Business Modelling Infrastructure" that supports those actors during configuring their value propositions and business models, with knowing which characteristics of which market segment they are targeting and what kind of intellectual properties do they need to use and what are their dependencies and limitations. The work in the hand presents also a business modelling case for additive manufacturing, where the Business Modelling Infrastructure is applied. Finally, the work evaluates the Business Modelling Infrastructure with giving preliminary results from that business modelling case.

Keywords: Business Modelling, Digital Service Design, Intellectual Property Management, Meta-modelling

1 Introduction

Digitalization triggers change and transforms businesses. Most future disruptive technologies relate to digital business transformation [12]. Industry 4.0, which originates from [10], indicates fourth industrial revolution based on Cyber Physical Systems [28], which is triggered by digitalization of manufacturing industries, where physical objects are seamlessly integrated in an information network, decentralized production and real-time adaptation are possible [20]. According to results of a global survey [39], Industry 4.0 is digital transformation of complete value chain and this development will change individual companies, transform market dynamics across range of industries. According to same survey results, through to new industrial revo-

© Springer International Publishing AG 2017
Y. Hara and D. Karagiannis (Eds.): ICServ 2017, LNCS 10371, pp. 153–163, 2017.
DOI: 10.1007/978-3-319-61240-9_15

lution, over five years, it is expected, that US$ 493 billion annual revenue increase and US$ 421 billion cost reduction.

The Additive Manufacturing (AM) is one of the main trends in Industry 4.0 and it might be the game changer in industry [42]. The market for systems, services and materials for AM currently totals EUR 1.7 billion and is expected to quadruple over the next 10 years. AM is on the verge of shifting from a pure rapid prototyping technology to series production readiness and is therefore opening up new market opportunities for actors such as machine suppliers, manufacturing service providers and designers/OEMs [42].

According to [20] and [39] keys for success of those developments are (1) digital transformation of individual enterprises with configuring their business models based on revolutionary digital product & services portfolios offered by those digital enterprises individually or in collaboration and incrementally adapted with sensing market needs, and (2) protection of their Know-how, with other words their intellectual properties (IP).

Consequently, two questions arise (1) how can above-mentioned actors keep up with digital business transformation, sense market needs and configure their businesses accordingly?, and (2) how can they manage intellectual properties.

Based on our experience gained during following EU Research projects dealing with Factory of Future; BIVEE [9], ComVantage [14], e-SAVE [19], Adapt4ee[1], CAxMan[13], DISRUPT[16] and GO0D MAN[24] -digital transformation of enterprises and management of digital enterprises starts with documentation of AS-IS situation with creating digital/virtual counterpart of real environment with certain abstraction level. Another point we experienced is aspects shall be considered from three distinctive viewpoints (1) Enterprise Strategic View point, where enterprise defines its business models, business goals and product and service offerings, their value creation chains, (2) Business Process View Point, where enterprise define, how those product and services are produced, and (3) Infrastructure View point, where enterprise define, which infrastructure it needs to run business, produce product and services.

The work at hand targets first view point and proposes a model-based holistic approach and its corresponding tool so-called "Business Modelling Infrastructure". Aim of the Business Modelling Infrastructure is to support enterprises to keep up with new industrial revolution by easing digital service design as well as management of IPs and their dependencies. Hence, Business Modelling Infrastructure offers conceptual model-based features to create and configure, -human and machine interpretable-business models, product and service portfolios, IP portfolios, and value-creation – chains, so the enterprises can be empowered with certain computer-aided business opportunity and risk analysis abilities. The Business Modelling Infrastructure is developed within an EU research project "CAxMAn", which aims to establish cloud based toolboxes, workflows and a One-Stop-Shop for Computer-aided-technologies (CAx) supporting the design, simulation and process planning for Additive Manufacturing integrated seamlessly.

In this respect, the remainder of the paper is structured as follows; Section 2 briefly introduces the business modelling case in CAxMan Project. Section 3 introduces the Business Modelling Infrastructure, which is used for the case. Section 4 concludes the paper with giving some preliminary results from CAxMAn business modelling case and gives an outlook on future work

2   CAxMan Case

As aforementioned, The H2020-FoF project CAxMan aims to establish cloud based toolboxes with (1) transforming existing CAx-product and services, and adding new features, (2) integrating and orchestrating those product and services in form of AM workflows and (3) offer them through a One-stop-shop.

CAxMan consortium offers product and services in very large spectrum; from design and simulation to process planning and 3D printing, as well from data interoperability and workflow management to High Performance Computing (HPC) services. These product and services are offered by different vendors in the consortium, which again have different legal status, business objectives and motivations. In addition to that, all those product and services consist of several IPs, which have different protection type (IP Rights), owners, dependencies and limitations.

On the other hand CAxMan targets a very large market; the whole manufacturing industry using AM technologies, which bring challenges, such as identification and definition of market structure and characteristic of the market.

CAxMan consortium requires an infrastructure, where (1) they can identify, virtualize their IPs, their protection type, owner, dependencies and limitation, so they can create and manage their IP portfolio, (2) they can configure their product and services with composing IPs conceptually, so they can create and manage their product and service portfolio, (3) identify their potential vendors and partners in their eco-system, (4) identify market structure, potential customers and their characteristics in sense of goal and needs of actors in the market segments, (5) Build and manage value creation chains considering whole life-cycle of their product and services, (6) design and configure their business models reflecting targeted market, value proposition, value flow, key partners and resources, (7) to know relations from business models to value creation chains down to product and service, and IPs and last but not least (8) to evaluate success of designed business models after execution.

3   Business Modelling Infrastructure

3.1   Related Work

An extensive state-of-the-art analysis on current business modelling approaches and frameworks in [27] shows that there are several components suggested by literature to be considered as part of business models; such as "Value Proposition" that is suggested by 97% of scanned literature, "Cooperation Structure" and "Revenue Model" 91%, "Customer and Market Segment" 88%, "Value Creation" %79, "Product and Service Structure/Offerings" %74. According to the state-of-the-art analysis, concepts suggested in [37], [38], [45], [8], [26], [35], [44], [7], [41] cover aspects in abovementioned components.

There are well-accepted conceptual modelling (de-facto-) standards such as "Business Model Canvas"[38] as entry point for design and configuration of business model, "e³-Value Model[25] for description of value creation, cooperation structures and value flows between actors, "Product Structure model" and "Market Structure Model" from [30], [17] for definition of market structure and characteristics as well as for definition of product and service components according to market needs.

Besides realization of conceptual models, another issue is definition of interdependencies among those conceptual models. The meta-modelling is a well-known approach to provide concepts and instruments for (a) realization of conceptual models as well as (b) the realization of weaving mechanisms to define interdependencies among those conceptual models.

Meta-modelling [31] is introduced as a realization approach to develop domain specific IT-supported concept modelling. Based on Strahringer [46], Karagiannis and Kühn [32] a layered approach for conceptual modelling is used. Most prominent meta-meta-models based on Kern [47] are mentioned: (a) Ecore from the Eclipse platform [11], (b) GOPRR from MetaEdit+ Platform [33] and (c) MS DSL Tools and MS Visio [15]. Additionally the following meta-meta-models are introduced: (d) MOF [34], which is realized on different UML Profile platforms (e) ADOxx based on the equally named platform ADOxx [2], (f) Obeo Designer on Eclipse [36] and (g) Generic Model Environment GME [23].

Besides the technical functionality, the provision of a model repository, as well as the flexible adaptation approach, the Business Modelling Infrastructure is collaboratively developed via the ADOxx.org [17] community with more than 1300 developers and more than 3500 stakeholders world-wide. Hence, in order to guarantee sustainability after the project period, the whole conceptual implementation is performed on the open collaborative CAxMan Developers Space on ADOxx.org [3].

3.2   Business Modelling Infrastructure Meta-Model

The work at hand proposes a model-based holistic approach and its corresponding tool so-called "Business Modelling Infrastructure". The Business Modelling Infrastructure supports both (1) top-down; business modelling scenarios beginning with identification of market structure and needs down to creation business models, configuration product and services, and identification required intellectual properties, (2)bottom-up; creation of business models with beginning exiting intellectual properties and composing product and services with those intellectual properties corresponding to the market needs, building value creation chains and creation of business models based on that. The modelling method proposed in this context is presented with introducing its meta-model and modelling stack.

The modelling method of Business Modelling Infrastructure is a hybrid modelling method coupling several modelling languages based on (defacto-) standards and best-practices for above-mentioned aspects. Following the state-of-the-art analysis in [27] and based-on our experience gained from aforementioned EU Research project we decided to implement the meta-model of Business Modelling Infrastructure on ADOxx based on following standards;

- "Business Model Canvas"[38] and "Lean Canvas" [48] for design and configuration of business model,
- "e³-Value Model" [25] for description of value creation, cooperation structures and value flows between actors,
- "Product Structure model" and "Market Structure Model" from [30], [17] for definition of market structure and characteristics as well as for definition of product and service components according to market needs
- Part of "Cause and Effects model" based on [17], [29] for definition of Key Performance Indicators.
- On the other hand, to the best of our knowledge, there is no model-based standard or best-practice for neither definition of IP nature and dependencies nor creation of IP portfolios. Based on experience gained from business modelling and innovation management workshops, which we hold with business developers from beneficiaries of CAxMan Consortium, as well as based on knowledge resources provided by European Patent Office [21], we propose a new model type, so-called "Intellectual Property Model".

The meta-model overview of Business Modelling Infrastructure is provided in FDMM form (Formalism for Describing ADOxx Meta Models and Models) [22].

According to FDMM, a meta-model is a tuple $\mathbf{MM} = \langle \mathbf{MT}, \preccurlyeq, \text{domain}, \text{range}, \text{card} \rangle$ where MT is the set of the defined model types, i.e. for i=1,...,m we have $\mathbf{MT} = \{MT_1, MT_2, ..., MT_m\}$. The $\mathbf{MT_i}$'s (i=1,...,m) are themselves tuples $\mathbf{MT_i} = \langle O_i^T, D_i^T, A_i \rangle$, where:

- O_i^T is the set of object types or classes,
- D_i^T is the set of data types, and
- A_i is the set of the attributes.

The Business Modelling Infrastructure Meta-model is composed of following model types:
- MT_{BMC} Business Model Canvas/Lean Canvas (BMC based on [38]),
- MT_{EVM} e3 Value Model (EVM based on [25])
- MT_{VM} Value Structure Model (VM based on [17], [30])
- MT_{IPM} Intellectual Property Model (IPM based on [21])
- MT_{MSM} Market Structure Model (MSM based on [30])
- MT_{PPM} Partner Pool Model (PPM based on [17], [30]))
- MT_{KPI} Key Performance Indicators model (KPI based on [17],[29])

And model types consist of following objects:
- $O_{BMC}^T = \{ BuildingBlock, Element, IsInside\}$
- $O_{EVM}^T = \{MarketSegment, Actor, ValueActivity, ValueInterface, ValueObject, StartStimulus, EndStimulus, And, Or, ValueExchange, Dependency\}$
- $O_{VSM}^T = \{Product/Service, Sub-Product/Service, Value, Requires\}$
- $O_{IPM}^T = \{IntellectualProperty, Requires\}$
- $O_{MSM}^T = \{Segment, Organization, Role, Characteristic, BelongsTo, HasCharacteristic\}$
- $O_{PPM}^T = \{Organization, Scope\}$

- O_{KPI}^T = {*Perspective, StrategicGoal, OperationalGoal, KPI, Influences, Operationalizes, Quantifies*}

The **Fig. 1** depicts Business Modelling Infrastructure Meta-model graphically with using MMDE notation [18]. In the figure, relations among modelling objects and model types can be seen. The most relevant relations for the work at hand are inter-model type relations, which are defined and realized with weaving concept (for details about weaving concept used in this work, please refer to [18]). As depicted in the figure Product/Service is composed of Sub-Product/Service and/or Value, where value has corresponding Intellectual Property defined in an IPM, as well as each Value and Intellectual Property has an owner corresponds to a Partner in a PPM, moreover each Value targets a certain Characteristic of a targeted Market Segment defined in a MSM. Besides that, each Value Object subject to value exchange in a value creation chain described by an EVM corresponds to Product/Service in a VSM. On the other hand, each value creation chain is abstracted and reflected in a BMC. And finally evaluation perspectives and criterion for each Business Model is defined in a KPI Model.

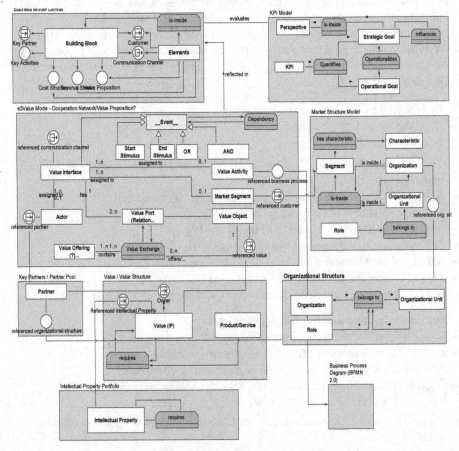

Fig. 1. Business Modelling Infrastructure Meta-model

Implemented modelling stack of Business Modelling Infrastructure corresponding to meta-model is depicted in **Fig. 2**. The full prototype (depicted in**Fig. 3**) can be downloaded from [3]

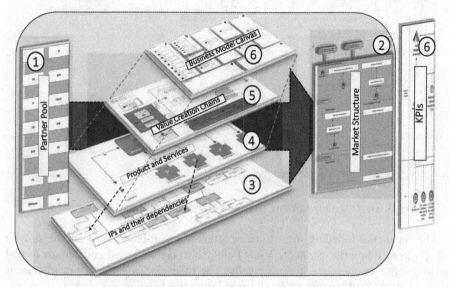

Fig. 2. Modelling Stack of Business Modelling Infrastructure

The modelling stack basically supports the both aforementioned top-down and bottom scenarios; (1) users of BMI can identify possible partners in a pool with their capabilities and contact points, (2) they can identify targeted market segments, structure of market with defining relation among market segments, their needs and goals, (3) They can identify existing and / or required IPs in the IP portfolio, (4) they can configure product and services with using IPs in the IP portfolio, (5) they can build value creation chains with using e3-Value Models for configured product and services, (6) describe high-level business model(s) reflecting value creation chains of product and services with using Business Model Canvas and last but not least (7) they can identify KPIs, match them to their strategic- and operational-goals to monitor success of the business model.

4 Conclusion and Outlook

In this paper, we introduced a model-based approach and its corresponding modelling software, so called "Business Modelling Infrastructure"(as depicted in **Fig. 3**), which should support actors dealing with business modelling in manufacturing industry towards Industry 4.0.

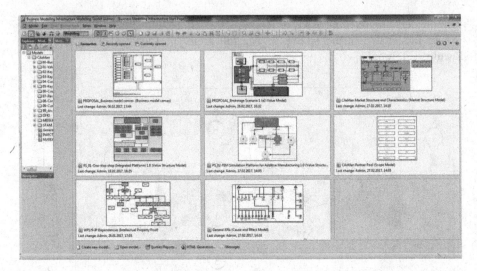

Fig. 3. The modelling software "Business Modelling Infrastructure version 2.2"

The Business Modelling Infrastructure offers a model-based approach to abstract aspects from Enterprise Strategic View Point, so to create digital counterpart of real environment and configure it conceptually. The Business Modelling Infrastructure is being used in CAxMan and 92 Intellectual Properties existing in CAxMan, their nature, dependencies, owners and limitations are identified, 25 Product and Services for CAxMan Product and Service Portfolio, and 2 possible Business Models for joint exploitation are identified, so far. The feedback coming from actors involved in CAxMan case showed, that having a modelling software based on certain and commonly accepted formalisms, ease (1) documentation of AS-IS situation, (2) sharing that with stakeholders, (3) making decisions, configurations on it, define TO-BE situation. As an outlook the following items derived from the feedback; (1) simulation of value flow based on different business model- and value chain-configurations, (2) completeness check of model content and (3) centrally accessible web-based infrastructure are desired additional features.

Acknowledgement

This work has been partly supported by European Union's Horizon 2020 research and innovation programme under grant agreement No 680448, project CAxMan.

References

1. Adapt4ee Consortium, Adapt4ee (FP7-ICT) Project: Occupant Aware, Intelligent and Adaptive Enterprises http://www.adapt4ee.eu
2. ADOxx, [Online www.adoxx.org, Accessed: 07.02.2017

3. ADOxx.org,   CAxMan   Developers   Space   [Online https://www.adoxx.org/live/web/caxman/space, Accessed 07.02.2017]
4. Afuah, A. and Tucci, C. L. Internet Business Models and Strategies: Text and Cases, McGraw-Hill/Irwin, New York City, NY, USA., 2013
5. Afuah, A. and Tucci, C. L., Internet Business Models and Strategies: Text and Cases, McGraw-Hill/Irwin, 2003
6. Amit, R. and Zott, C., Value Creation in E-Business, Strategic Management Journal, 22, 6-7, 493-520., 2001
7. Aziz, S., Fitzsimmons, K., and Douglas, E., Clarifying the Business Model Construct, in AGSE International Entrepreneurship Research Exchange, pp. 795-813, 2008.
8. Bieger, T., Rüegg-Stürm, J., and von Rohr, T. Strukturen und Ansätze einer Gestaltung von Beziehungskonfigurationen – Das Konzept Geschäftsmodell, in Bieger, T., Bickhoff, N., Caspers, R., zu Knyphausen-Aufseß, D., and Reding, K. (Eds.) Zukünftige Geschäfts-modelle – Konzepte und Anwendung in der Netzökonomie, Springer-Verlag, Berlin et al., pp. 35-62, 2002.
9. BIVEE Consortium, BIVEE (FP7-FoF) Project: Business Innovation and Virtual Enter-prise Environment http://www.bivee.eu
10. BMBF, Zukunftsprojekt Industrie 4.0 – BMBF, in German [Online https://www.bmbf.de/de/zukunftsprojekt-industrie-4-0-848.html Accessed : 07.02.2017]
11. Budinsky F., Steinberg. D., Merks E., Ellersick R. and Grose T.J., Eclipse modelling Framework. The Eclipse Series. Addison Wesley, 2004
12. Capgemini Consulting, Digital Transformation, [Online https://www.de.capgemini-consulting.com/resources/digital-transformation Accessed:07.02.2017]
13. CAxMan Consortium, CAxMan (H2020-FoF) Project: Computer Aided Technologies for Additive Manufacturing
14. ComVantage Consortium, ComVantage (FP7-FoF) Project: Collaborative Manufacturing Network for Competitive Advantage http://www.comvantage.eu
15. Cook S., Jones G., Kent S., und Wills A.C. Domain Specific Development with Visual Studio DSL Tools (Microsoft .Net Development). Addison-Weseley Longman, 2007
16. DISRUPT Consortium, DISRUPT (H2020-FoF) Project: Decentralised architectures for optimised operations via virtualised processes and manufacturing ecosystem collaboration http://disrupt-project.eu
17. Efendioglu, N., Utz, W., Woitsch, R., The Misson Control Room, in Enterprise Innova-tion: From Creativitiy to Engineering, pp.125-143, Wiley, 2015.
18. Efendioglu, N., Woitsch, R., Karagiannis, D., Modelling Method Design: A Model-driven Appraoch, in Proceedings of the 17th International Conference on Information Integration and Web-based Applications \& Services series (iiWAS'15), 2015.
19. e-SAVE Consortium, e-SAVE (FP7-ICT) Project, Energy Efficiency in the Supply Chain through Collaboration, Advanced Decision Support and Automatic Sensing http://www.e-save.eu
20. European Parliament Policy Department A: Economic and Scientific Policy, "Industry 4.0", 2016.
21. European Patent Office, IP Teaching Kit [Online http://www.epo.org/learning-events/materials/kit, Accessed 07.02.2017]
22. Fill, H., Redmond, T., Karagiannis, D., Formalizing Meta Models with FDMM: The ADOxx Case, in: Cordeiro, J., Maciaszek, L., Filipe, J.: Enterprise Information Systems, LNBIP, Vol. 141, 429-451
23. Generic Model Environment GME, [Online www.isis.vanderbilt.edu/Projects/gme, Ac-cessed07.02.2017]

24. GO0D MAN Consortium, GO0D MAN (H2020-FoF) Prject: Agent oriented zero defect multi-stage manufacturing [http://go0dman-project.eu
25. Gordijn, Jaap and Akkermans, Hans, Designing and Evaluating E-Business Models, in IEEE Intelligent Systems vol.14 num.4, pp. 11-17, IEEE Educational Activities Department, 2001
26. Haaker, T., Bouwman, H., and Faber, E. Customer and Network Value of Mobile Services: Balancing Requirements and Strategic Interests, in Proceedings of the 25th International Conference on Informations Systems (ICIS 2004), Association for Information Systems, pp. 1-14, 2004.
27. J. Krumeich, T. Burkhart, D. Werth, and P. Loos. Towards a Component-based Description of Business Models: A State-of-the-Art Analysis., AMCIS, Association for Information Systems, 2012
28. Kagermann H., Wahlster W., Helbig, J., Recommendations for implementing the strategic initiative INDUSTRIE 4.0, Final report of the Industrie 4.0 Working Group, 2013
29. Kaplan, R. S., Norton, D. P.: The Balanced Scorecard – Measures that Drive Performance. In: Harvard Business Review., Januar/Februar 1992
30. Karagiannis, D., Buchmann, R., Burzynski, P., Brakmic, J., D3.1.1 –Specification of Modelling Method Including Conceptualisation Outline, ComVantage Project Deliverable, 2012.
31. Karagiannis, D., Höfferer, P. , Metamodels in Action: An overview, In: J. Filipe, B.Shishkov, M. Helfert, ICSOFT 2006 - First Int. Conf. on Software and Data Technologies: IS27-36. Setúbal: Insticc Press, 2006.
32. Karagiannis, D.; Kühn, H.: Metamodelling Platforms. Invited Paper. In: Bauknecht, K.; Min Tjoa, A.; Quirchmayer, G. (Eds.): Proceedings of the Third International Conference EC-Web 2002 – Dexa 2002, Aix-en-Provence, France, September 2-6, 2002, LNCS 2455, Springer-Verlag, Berlin, Heidelberg, p. 182, 2002.
33. Kelly S., Tolvanen J.-P., Doamin-Specific Modelling: Enabling Full Code Generation, John Wiley & Son, Inc. 2008
34. Meta Object Facility [Online http://www.omg.org/mof/, Accessed: 07.02.2017
35. Morris, M., Schindehutte, M., and Allen, J., The entrepreneur's business model: toward a unified perspective, Journal of Business Research, 58, 6, 726-735, 2005
36. Obeo Designer, [Online https://www.obeo.fr/en/products/eclipse-sirius, Accessed 07.02.2017]
37. Osterwalder, A. and Pigneur, Y, and Tucci, C., Clarifying Business models: Origins, Present and Future of the Concept, Communications of Association for Information Systems, 16, 1, pp. 1-25, 2005.
38. Osterwalder, A. and Pigneur, Y., Business Model Generation, John Wiley & Sons, Inc., Hoboken, New Jersey, USA., 2010
39. PwC, 2016 Global Industry 4.0 Survey: Building the digital enterprise, 2016
40. Rappa, M. A. The utility business model and the future of computing services, IBM Systems Journal, 43, 1, 32-42, 2004.
41. Richardson, J., The business model: an integrative framework for strategy execution, Strategic Change, 17, 5-6, pp. 133-144, 2008.
42. Ronald Berger Strategy Consultants, Additive Manufacturing A game changer for the manufacturing industry? 2014.
43. Schweizer, L., Concept and evolution of business models, Journal of General Management, 31, 2, 37-56, 2005.
44. Schweizer, L., Concept and evolution of business models, Journal of General Management, 31, 2, pp. 37-56, 2005.

45. Stähler, P. Merkmale von Geschäftsmodellen in der digitalen Ökonomie. Dissertation, in German, Josef Eul Verlag, 2001.
46. Strahringer S ,Metamodellierung als Instrument des Methodenvergleichs: eine Evaluierung am Beispiel objektorientierter Analysemethoden, in German, Shaker, Aachen, 1996
47. Vgl. Kern H., Hummel A., Kühne S. Towards a Comparative Analysis of Meta-Metamodels, In The 11th Workshop on Domain-Specific Modeling, Portland, ISA. [Online www.dsmforum.org/events/DSM11/Papers/kern.pdf, Accessed. 07.02.2017)
48. Maurya, A., Running Lean, Iterate from Plan A to a Plan That Works, 2nd Edition, O'Reilly, 2012

Service-Driven Enrichment for KbR in the OMiLAB Environment

Michael Walch and Dimitris Karagiannis

Research Group Knowledge Engineering,
Faculty of Computer Science, University of Vienna,
Währinger Straße 29, 1090 Vienna, Austria
{michael.walch,dk}@dke.univie.ac.at
https://informatik.univie.ac.at/ke/

Abstract. In this paper, details are presented on how physical objects interact with conceptual models in Factory of the Future (FoF) scenarios. For this reason, a hierarchical three layer structure - for physical objects, models and concepts - is described as part of the Knowledge-based Robotics (KbR) approach. Focusing on the integration of physical objects and models, the need for service-driven enrichment emerges. Thereby, the extension of physical objects with cyber twins is realized for enabling service capabilities like monitoring and control. For their development, an architecture is introduced based on the integration of logical and physical components. This is validated in the OMiLAB environment using the OMiRob case. The conceptual approach proves the capability of applying service-driven enrichment to physical objects using metamodeling techniques.

Keywords: Knowledge-based Robotics, service-driven enrichment, (micro)service architecture, embedded computation

1 Introduction

At least 40% of all businesses will die in the next 10 years [1, 2]. The motivation for this bold prediction is rooted in the disruptive impact of *digitalization*, which describes the conversion from physical to digital that is having a fundamental effect on businesses [3]. Thereby, the transformation from manual work performed by humans towards automated tasks performed by machines and in particular by robots is currently revolutionized by the availability and advancement of information technology.

The applications scenarios are promising, like, but not limited to, (i) raising efficiency, reducing time and costs with equal quality, (ii) enabling new product-service system possibilities like data economy or mass individualization, and (iii) introducing new management approaches for zero defect manufacturing, better forecasting and reaction to interruptions. Conceptual models are used to describe, simulate and execute these scenarios [4].

This leads to a massive increase in complexity because of a deviation between *physical objects that operate at run-time* and *conceptual models that are formed*

© Springer International Publishing AG 2017
Y. Hara and D. Karagiannis (Eds.): ICServ 2017, LNCS 10371, pp. 164–177, 2017.
DOI: 10.1007/978-3-319-61240-9_16

at design-time. Bridging the gap facilitates a revolution for, e.g., (i) production processes, (ii) production technology, (iii) products, (iv) information flows as well as (v) the cooperation with human workers.

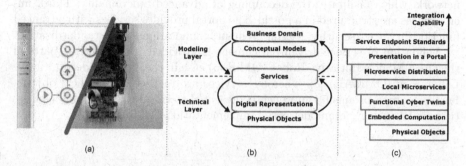

Fig. 1. (a) Conceptual model (left) and physical object (right), **(b)** bridging the gap using service-driven enrichment, **(c)** service development.

To exploit the potential of digitalization[1], the integration of physical objects and conceptual models is required, as shown in Fig. 1 (a). Thereby, the problem is to bring together different engineers, skills, methods, solutions and the like. To solve this problem, the Knowledge-based Robotics (KbR) approach can be employed to support the integration of physical objects and conceptual models, as shown in Section two. Following the KbR approach, a (micro)service architecture is proposed in this paper that revolves around services[2], as shown in Fig. 1 (b). Thereby, service-driven enrichment describes

  (i) cyber-physical system (CPS) conceptualization: the extension of physical objects with functional services to model operations (low-level abstraction on a technical layer); and

 (ii) scenario conceptualization: the specialization of conceptual models with capabilities for intelligent behaviour (high-level abstraction on a modeling layer using services).

Focusing on the first point, **this study introduces details on a (micro)service architecture that supports the extension of physical objects with services**, as shown in Fig. 1 (c). Additional studies on the second point have to clarify how services can be fully integrated in conceptual models.

In detail, the (micro)service architecture is conceptualized using three building blocks. First, computational capability is embedded in physical objects to

---

[1] Digitalization results in competitive advantages, as, e.g., real-time operations are improved by efficient decision making, stakeholder experiences are cultivated by improved networking, and creative innovations are stimulated by a deeper understanding of value chains. This leads to competition among businesses, which promotes consumer well being [5], thus fulfilling the requirements for critical research [6].

[2] Service engineering is able to bridge the gap between physical objects and conceptual models [7].

host cyber twins. Cyber twins are digital models of physical objects that provide functionality to monitor and control the physical objects' sensing and acting capabilities. Second, the functionality of cyber twins is enhanced by microservices. Microservices enable cyber twins to communicate information in a network, which facilitates the decoupling of advanced functionality. Third, microservices are structured in a portal. The portal provides services with advanced functionality, e.g., security, logging, semantic annotations, and standardization.

Validation of service-driven enrichment is provided by performing parts of the Open Models Initiative Robot (OMiRob) case in the Open Models Initiative Laboratory (OMiLAB) [8]. Thereby, services are realized for physical objects. Furthermore, a promising approach is presented to integrate services in conceptual models using metamodel-based implementation (MMbI) [9].

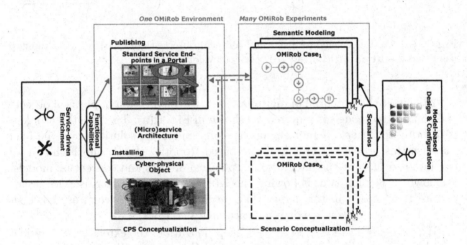

Fig. 2. KbR approach for service-driven enrichment.

Fig. 2 shows the deployment of systems using service-driven enrichment. Labour intensive tasks are required to engineer cyber-physical systems, the (micro)service architecture, and the integration of services in conceptual models. The process can be improved in the future using model-based design and configuration, which eases the engineering complexity and effort for human developers.

Section two introduces the approach on which this study is based. Section three defines details of the (micro)service architecture. Section four describes the validation of service-driven enrichment. Section five concludes the study.

2   Foundations: Knowledge-based Robotics (KbR)

Service-driven enrichment as proposed in this study is realized using the Knowledge-based Robotics (KbR) approach. KbR essentially is a modeling framework in the field of robotics with a specialized focus on modeling knowledge that generates intelligent behaviour. The term "smart models" is coined for the models resulting from this approach. The benefit of KbR is that robots gain increased flexibility through "smart models", as the engineering burden of domain-specific solutions is lifted from human programmers.

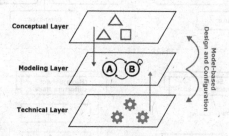

Fig. 3. An abstract visualization of the KbR approach.

The idea of KbR is to integrate concepts and technical systems, as shown in Fig. 3. Using design-oriented [10] thinking, the desired integration is facilitated on a modeling layer using model-driven engineering [11–13]. Thereby, models are treated as first-class citizen that specialize the conceptual layer and that extend the technical layer, with respect to the goal of modeling knowledge that generates intelligent behaviour of robots.

In order to achieve the goal of KbR, models are required to specialize *actions* and *semantics*, as shown in Fig. 4. The first is used in modeling behaviour and the second in modeling knowledge. Models of semantics can be extended by knowledge representation schemes, artificial intelligence technologies, and conceptual models, which leads to "smart models". Models of actions can be extended by different fields in robotics (with individual foci on, e.g., humanoid, industrial, and other kinds of robots), which leads to executable models.

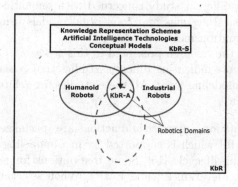

Fig. 4. Fields in robotics and their relation to semantics (KbR-S) and actions (KbR-A).

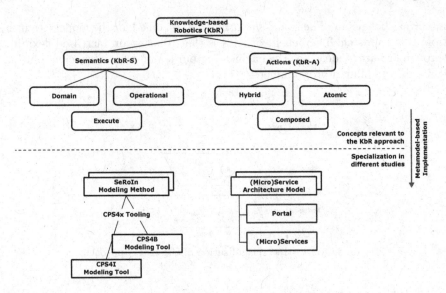

Fig. 5. KbR concept and possible instantiation.

Fig. 5 shows the separation between the KbR approach and different studies that realize parts of the approach. In detail, the top part of Fig. 5 shows the concepts for semantics and actions. Subconcepts of semantics are concerned with domain knowledge, knowledge that is used in behaviour execution, and operational knowledge (e.g., goals and plans). Subconcepts of actions are atomic and composed actions (describing scripted behaviour), and hybrid actions (describing intelligent behaviour using knowledge). The bottom part of Fig. 5 shows studies that specialize concepts of the KbR approach on the modeling layer, where individual studies may focus on different concepts. For example, the bottom part of Fig. 5 shows:

(i) To the left, a different study concerned with semantic-driven integration of cyber-physical systems and conceptual models using tooling support for industry and business settings.

(ii) To the right, the research presented in this study.

(iii) Hidden elements indicating different studies that research different artefacts on the modeling layer. All these studies are related by some dependency structure.

In detail, concepts for semantics and actions are specialized on the modeling layer [14] using MMbI which is supported by metamodeling platforms [9] in a dedicated engineering lifecycle [15]. Some free options for metamodeling platforms are ADOxx[3], MetaEdit+[4], and EMF[5]. When selecting a metamodeling

---

[3] www.adoxx.org

[4] www.metacase.com/mep

[5] www.eclipse.org/emf

platform, one has to take into account how components of the platform support the engineering of the modeling layer [9]. In addition, the modeling layer is extended by a technical layer. Therefore, new core technologies are observed:

- The introduction of smartness via **AI and cognition** enables "smart" behaviour of machines.
- **Cognitive mechatronic** enables a "learning" combination of mechanical, electronic and cognitive information technology.
- Humanoid robots imitate human related mobility and cooperation behaviour and hence enable a new form of interaction known as **socially cooperative human robot interaction**.
- To manage the complexity and to accelerate development and deployment of robot capabilities, approaches for (automated) **model-based design and configuration** are required as the low-level implementation of robots by humans does not scale to advanced requirements.

The following two subsections provide additional information on KbR concepts for semantics and actions, their specialization in models, and their technical extensions.

2.1 Semantics: relevant Concepts and selected Studies

Semantics is used to infuse systems and especially robots with characteristics that are related to intelligence. Therefore, different concepts enable the representation of semantic-rich information, reasoning and adaptation, and interaction with humans. These concepts are specialized by knowledge representation schemes, artificial intelligence technologies, and conceptual models. Some of the resulting artefacts are rich in formalisms (e.g., as found in the Semantic Web Stack[6,7]), while others focus on data (e.g., neural networks, evolutionary algorithms and statistical analysis). Several studies using KbR exist that extend these artefacts in the field of robotics.

For example, semantic-rich artefacts can be extended using existing robot technologies like ROS[8] and AutomationML[9] [16, 17]. Such artefacts describe domain knowledge and its operationalization in executable behaviour [18, 19]. Thereby, a focus is the integration of semantics and actions [20, 21] and on improving the capabilities of semantic models and technologies [22, 23].

Fig. 6 shows a possible model that specializes semantics concepts for knowledge representation. Thereby, an ontology formalizes knowledge about entities and behaviours relevant to FoF scenarios. Listing. 1.1 shows a technical detail in that ontology that relates entities with behaviour.

---

[6] www.w3.org/standards/semanticweb/
[7] www.w3.org/Consortium/techstack-desc.html
[8] http://www.ros.org/
[9] www.automationml.org

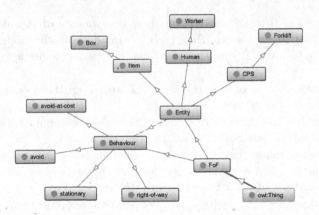

Fig. 6. Example for an ontology that is relevant to the OMiRob case.

Listing 1.1. Excerpt of the ontology in Fig. 6

```
###   OMiRob–Case–Ontology#hasBehaviour
:hasBehaviour  rdf:type  owl:ObjectProperty  ;
rdfs:range  :Behaviour  ;
rdfs:domain  :Entity  .
```

2.2   Actions: The OMiRob Case

An illustrative scenario can be considered as follows: In a Factory of the Future (FoF) scenario, a self-driving forklift operates in close proximity to human workers. In case of a fault in the self-driving forklift's braking system, a moral dilemma occurs when lives are in danger, as seen in in Fig. 7 (a). Even though it is reasonable for humans to choose option 1 as it avoids human casualties, the choice is not intuitive for machines.

Solving the dilemma by machines requires the transformation and specialization of concepts used in human reasoning into models that can be interpreted by machines. E.g., a rule could be formalized to express that option 1 is preferred over option 2. However, machine-interpretable models solve only a part of the problem, as the forklift has to move in the right direction in the end to avoid human casualties. A pragmatic real-world execution of the machine-interpretable models is required as well. In other words, an architecture is needed that enables physical objects to execute functionality. To fulfil the requirements for this architecture, service-driven enrichment extends physical objects with services. Thereby, services facilitate the transformation of robot functionality to machine-interpretable models, which enables advanced capabilities (e.g., the automated start of a maintenance process upon fault detection while the physical object executes emergency behaviour).

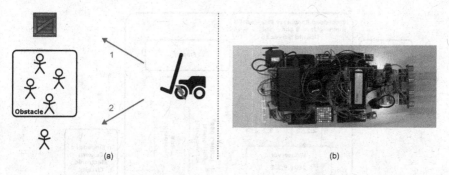

Fig. 7. (a) Pictorial conceptualization of the OMiRob Case. **(b)** The physical object used to simulate a self-driving forklift in the OMiRob Case.

3 The (Micro)Service Architecture

For service-driven enrichment of physical objects, three building blocks are proposed. First, computational capabilities are embedded in physical objects, which allow the former to host the cyber twins of the latter. Second, the cyber twins are enhanced with microservices which enable communication in a network. Third, microservices are structured and enhanced in a portal.

Regarding the first building block, embedding custom electronic circuits in physical objects enables basic functionality that is defined by low level program code. By implementing low level program code, it is possible to monitor and control sensing and acting capabilities of physical objects. However, custom electronic circuits are severely limited in their computational capabilities, which renders them inadequate to enhance cyber twins with complex services. Therefore, the proposal is to embed custom electronic circuits in combination with ready made computer boards, e.g., the Raspberry Pi 2 Model B. Ready made computer boards interface with custom electronic circuits using, e.g., the Inter-Integrated Circuit (I^2C) bus, while being capable of enhancing cyber twins with complex services.

Regarding the second building block, the proposed design choices expressed in terms of java and python (different languages offer similar concepts) can be seen in Fig. 8. Thereby, custom electronic circuits interface locally with ready made computer boards, e.g., the former act as slaves and the latter act as master on the (I^2C) bus. Data exchange with ready made computer boards running high level program code results in cyber twins. Microservices enhance the functionality of cyber twins and allow for information exchange in a network. Thereby, a system of communicating microservices enables the decoupling of functionality. Decoupling is archived, e.g., as microservices provide TCP interfaces for binding[10], which results in functionality that can be embedded or distributed based on requirements.

---

[10] Different Internet of Things (IoT) protocols can be used to provide various interfaces.

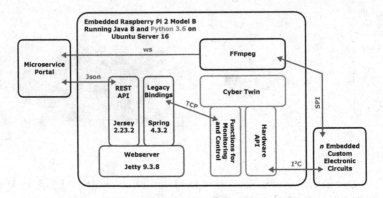

Fig. 8. The (micro)service architecture model.

Regarding the third building block, microservices are structured in a portal that extends service capabilities. Therefore, microservices have to fulfil certain requirements of the portal. A suitable portal is described in [24] and implemented in [25]. Its requirements can be fulfilled, e.g., by binding the microservices' TCP interfaces and autowiring them in servlets using the Spring Framework. These servlets extend the capabilities of a webserver, e.g., jetty. The webserver again provides microservices via the representational state transfer (REST) architecture. These microservices support in and outgoing connections via standard APIs using different protocols as required by the portal, e.g., HTTP or WebSocket. Depending on the protocol, different data exchange formats are supported, e.g., JavaScript Object Notation (JSON). A technical difficulty in this building block is the cross domain issue resulting from the distributed architecture in combination with the same-origin policy, which can be solved by configuring a reverse proxy like NGINX.

An example for machine-readable service endpoints as provided by the portal is shown in Listing. 1.2 and Fig. 9. Human-readable services are provided by the portal as well [26].

Listing 1.2. Service endpoint generator

```
public final class DeviceREST {
  @GET
  @Path("/device/{devicename}")
  @Produces(MediaType.APPLICATION_JSON)
  public String getRequests(@PathParam("devicename")
    String deviceName,
    final @Context
    HttpServletRequest servletRequest) {

    return deviceService.getRequest(deviceName,
      auth(servletRequest)).toString();
    }}
```

Fig. 9. Accessing atomic services.

4   Validation in the OMiLAB Environment

Naturalistic ex post evaluation of the architecture as introduced in section three is provided by performing a specific scenario [27]. The scenario used for evaluation is inspired by the OMiRob case presented in section two, where functionality of physical object is transferred to machine-interpretable models. These models interact with physical objects using the services that the latter provide. For evaluation, service-driven enrichment is performed for the physical object in Fig. 7 (b) using the three building blocks of the introduced architecture. Human- and machine-readable endpoints of the resulting services can be found in [26].

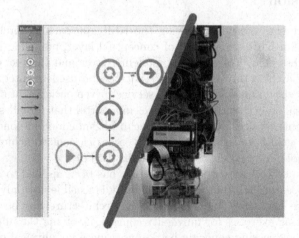

Fig. 10. A model that is integrating services provided by physical objects. Additional information can be found on www.omilab.org/psm/omipob

Additionally, a first prototype is implemented that demonstrates the potential of MMbI for the integration of services in conceptual models. Thereby, models are constructed for inferring the control of actuator output, i.e., steering to the left or to the right, from monitored sensory input, i.e., fault detection and image recognition. The model with service integration capabilities was engineered using the ADOxx metamodeling platform [28].

Validation is performed by constructing cyber twins to monitor and control physical objects, by enhancing cyber twins with microservices for communication, by organizing microservices in a portal to provide services, and by integrating services in a machine-interpretable conceptual model. The implementation is shared in [29]. A video of the system in action can be found in [30].

As a result of the validation, some key features of service-driven enrichment can be stressed in a nutshell:

(i) Where possible, abstract capabilities from technical components to a standardized level of functional abstraction, i.e., to services. This is a trade-off between performance (functional abstraction implies additional overhead which is problematic for, e.g., time sensitive, computation & bandwidth constrained, and energy critical applications) and integration capability (services enable the integration of physical objects with, e.g., semantic reasoning, business logic, and agent systems).

(ii) If functional abstraction is not possible, at least have semantic-rich artefacts, describing the capabilities of technical components and their aggregations. Provide services using these semantic-rich artefacts.

(iii) The combination of (i) and (ii) enables the vision of KbR, where physical objects are integrated with conceptual models (as shown in Fig. 10) and semantic reasoning (as presented in [22]).

5   Conclusion

This paper presents a study following the KbR approach. Thereby, the three layer structure of KbR - consisting of conceptual layer, modeling layer, technical layer - is dissected. To relate the modeling layer and the technical layer, a (micro)service architecture is proposed that can be used to integrate physical objects in conceptual models. In detail, service-driven enrichment extends cyber twins of physical objects with microservices in a portal that provides human- and machine-readable services. These services can be embedded in conceptual models, where the goal is to utilize service-driven enrichment to achieve intelligent behaviour of robots based on requirements in the FoF.

The developed (micro)service architecture has been applied to different FoF scenarios, as seen in [31]. Its technical difficulty is feasible not only for FoF scenarios but also for other domains. E.g., the architecture has been applied to create motivating exercises for university courses, involving the implementation of knowledge engineering concepts based on services for physical objects. However, more complex scenarios are also possible by extending the capabilities of physical objects [32].

Furthermore, an implemented prototype suggests that services provided by the architecture can be integrated in conceptual models. To facilitate this integration, domain-specific modeling methods are constructed using metamodeling frameworks [33]. Additional studies are planned to research the integration of services in conceptual models that represent business aspects in more detail.

However, constructing services for physical objects is shown to be a manual and labour intensive task. Managing the complexity and accelerating the development and deployment in application areas, like, but not limited to, (a) healthcare, (b) inspection of infrastructure, (c) agri-food, or (d) industrial, requires dedicated concepts, methods and tools. The difficulty thereby is that particular application scenarios require flexible compose-able support for (i) the application domains (e.g., health), (ii) the production process (e.g., additive vs. subtractive; mechanical vs. chemical), (iii) the production technology (e.g., automated vs. semi-automated lines), (iv) the externalization of knowledge (e.g., extraction from data analysis vs. human externalization), (v) the technology that interprets the knowledge (e.g., agent vs. ontologies), (vi) the type of interaction and communication (e.g., human - machine vs. machine - machine communication), (vii) the data format (standards), the information flow (e.g., low level event and information bus vs. edge computing vs. high level application in the cloud), (viii) the requested support (e.g., development of serverless applications), and many more. A possible approach to solve the problem is model-based design and configuration, which implies transferring some of the complexity to "smart models".

References

1. John Chambers and Rik Kirkland. Cisco's John Chambers on the digital era. http://www.mckinsey.com/industries/high-tech/our-insights/ciscos-john-chambers-on-the-digital-era (visited on 01.03.2017), 2015.
2. John Chambers and Zoelle Egner. Advice from John Chambers to CIOs - and the world. https://blog.box.com/blog/advice-john-chambers-cios-and-world/ (visited on 01.03.2017), 2015.
3. Shahyan Khan. Leadership in the digital age: A study on the effects of digitalisation on top management leadership, 2016.
4. Christian Schlegel, Andreas Steck, Davide Brugali, and Alois Knoll. *Design Abstraction and Processes in Robotics: From Code-Driven to Model-Driven Engineering*, pages 324–335. Springer Berlin Heidelberg, Berlin, Heidelberg, 2010.
5. Maurice E. Stucke. Is competition always good? *Journal of Antitrust Enforcement*, 1(1):162, 2013.
6. Michael D. Myers and Heinz K. Klein. A set of principles for conducting critical research in information systems. *MIS Q.*, 35(1):17–36, March 2011.
7. Kentaro Watanabe, Masaaki Mochimaru, and Yoshiki Shimomura. Service engineering research in Japan: Towards a sustainable society. In *Services and the Green Economy*, pages 221–244. Springer, 2016.
8. The OMiLAB Community. OMiLAB Europe. http://www.omilab.org/psm/about (visited on 01.03.2017), 2017.

9. Hans-Georg Fill and Dimitris Karagiannis. On the conceptualisation of modelling methods using the ADOxx meta modelling platform. *Enterprise Modelling and Information Systems Architectures - An International Journal*, 8(1):4–25, 2013.

10. Hubert Österle, Jörg Becker, Ulrich Frank, Thomas Hess, Dimitris Karagiannis, Helmut Krcmar, Peter Loos, Peter Mertens, Andreas Oberweis, and Elmar J Sinz. Memorandum on design-oriented information systems research. *European Journal of Information Systems*, 20(1):7–10, 2011.

11. Alberto Rodrigues da Silva. Model-driven engineering: A survey supported by the unified conceptual model. *Computer Languages, Systems & Structures*, 43:139 – 155, 2015.

12. Christian Schlegel, Andreas Steck, and Alex Lotz. Robotic software systems: From code-driven to model-driven software development. In *Robotic Systems-Applications, Control and Programming*. InTech, 2012.

13. Bernd-Holger Schlingloff. *Cyber-Physical Systems Engineering*, pages 256–289. Springer International Publishing, Cham, 2016.

14. Dimitris Karagiannis and Harald Kühn. *Metamodelling Platforms*, pages 182–182. Springer Berlin Heidelberg, Berlin, Heidelberg, 2002.

15. Dimitris Karagiannis. Agile modeling method engineering. In *Proceedings of the 19th Panhellenic Conference on Informatics*, PCI '15, pages 5–10, New York, NY, USA, 2015. ACM.

16. Yingbing Hua, Stefan Zander, Mirko Bordignon, and Björn Hein. From automationml to ros: A model-driven approach for software engineering of industrial robotics using ontological reasoning. In *Emerging Technologies and Factory Automation (ETFA), 2016 IEEE 21st International Conference on*, pages 1–8. IEEE, 2016.

17. Stefan Zander, Georg Heppner, Georg Neugschwandtner, Ramez Awad, Marc Essinger, and Nadia Ahmed. A model-driven engineering approach for ros using ontological semantics. *arXiv preprint arXiv:1601.03998*, 2016.

18. Ashutosh Saxena, Ashesh Jain, Ozan Sener, Aditya Jami, Dipendra Kumar Misra, and Hema Swetha Koppula. Robobrain: Large-scale knowledge engine for robots. *CoRR*, abs/1412.0691, 2014.

19. Moritz Tenorth and Michael Beetz. Knowrob: A knowledge processing infrastructure for cognition-enabled robots. *The International Journal of Robotics Research*, 32(5):566–590, 2013.

20. Shotaro Kobayashi, Susumu Tamagawa, Takeshi Morita, and Takahira Yamaguchi. Intelligent humanoid robot with japanese wikipedia ontology and robot action ontology. In *Human-Robot Interaction (HRI), 2011 6th ACM/IEEE International Conference on*, pages 417–424. IEEE, 2011.

21. Hiroshi Asano, Takeshi Morita, and Takahira Yamaguchi. Development and evaluation of an operational service robot using wikipedia-based and domain ontologies. In *Web Intelligence (WI), 2016 IEEE/WIC/ACM International Conference on*, pages 511–514. IEEE, 2016.

22. Takeshi Morita, Yu Sugawara, Ryota Nishimura, and Takahira Yamaguchi. Integrating symbols and signals based on stream reasoning and ros. In *Pacific Rim Knowledge Acquisition Workshop*, pages 251–260. Springer, 2016.

23. Stefan Zander and Ramez Awad. Expressing and reasoning on features of robot-centric workplaces using ontological semantics. In *Intelligent Robots and Systems (IROS), 2015 IEEE/RSJ International Conference on*, pages 2889–2896. IEEE, 2015.

24. David Götzinger, Elena-Teodora Miron, and Franz Staffel. *OMiLAB: An Open Collaborative Environment for Modeling Method Engineering*, pages 55–76. Springer International Publishing, Cham, 2016.

25. The OMiLAB Community. OMiLAB core infrastructure. `https://gitlab.dke.univie.ac.at/omilab-core-infrastructure` (visited on 01.03.2017), 2017.

26. The OMiLAB Community. OMiROB proof of concept. `http://austria.omilab.org/psm/content/omicarpoc1/info` (visited on 01.03.2017), 2017.

27. John Venable, Jan Pries-Heje, and Richard Baskerville. A comprehensive framework for evaluation in design science research. In *Proceedings of the 7th International Conference on Design Science Research in Information Systems: Advances in Theory and Practice*, DESRIST'12, pages 423–438, Berlin, Heidelberg, 2012. Springer-Verlag.

28. The OMiLAB Community. The ADOxx metamodelling platform. `http://www.adoxx.org` (visited on 01.03.2017), 2017.

29. The OMiLAB Community. OMiROB proof of concept infastructure. `https://gitlab.dke.univie.ac.at/OMiROB/RobotCarPoC` (visited on 01.03.2017), 2017.

30. The OMiLAB Community. Conceptual Models for Robot Control and Robot Monitoring. `https://www.youtube.com/watch?v=n4AqAxfHxJk` (visited on 01.03.2017), 2016.

31. The OMiLAB Community. OMiRob experiments. `http://austria.omilab.org/psm/omirob` (visited on 01.03.2017), 2016.

32. Yu Sugawara, Takeshi Morita, S Saito, and Takahira Yamaguchi. An intelligent application development platform for service robots. In *MuSRobS@ IROS*, pages 16–20, 2015.

33. Dimitris Karagiannis, Robert Andrei Buchmann, Patrik Burzynski, Ulrich Reimer, and Michael Walch. *Fundamental Conceptual Modeling Languages in OMiLAB*, pages 3–30. Springer International Publishing, Cham, 2016.

Modeling Digital Enterprise Ecosystems with ArchiMate: A Mobility Provision Case Study

Benedikt Pittl and Dominik Bork

Research Group Knowledge Engineering
Faculty of Computer Science
University of Vienna, Austria
{firstname.lastname}@univie.ac.at

Abstract. Currently there is a shift from product centered enterprises to product-service centered enterprises which rely on a network of customers, suppliers and partners called enterprise ecosystems. This trend also affects the underlying IT architecture which has to integrate and provide software components (e.g. services) as well as hardware components (e.g. sensors) leading to a digital enterprise ecosystem. This digital ecosystem is complex so that modeling approaches which aim on simplifying complexity are eligible for their design and management. In the paper at hand, we show that existing enterprise modeling approaches are inappropriate for modeling digital enterprise ecosystems comprehensively. By using a case-based analysis we sketch extension points for a digital enterprise ecosystem modeling method based on ArchiMate.

Keywords: Domain-Specific Modeling, Enterprise Ecosystem, Enterprise Modeling

1 Introduction

Currently, there is a shift from a *product* oriented to a *product-service* oriented economy [10]. Thereby enterprises face challenges in creating new value streams, business models, and IT architectures. Hilti's *Tools on Demand* business model as well as new enterprises trading services such as Uber or Airbnb are results of this trend. According to [32], the service trend leads to enterprises which rely on a tight network of stakeholders such as customers, suppliers and cooperation partners. This network is referred to as enterprise ecosystem. A vital part of such ecosystems is the tight integration of the underlying IT infrastructure (e.g. servers, cloud services, third party applications). To reflect this distinguishing character, the term *digital enterprise ecosystem* is used. This paper elaborates the importance of models for designing digital enterprise ecosystems which encompass the integration and provisioning of software components as well as hardware components. The design as well as the coordination of such ecosystems is complex and can be considered as a key challenge of enterprises in the future. Modeling approaches, with the aim on simplifying complex systems, are an appropriate instrument for describing them.

© Springer International Publishing AG 2017
Y. Hara and D. Karagiannis (Eds.): ICServ 2017, LNCS 10371, pp. 178–189, 2017.
DOI: 10.1007/978-3-319-61240-9_17

Enterprise modeling approaches integrate multiple perspectives or views to derive a coherent and comprehensive description (cf. [6]). See for example 4EM [33], ArichMate [18], Semantic Object Model [12], or Integrated Enterprise Balancing [15]. All these enterprise modeling approaches where designed with the aim on generality: any enterprise can be described with them. However, the description of digital enterprise ecosystems with enterprise modeling approaches is unfeasible. This is because they currently lack in expressiveness when describing digital enterprise ecosystems. Existing enterprise modeling approaches need to evolve in order to comprehend current developments. In this paper, the ArchiMate modeling approaches serves as a starting point to identify current weaknesses and propose extensions for modeling digital enterprise ecosystems.

Our research endeavour is to create domain-specific conceptual modeling methods for digital enterprise ecosystems. Thereby we use the term conceptual model as defined in [29], which describes them as models used for communication and understanding by human beings. In the paper at hand, we analyze the appropriateness of ArchiMate to express the specifics of digital enterprise ecosystems and propose first ideas of how an extension of ArchiMate could be achieved to meet the aforementioned requirements.

The remainder of the paper is structured as follows: Section 2 describes foundations of modeling methods in context of the service-product trend and some related work. A mobility provision case study is described in section 3. Along this case study we develop requirements as well as a sketch of a domain-specific language for digital enterprise ecosystems. The paper is closed with a conclusion in section 4.

2 Foundations

2.1 Conceptual Modeling Methods

The authors of [20] define a modeling method as consisting of a modeling language, modeling procedure, and modeling algorithms. An overview of a modeling method is depicted in Figure 1. The modeling language consists of syntax, semantics, and notation. The modeling algorithms are algorithms which are executed on the modeling language. They range from generic algorithms (e.g. shortest path algorithms) to specialized algorithms (e.g. process and capacity simulations). The modeling procedure describes concrete steps which the modeler has to follow in order to create valid models.

According to this definition of a modeling method, most of the popular modeling approaches like BPMN or UML can be considered as modeling languages as they do neither define a modeling procedure nor modeling algorithms.

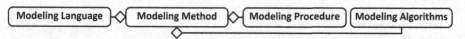

Fig. 1: Core components of modeling methods (excerpt from [20])

While enterprises and their environments require agility, modeling approaches seem to remain nearly unchanged. Prominent modeling methods like BPMN and ArchiMate are heavily used in science and industry, even if their update cycles are rather long: The update from BPMN 1.2 to the current version 2 took about two years[1], while ArichMate 3.0 was released three years after its predecessor ArichMate 2.1[2]. Similarly, the latest UML specification was released approximately four years after the previous specification[3]. The stability of these so-called general purpose modeling languages is based on a rather high abstraction level implying limited semantic specificity. For example, an activity in BPMN can be used for describing processes using different levels of abstraction in almost all domains. Contrary to general purpose modeling languages, domain-specific modeling languages have a high expressiveness in a certain domain. Due to their strong domain focus such languages are usually not standardized and their awareness is low.

2.2   Related Work

The related work analysis is structured into two parts: the first part summarizes literature relevant for enterprise ecosystems while the second part summarizes existing enterprise modeling approaches which might be promising starting points for modeling digital enterprise ecosystems.

In [30], the authors elaborate the importance of currently emerging ecosystems which leads to a tight integration of different stakeholders. This integration requires a harmonization of software systems. Therefore, different approaches are summarized in [3]. Further enterprise integration aspects, beyond software system integration aspects, have been investigated in [32]. The author of [22] analyzes how the model quality framework Semiotic Quality Framework (SEQAL) can be used for evaluating models in the domain of digital ecosystems.

A generic reference architecture for modeling enterprises was described in [25], where the author introduces a business rule-, an activity-, a resource-, a business process- as well as an organisational view. All the enterprise modeling methods which we describe in the following have a comparable structure. The Multi-Perspective Enterprise Modeling (MEMO) method, introduced in [14] tool support described in [4], has a strategy, a organisational as well as an information system perspective whereby each perspective is organized along the four aspects structure, process, resources, goals. The 4EM modeling method [33] has the vision of a holistic description of enterprises. It encompasses a process model, a goal model, a rule model, a concept model, an actors and resource model as well as a technical component model. There are also research initiatives using the Unified Modeling Language (UML) for modeling enterprises [27]. The Open Group Architecture Framework (TOGAF) is a framework which aims on capturing enterprise architectures [16]. Thereby, TOGAF distinguishes between a

---

[1] http://www.omg.org/spec/BPMN/
[2] http://opengroup.org/standards/ea
[3] http://www.omg.org/spec/UML/

business architecture, an application architecture, a data architecture as well as a technical architecture.

ArchiMate is a modeling method which distinguishes between a business layer, an application layer as well as a technology layer [18]. The business layer is about to describe business processes, the application layer describes software applications, and the technology layer allows to describe hardware as well as software infrastructures. It is designed for modeling enterprise architectures.

ArchiMate served as extension point for a couple of other modeling methods such as [11, 1]. In [15], the authors designed a modeling method for Integrated Enterprise Balancing with the aim of generating a common data structure. The Integrated Enterprise Modeling method was introduced in [28], it has a strong focus on processes of manufacturing enterprises.

All of theses modeling approaches focus on an isolated description of enterprises. What is missing is an approach for modeling digital enterprise ecosystem-specific concepts in a comprehensive and integrated manner.

3 Case Study: Digital Enterprise Ecosystem for Mobility Provision in the Automotive Industry

The trend towards product-services is a result of the digital transformation. For a better analysis of the effects, we follow the classification of [23], which describes that an enterprise architecture consist of a business architecture, an information systems architecture and a technology architecture as shown in Figure 2a. The information systems architecture forms together with the technology architecture the IT architecture.

Product-service centered enterprises have to redesign their business architecture, requiring also a redesign of the underlying IT architecture. Thus, in the information systems architecture layer, enterprises face challenges in integrating and provisioning of software components. Further, flexible application architectures are required which allow modifications immediately after changes occur in the environment. The technological architecture is increasingly distributed due to the usage of clouds as well as of other hardware components such as sensors. Their integration and coordination becomes a key challenge in the future.

The described enterprise architecture does not only allow a top-down approach where changes of the business model are propagated down to the IT architecture level. Disruptive technologies like the IoT [2] which belong to the IT architecture layer may force enterprises to modify their business architecture

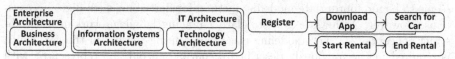

(a) Enterprise architecture and IT architecture

(b) Simplified scenario for renting a car at Car2Go

Fig. 2: Overview over enterprise architecture and mobility provision scenario

which represents a bottom-up approach [26]. The digital photography is an example of such a disruptive technology where corporations like Kodak failed to adapt their business models.

In the case study we describe the digital enterprise ecosystem for a car-rental scenario on a very high level of abstraction using the example of Car2Go (www.car2go.com). The scenario of renting a car is visualized in Figure 2b:

1. **Register.** New costumers have to enter their personal data including payment relevant information.
2. **Download App.** Customers have to download the Car2Go app to access all Car2Go services.
3. **Search for Car.** Customers have to find an available car in proximity to their current location. Therefore the app can be used as a route planer to find the next car.
4. **Start Rental.** The rental process of a car is triggered after the consumer found a car, opened it, and started it with the app.
5. **End Rental.** The rental ends when the customer leaves the car. Therby the customer is charge based on the chosen pricing model.

For executing such a scenario, services and devices are required belonging to the digital enterprise ecosystem as summarized in Table 1: The registration step requires a web application while the app store is required so that consumers can download the app. The search of cars requires communication with geographical services as well as with a car sensor. For initiating the rental process a communication to car sensors e.g. for unlocking the car as well as for tracking the car trip is necessary. The end rental process step requires an integration with payment services. Overall, parts of the data are stored on an external cloud.

3.1 Modeling the Mobility Provision Scenario with existing Approaches

Modeling of digital enterprise ecosystems such as described in the scenario is not trivial: For the overall process we could use BPMN which fails to model the technical aspects. Process modeling with enterprise modeling methods like 4EM are approximately on the same level of abstraction as the BPMN. Hence, they face similar problems. Contrary, the technical modeling languages grouped into the UML might be more appropriate for modeling the technical aspects even if the semantics of the resulting models is limited. However, the UML is inappropriate for modeling the business aspects.

ArchiMate with its business layer, application layer and technology layer seems to be an appropriate modeling method for describing such digital ecosystems. However, ArchiMate is a standard modeling language working with abstract concepts [24]. The modeling class representing sensors in the car, which is required in the previously described scenario, can only be represented with ArchiMate's device modeling class. The (informal) semantics of the device class is described in the standard [31]: *A device models a physical computational resource, upon which artifacts may be deployed for execution.* It is obvious that modeling sensors with the device class is generally possible, however, the expressiveness of such modeling constructs is limited. Even prefixing the names of modeling elements of the type device with *'sensor'* leads only to limited expressiveness improvements for humans while the expressiveness for machines remains unchanged.

Step	Service	Sensors
1 Register	WebApp-Cloud	-
2 Download App	WebApp-Cloud	-
3 Search for Car	Geo-Service	Car GPS Sensor
4 Start Rental	Tracking-Service	Car Lock Sensor
5 End Rental	Payment-Service	Car Lock Sensor

Table 1: Summary of the scenario with its required services and sensors

An excerpt of a model for this scenario created with ArchiMate is depicted in Figure 3. The process model (shown on the top of the figure) seems to be appropriate for our purpose. The application model (shown in the center of the figure) is on a very abstract level of detail: We used ArchiMate's application component class for modeling the Car2Go Registration Site, the AppStore as well as the Car2Go App. The car information system which belongs to ArchiMate's technical layer is depicted on the lower left corner: Here, we used the device class for modeling the sensors. Further, we used the generic technology interface modeling class to elaborate that there are well defined interfaces for accessing the sensors. On the lower right corner, we modeled an excerpt of the server-side system which is used by the Car2Go App. The Car2Go server system uses an external Data Cloud which was modeled by using the generic node class. The Car2Go server accesses the cloud. Thereby we connected the cloud with the server system via the network model element which we named Car2Go App Server System. The server offers a tracking service which is accessed by the app. The tracking service is modeled by using a generic technical service class.

The described example elaborates that we have to improvise for modeling such a simple scenario using ArchiMate. ArchiMates limitations in modeling precisely use cases is a well known fact [24]. Looking at the model without showing the name labels reveals that semantics of the model itself is very low due to the high level of abstraction of the ArchiMate modeling language. The names of the model elements such as 'External Data Cloud' contain the majority of the semantics. Simply placing information into the name labels works only for a limited amount of information. For example the name label of the 'External Data Cloud' is insufficient to describe the service level agreement which the Car2Go system has with the external cloud. Therefore, further classes or class attributes are necessary.

3.2 Requirements for Modeling a Digital Enterprise Ecosystem with ArchiMate

For an adequate modeling of the product-service scenario additional domain-specific concepts have to be introduced to ArchiMate. For the scenario model, classes such as 'Lock Sensor' and 'GPS Sensor' are necessary which have inter

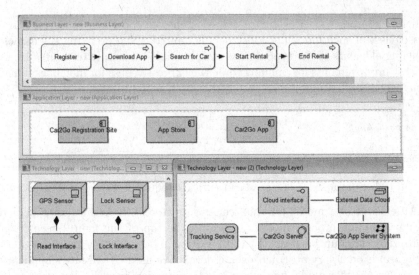

Fig. 3: Excerpt of the scenario model created with ArchiMate

alia the attributes 'communication protocol', 'status' as well as 'interface'. The expressiveness of the ArchiMate interface class is limited. Due to the high level of abstraction it is not clear if the interface is a hardware interface or a software interface. For the purpose of our scenario, it would be necessary to describe interfaces in more detail, e.g. by introducing a modeling class for expressing REST interfaces. ArchiMate is continuously extended by introducing new elements - in the current version 3.0, 56 different elements are existing[4]. However, due to ArchiMates broad domain it is unfeasible to reach a semantic richness compared to particularly designed domain-specific languages.

A major drawback of ArchiMate is that it does not foresee attributes of modeling classes (except the name). So it is not possible to distinguish between external and internal nodes to e.g. model the external cloud. From ArchiMate's point of view the ignorance of attributes is clear: attributes describe details of classes. However, ArchiMate's classes are generic which simply do not have any details. Hence, all kinds of class-related information which would be appropriate to be a class attribute have to be expressed as a separate modeling classes.

An exemplary list of domain-specific classes and attributes required for modeling our scenario is shown in Table 2. This table is not a prime solution which allows to model the described scenario adequately. Instead it should elaborate that further modeling classes are necessary to model the scenario adequately. For creating these additional modeling classes ArchiMate's profiling and specification extension mechanisms can be used [31].

For fully leveraging the expressive power of ArichMate, a formal description of how the model elements of different layers e.g. the application and technical layer can be connected is necessary [5]. This is for example necessary to describe that a certain sensor is used for an application which is executed for running

---

[4] https://masteringarchimate.com/2016/06/26/archimate-3-0-the-good-the-bad-and-the-ugly/ for a discussion

a certain process step. Currently, the standard is very vague regarding such inter-model connections. It describes for example that the interface model class which belongs to the technology layer *[...] can be accessed by other nodes or by application components from the Application Layer.*

Layer	Class	Attributes
Technology Layer	Lock Sensor	Name, Communication protocol, Status, Interface
Technology Layer	GPS Sensor	Name, Communication protocol, Precision, Interface
Technology Layer	WebService Interface	Name, WebService type, Parameter, Functional description
Technology Layer	Cloud component	Name, Service type
Application Layer	Application Component	Name, Application type, External/Internal component

Table 2: Additional/extended model classes including attributes

3.3   Design of a Domain-Specific Modeling Language

In this section an excerpt of a modeling language for the description of the use case shown on the lower left corner of Figure 3 is introduced. The model elements, its notation as well as its semantics are described in Table 3. In total the domain-specific language contains three classes and one connector. For each of these elements we described the semantics informally using natural language (following the formalization framework as proposed by [5]). Additionally, we added the corresponding ArchiMate modeling element - which we used for modeling the use case in Figure 3 - as well as its semantics to the table. We took the semantic description of the ArchiMate elements from the standard [31].

Concept	ArchiMate Element	Domain-Specific Element
Lock Sensor	Device	<<LockSensor>>
	A device is a physical IT resource upon which system software and artifacts may be stored or deployed for execution.	A lock sensor is a physical device in a car for locking an unlocking it. It might offer digital interfaces for controlling it.
GPS Sensor	Device	<<GPSSensor>>
	A device is a physical IT resource upon which system software and artifacts may be stored or deployed for execution.	A GPS sensor is a physical device which tracks the position. It might offer digital interfaces for accessing the current position.
Interface	Technology interface	<<Interface>>
	A technology interface represents a point of access where technology services offered by a node can be accessed.	An interface represents a technical interface (REST or SOAP) through which other applications can communicate, guide or control the system which offers the interface.
OffersInter-face	◆- -▶	
	A path represents a link between two or more nodes, through which these nodes can exchange data or material.	The offersInterfaces connector is used by sensors to describe that they offer an interface.

Table 3: Comparison of the elements of the domain-specific language with the corresponding elements in ArchiMate

To emphasize that the domain-specific modeling language is not only the introduction of a user-defined notation, we created an example which is depicted in Figure 4. It shows the model layer as well as the metamodel layer from the classical metamodeling stack (see e.g. [17] for more information). In the paper at hand we analyzed ArchiMate and the domain-specific language. Excerpts of their metamodels are shown on layer 2, the metamodel layer. On layer 1 there are two identical models which we created for a better readability of the figure. With both metamodels we are able to create the model elements used in the two models. From a syntactical point of view the introduced domain-specific modeling language is similar to the excerpt created with ArchiMate. The most obvious syntactical difference is that the domain-specific modeling language distinguishes between two sensor classes - in ArchiMate we used the device class for representing both sensors. Furthermore, as shown in Table 2 we enriched e.g. the interface class with attributes.

While the syntax of the two languages is similar, a comparison of the semantic description of the domain specific language and ArchiMate - see Table 3 - reveals that their semantics is different. In the right model (referenced with 1 in Figure 4) the sensors are represented by instances of the device class and the interfaces were created by instancing the technology interface class. Thereby, the instances like the GPS Sensor and the Lock Sensor inherit the semantics of the class *Device*. The semantics gained through this kind of inheritance is known as the *type semantics* [17]. As already described, the semantics of the classes in ArchiMate is limited and consequently, the inherited semantics of the corresponding instances is limited, too. Contrary, by using domain-specific languages the type semantics is richer. This semantic richness comes at the price of limited applicability for other domains. For example, the appliance of the previously introduced lock sensor class is limited to cars.

We will further develop the introduced language within the Open Models Initiative Laboratory (OMiLAB). OMiLAB is a research initiative for *conceptualization, development, and deployment of modeling methods and the models designed with them*[5]. OMiLAB hosts already projects in domains such as semantic alignment of models [13], multi-view modeling [7] and industry related domain-specific modeling [8]. For more information about the OMiLAB please see [19]. An overview of existing open modeling tools realized within the OMiLAB is given in [21].

4   Conclusion and Further Research

The trend towards a product-service driven economy leads to ecosystems where enterprises are tightly connected with other stakeholders and service providers. These connections lead to complex IT infrastructures that need to be integrated and managed in a digital enterprise ecosystem. Existing enterprise modeling methods have the problem that their expressiveness is limited. In this paper

---

[5] http://www.omilab.org/psm/about

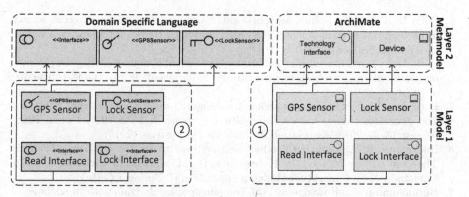

Fig. 4: Excerpt of the scenario model created with ArchiMate

we elaborate this problem by developing a scenario in the mobility provision domain. Based on the Car2Go scenario, we proposed domain-specific extensions for ArchiMate in order to increase its expressiveness and adequacy. In our future work we will develop a comprehensive digital enterprise ecosystem modeling method within the Open Models Initiatve Laboratory (OMiLAB, www.omilab. org). moreover, we plan to design and develop an open modeling tool to support design and management of complex digital enterprise ecosystems. In this regard, we plan to investigate how we can use the created models as a diagrammatic source for knowledge engineering (cf. [9]).

Acknowledgement

Part of this research has been funded through the South Africa / Austria Joint Scientific and Technological Cooperation program with the project number ZA 11/2017.

References

1. Al-Fedaghi, S.: Enterprise architecture: An alternative to archimate conceptualization. In: Silhavy, R., Silhavy, P., Prokopova, Z., Senkerik, R., Kominkova Oplatkova, Z. (eds.) Software Engineering Trends and Techniques in Intelligent Systems: Proceedings of the 6th Computer Science On-line Conference 2017 (CSOC2017), Vol 3, pp. 68–77. Springer International Publishing, Cham (2017)
2. Asghar, M.H., Negi, A., Mohammadzadeh, N.: Principle application and vision in internet of things (iot). In: Computing, Communication & Automation (ICCCA), 2015 International Conference on. pp. 427–431. IEEE (2015)
3. Barbosa, O., Alves, C.: A systematic mapping study on software ecosystems. In: Proceedings of the Third International Workshop on Software Ecosystems, Brussels, Belgium, June 7th, 2011. pp. 15–26 (2011)
4. Bock, A., Frank, U.: Multi-perspective enterprise modeling - conceptual foundation and implementation with adoxx. In: Karagiannis, D., Mayr, H.C., Mylopoulos, J. (eds.) Domain-Specific Conceptual Modeling, Concepts, Methods and Tools, pp. 241–267. Springer (2016)

5. Bork, D., Fill, H.G.: Formal aspects of enterprise modeling methods: a comparison framework. In: System Sciences (HICSS), 2014 47th Hawaii International Conference on. pp. 3400–3409. IEEE (2014)
6. Bork, D.: A Development Method for the Conceptual Design of Multi-View Modeling Tools with an Emphasis on Consistency Requirements. Ph.D. thesis, University of Bamberg (2015)
7. Bork, D.: Using conceptual modeling for designing multi-view modeling tools. In: 21st Americas Conference on Information Systems, AMCIS 2015, Puerto Rico, August 13-15, 2015. Association for Information Systems (2015)
8. Buchmann, R.A.: Modeling Product-Service Systems for the Internet of Things: The ComVantage Method. In: Karagiannis, D., Mayr, H.C., Mylopoulos, J. (eds.) Domain-Specific Conceptual Modeling, pp. 417–437. Springer (2016)
9. Buchmann, R.A., Karagiannis, D.: Domain-specific diagrammatic modelling: a source of machine-readable semantics for the internet of things. Cluster Computing 20(1), 895–908 (2017)
10. Chew, E.K.: Service innovation for the digital world. Enterprise Modelling and Information Systems Architectures 9(1), 70–89 (2015)
11. Engelsman, W., Jonkers, H., Quartel, D.: Archimate® extension for modeling and managing motivation, principles, and requirements in togaf®. White paper, The Open Group (2011)
12. Ferstl, O.K., Sinz, E.J., Bork, D.: Tool support for the semantic object model. In: Dimitris Karagiannis, Heinrich C. Mayr, J.M. (ed.) Domain-Specific Conceptual Modeling, pp. 291–310. Springer (2016)
13. Fill, H.G.: Semantic evaluation of business processes using semfis. In: Dimitris Karagiannis, Heinrich C. Mayr, J.M. (ed.) Domain-Specific Conceptual Modeling, pp. 149–170. Springer (2016)
14. Frank, U.: Multi-perspective enterprise modeling (memo) conceptual framework and modeling languages. In: System Sciences, 2002. HICSS. Proceedings of the 35th Annual Hawaii International Conference on. pp. 1258–1267. IEEE (2002)
15. Gericke, A., Fill, H.G., Karagiannis, D., Winter, R.: Situational method engineering for governance, risk and compliance information systems. In: Proceedings of the 4th international conference on design science research in information systems and technology. p. 24. ACM (2009)
16. Haren, V.: TOGAF Version 9.1. Van Haren Publishing (2011)
17. Höfferer, P.: Achieving business process model interoperability using metamodels and ontologies. In: ECIS. pp. 1620–1631 (2007)
18. Iacob, M.E., Jonkers, H., Lankhorst, M.M., Proper, H.A.: ArchiMate 1.0 Specification. Zaltbommel: Van Haren Publishing (2009)
19. Karagiannis, D., Buchmann, R.A., Burzynski, P., Reimer, U., Walch, M.: Fundamental conceptual modeling languages in omilab. In: Dimitris Karagiannis, Heinrich C. Mayr, J.M. (ed.) Domain-Specific Conceptual Modeling, pp. 3–30. Springer (2016)
20. Karagiannis, D., Kühn, H.: Metamodelling Platforms. In: Bauknecht, K., Tjoa, A.M., Quirchmayr, G. (eds.) E-Commerce and Web Technologies, Third International Conference, EC-Web 2002, Aix-en-Provence, France, Proceedings. Lecture Notes in Computer Science, vol. 2455, p. 182. Springer (2002)
21. Karagiannis, D., Mayr, H.C., Mylopoulos, J. (eds.): Domain-Specific Conceptual Modeling, Concepts, Methods and Tools. Springer (2016), http://dx.doi.org/10.1007/978-3-319-39417-6
22. Krogstie, J.: Modeling of digital ecosystems: Challenges and opportunities. In: Working Conference on Virtual Enterprises. pp. 137–145. Springer (2012)

23. Kurbel, K.E.: Developing Information Systems. Springer (2008)
24. Lankhorst, M.: Introduction to enterprise architecture. In: Enterprise Architecture at Work, pp. 1–10. Springer (2013)
25. Liles, D.H., Presley, A.R.: Enterprise modeling within an enterprise engineering framework. In: Proceedings of the 28th conference on Winter simulation. pp. 993–999. IEEE Computer Society (1996)
26. Lyytinen, K., Rose, G.M.: The disruptive nature of information technology innovations: the case of internet computing in systems development organizations. MIS quarterly pp. 557–596 (2003)
27. Marshall, C.: Enterprise modeling with UML: designing successful software through business analysis. Addison-Wesley Professional (2000)
28. Mertins, K., Jochem, R.: Integrated enterprise modeling: method and tool. ACM SIGGROUP Bulletin 18(2), 63–66 (1997)
29. Mylopoulos, J.: Conceptual modelling and Telos. Conceptual Modelling, Databases, and CASE: an Integrated View of Information System Development, New York: John Wiley & Sons pp. 49–68 (1992)
30. Nachira, F., Dini, P., Nicolai, A.: A network of digital business ecosystems for europe: roots, processes and perspectives. European Commission, Bruxelles, Introductory Paper (2007)
31. OpenGroup: Archimate standard (2016), http://pubs.opengroup.org/architecture/archimate3-doc/toc.html, accessed: 2017-02-23
32. Panetto, H., Jardim-Goncalves, R., Molina, A.: Enterprise integration and networking: theory and practice. Annual Reviews in Control 36(2), 284–290 (2012)
33. Sandkuhl, K., Stirna, J., Persson, A., Wißotzki, M.: Enterprise modeling. Tackling Business Challenges with the 4EM Method. Springer 309 (2014)

Serviceology-as-a-Service:
a Knowledge-Centric Interpretation

Robert Andrei Buchmann, Ana-Maria Ghiran

Business Informatics Research Centre,
Faculty of Economic Sciences and Business Administration,
Babeş-Bolyai University, Cluj Napoca, Romania
{robert.buchmann,anamaria.ghiran@econ.ubbcluj.ro}

Abstract. The paper proposes a knowledge-centric interpretation of the notion of Serviceology, as well as technical means of making this interpretation operational. On a theoretical level, the proposal mixes principles from the disciplines of Knowledge Management, Conceptual Modelling, Service Science and Artificial Intelligence in order to articulate a notion of Serviceology in the sense of "service knowledge", then to deploy this knowledge "as-a-service" through conceptual modelling and knowledge graph distribution platforms. The goal is to establish a service management support framework, labelled here as SERVaaS (Serviceology-as-a-Service), based on hybrid systems that maintain both human-oriented and machine-oriented representations of service knowledge. The human-oriented representations are enabled by agile, domain-specific service modelling methods, whereas the machine-oriented representations rely on distributed graph databases exposing knowledge graphs through RESTful APIs. The proposal is based on practical project experience, aiming towards the demonstration of enterprise semantics-awareness in information systems.

Keywords: Service Management, Knowledge Graphs, Service Modelling, Metamodelling

1   Introduction

The Society for Serviceology [1] is promoting the need for a scientific systematisation of services and their technological support, therefore the emphasis is placed on the convergence of services and technology, at least in a manufacturing context [2]. However the etymology of the "serviceology" term includes "logos", which may be considered more than just a suffix of "technology", suggesting that Serviceology may also be interpreted as "service knowledge" or "reasoning on services". This interpretation must be operationalised through technological means, therefore the technology facet is not lost, and is instantiated in the work at hand by a particular approach that mixes conceptual modelling and knowledge representation techniques within a common deployment environment.

© Springer International Publishing AG 2017
Y. Hara and D. Karagiannis (Eds.): ICServ 2017, LNCS 10371, pp. 190–201, 2017.
DOI: 10.1007/978-3-319-61240-9_18

In short, the technical proposal relies on agile service modelling languages to capture service knowledge in diagrammatic form and on Resource Description Framework (RDF) knowledge graphs to derive and enrich that knowledge. Graph databases are employed to store the content and Web services based on standard RESTful protocols are employed to expose the machine-readable service descriptions (and any data linked to them) to arbitrary apps that need to be "sensitive" to the domain-specific semantics of services and their enterprise context.

On a theoretical level, this vision is subordinated to the proposed "Serviceology-as-a-Service" (SERVaaS) concept - a service management support framework that converges from a particular perspective on Knowledge Management Systems and from disparate application cases originating in multiple projects that addressed the challenge of agile service modelling with varying degrees of domain-specificity. A work-in-progress proof-of-concept will be discussed here in the form of a domain-specific modelling language for Product-Service systems – an emerging business model that blurs distinctions between products and services in order to gain flexibility in covering the variability of customer needs and to improve their engagement.

The remainder of the paper is structured as follows: Section 2 introduces SERVaaS on a high abstraction level, foreshadowing its key enablers as well as the instantiation to be detailed later; Section 3 discusses background and related works; Section 4 grounds SERVaaS in a project-based case and provides insights about its instantiation. The paper ends with conclusions and an outlook to future developments of the SERVaaS vision, systematised in the form of a SWOT analysis.

2 Introducing the SERVaaS Concept

As suggested by **Fig. 1**, SERVaaS is the result of a convergence between enablers pertaining to *knowledge representation* (as understood in Artificial Intelligence), *knowledge conversion* (as understood in Knowledge Management), *enterprise modelling* (as a specialisation of Conceptual Modelling) and *service science* (as a source of domain-specific semantics for conceptualising the "service" concept). In terms of applicability, SERVaaS relies on a knowledge conversion cycle inspired by Nonaka's seminal "Socialisation-Externalisation-Combination-Internalisation" (SECI) cycle [3], popularised in the Knowledge Management literature. The SECI cycle is specialised by SERVaaS for "service knowledge" assets and for knowledge conversion mechanisms that combine diagrammatic modelling with the Resource Description Framework (RDF) [4].

The SECI cycle is enriched by the knowledge distilling steps suggested in **Fig. 2**, towards the goal of making service knowledge available "as-a-service" to two complementary classes of stakeholders – (i) decision-makers whose management practices involve enterprise modelling methods and (ii) those involved at operations level in the delivery of services. In the enriched version, the SECI phases are reinterpreted as follows:

— the *Externalisation* phase has been traditionally accomplished by acquiring knowledge in natural language form, through weakly structured documents and

mixed content types; the traditional approach is replaced here with a guided conceptual modelling effort, where a modelling language is tailored for capturing service knowledge and stakeholder statements in diagrammatic "phrases", according a
customised graphic vocabulary. The language can be agilely tailored to incorporate
both generic semantics from the serviceology domain and specific semantics from
the application domain (or even a single enterprise context, if language reusability
outside this context is not a requirement);

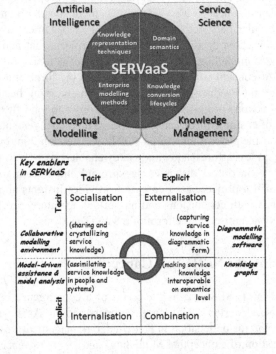

Fig. 1. Knowledge sources and conversion cycle in SERVaaS

- Next, the *Combination* phase takes into consideration the recent advances in semantic interoperability, which may be enabled by distilling (i.e., serialising) diagrammatic representations into machine-readable knowledge graphs. **Fig. 2** suggests this distillation process along the stages of (i) a procedural description in natural language (in this mock-up example, of some maintenance service delivery
  tasks), then (ii) the same procedural knowledge represented in diagrammatic form
  (using here the customised ComVantage notation [5]) and finally (iii) knowledge
  graphs written in RDF's Turtle syntax [6] for improved readability, ready for publishing and distribution with the help of a graph database management system;
- The *Internalisation* phase is further facilitated by the availability of service
  knowledge in both diagrammatic and machine-readable form - the first will support
  knowledge transfer between stakeholders, whereas the second will feed

knowledge-driven systems through a Web service-based architecture for which numerous technical solutions have been established.

The concept of modelling method [7] and the RDF data model [4] provide the conceptual and technological enablers for this new variant of the SECI model and for its knowledge distilling steps, whereas the Agile Modelling Method Engineering (AMME) framework [8] is the methodological enabler that makes it possible to tailor a modelling language for the serviceology domain, for the targeted enterprise case and its decision-making needs.

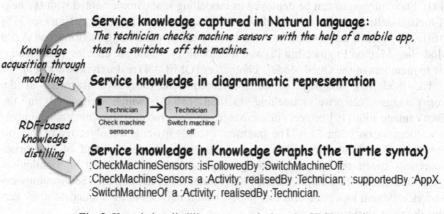

Fig. 2. Knowledge distilling steps grafted on the SECI model

3   Background and Related Works

As **Fig. 2** indirectly suggested, the technological support for SERVaaS is twofold: (i) a modelling language/tool is necessary to formulate "phrases" in diagrammatic form, with the help of graphical notations corresponding to well defined syntax and semantics customised for the application context; (ii) an RDF vocabulary and a serialisation mechanism are necessary to transfer the diagrammatic constructs to machine-readable statements (stripping them from the graphics that are irrelevant for machine interpretation and reasoning).

The knowledge-intensive nature of service design has been recognised in the serviceology literature [9] and is specialised here with a conceptual modelling approach that considers the notion of Service as an "artefact under study", aiming to capture its semantics and the factors contributing to value creation through services. A modelling method can be engineered to facilitate the knowledge acquisition and "synthesis" (an effort recognised by [10] as associated with service design).

Considering the definition of a *modelling method* [7], one key building block is a modelling language which must provide *notation* (graphical symbols), *abstract syntax* (structural constraints on how symbols may be combined in well-formed diagrammatic models) and *semantics* (the concepts assigned to each graphical symbol and their editable, domain-specific properties). *Domain-specific modelling languages* can be tailored for cases where knowledge acquisition and domain-specific mechanisms are favoured (i.e., required) to the detriment of reusability across domains (typically addressed by general purpose languages) – reasons for this may pertain to productivity, machine-interpretability or knowledge management goals, and the domain of service design provides ideal cases considering the importance of domain specific and contextual aspects. Several engineering methodologies have been established for tailoring modelling languages [8][11] and a wide palette of such languages have been overviewed in a first volume of a series dedicated to domain-specific modelling [12] (it also includes a few languages tailored for the service management domain – e.g., [13] [14]). Such languages can be deployed as modelling tools, implemented with the help of metamodelling platforms that allow a full diagrammatic language design (see [15] [16]). The work at hand employs ADOxx [15] as the underlying platform and Agile Modelling Method Engineering [8] as a methodology – both are enables made available to members of the Open Models Laboratory (OMiLAB) research network [17].

The modelling language to be showcased here evolves a fragment of the ComVantage enterprise modelling method [5][18] which originated in the ComVantage FP7 [19] project (in this stage we keep most of the ComVantage notation, focusing on semantics). The fragment evolves towards the objective of the follow-up project EnterKnow [20] – i.e., to demonstrate the concept of enterprise-awareness based on hybrid knowledge representations combining an ontological graph databases with a diagrammatic model base (thus fulfilling the "Serviceology-as-a-service" vision as outlined in this paper, which may serve as a foundation for service delivery platforms).

A key distinction between the language to be presented here and the service modelling languages referenced earlier in this section is the semantic interoperability with RDF knowledge graphs, thus making service knowledge available in dual representations, for multiple interpretations on the *Combination* and *Internalisation* phases from SECI. At the same time, it creates opportunities for evolving Web 2.0 service management systems (e.g., [21]) to the Web 3.0 stage through its use of semantic technologies.

Web 3.0 proposes *knowledge graphs* as a popular knowledge representation technique based on the RDF data model and popularised through initiatives such as Google's Knowledge Graph API [22] or DBPedia [23], which basically expose machine-readable conceptual graphs (representing knowledge of public interest) to arbitrary client applications. Arbitrary clients may retrieve graphs from such "knowledge services" through HTTP-based protocols [24] and graph query languages [25]. The technological space associated with knowledge graphs, originally employed for metadata publishing and semantic lifting, is repurposed by SERVaaS to distribute the service knowledge distilled from diagrammatic representations, which in turn are enabled by a customised service modelling language.

The knowledge distilling mechanism is based on a catalogue of diagrammatic patterns that have been investigated over time in various modelling languages (with implementations available in OMiLAB [17]). The patterns have been formally described in complementary publications such as [26] and [27]. Based on them, graph queries may be employed to retrieve the diagrammatic semantics (see [28] for a different application domain).

In the next section, the paper will focus on the service modelling language, to provide insights about the knowledge structures that may be provided "as a service", both in a service modelling environment and by graph publishing services for arbitrary client queries.

4   Proof-of-concept

4.1   The Modelling Language

The proposed service modelling language is summarised through **Fig. 3** (diagrammatic samples), **Fig. 4** (notation legend) and **Fig. 5** (the language vocabulary). Service descriptions are composed of three views that are semantically interlinked:

— The *Product-Service view* describes product-service mixtures through a flavour of feature-modelling [29] with specific semantics enabled for the otherwise generic "features" (here named "values"). The example in **Fig. 3** shows a Printer product class which may be offered in combination with one of several Service Level Agreements (SLAs), each with its distinct benefits: a Basic SLA (includes an on-demand toner replacement service, a contract for on-request corrective maintenance interventions), a Gold SLA and a Platinum SLA (both including the rental of the printer instead of buying, plus different classes of preventive interventions distinguished by the type of preventive processes – see the links from the process map);
— The *Technical view* describes the actual product to which services are associated, in a domain-specific decomposition (not only the "parts" but also the "part-of" relations have domain specificity) – here the printer is decomposed into printer parts and their relevant sensors; various "issue" classes have adequate maintenance services prescribed to them ("issues" may be defects signalled by combinations of sensors, but also explicit requests made by customers based on their acquired SLAs – e.g., toner replacement request);
— The *Procedural view* describes, in flowchart-like representations, how services are delivered for each issue class, how they are mapped to different SLAs, as well as other project-relevant properties (e.g., task responsibilities and skill requirements – reflected here only in the metamodel **Fig. 5** to keep the example easy to grasp).

The notation legend in **Fig. 4** leaves out certain relations that may be identified in the metamodel (**Fig. 5**). Some relations that are not available as visual connectors on the modelling canvas. Instead, they can be created as hyperlinks, enabling navigation between different diagrammatic models (suggested in the legend of **Fig. 3**). However, they differ from typical HTML hyperlinks by well-defined syntax and semantics – i.e., constrained domain, range, link-level attributes. Such "meaningful" hyperlinks are the basis for unifying the different views in a common knowledge graph, thus making it amenable to semantic queries and reasoning (e.g., graph queries using the SPARQL language [25] or rule-based reasoning systems).

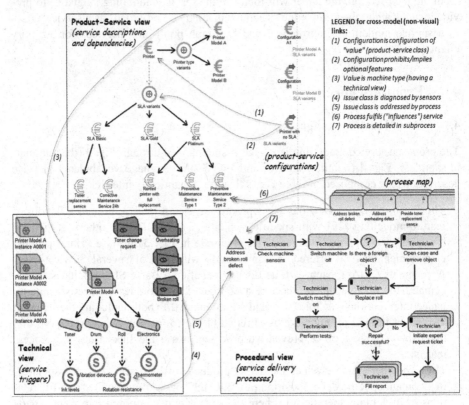

Fig. 3. Model samples

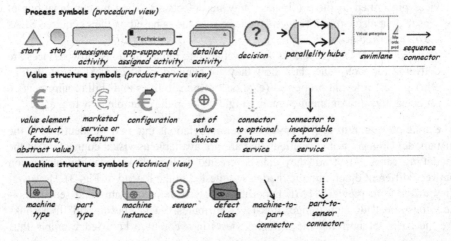

Fig. 4. Key notational elements

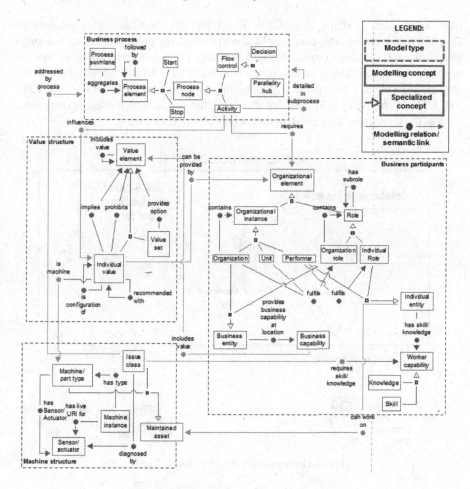

Fig. 5. The modelling language vocabulary

4.2   Deployment Architecture

The architecture for deploying SERVaaS is described in **Fig. 6**, which emphasises the dual nature of *service knowledge consumed as knowledge services*: (i) diagrammatic service models created and maintained in a modelling tool with shared use (or access to a common model base); (ii) the knowledge graphs distilled from those models are stored on graph database servers that provide RESTful endpoints for semantic queries (see [24] for a popular HTTP-based protocol).

The OMiLAB collaborative environment offers key pillars for such a deployment, with its internal architecture described in [30] and an example of modelling language hybridisation based on Agile Modelling Method Engineering in [31]. Graph database servers are widely available to fulfil the second requirement – e.g., GraphDB [32], RDF4J [33]. Besides scalable storage capabilities, they provide production-ready capabilities for reasoning (rule-based or ontology-based), for deriving data graphs from legacy data systems (e.g., CSV, Excel through the OntoRefine adapters of GraphDB), for performing data graphs analytics and for publishing graphs through standardised HTTP-based protocols and formats. The knowledge distilling mechanism for converting diagrammatic representations to RDF knowledge graphs is available at [34] - already incorporated in modelling tools such as BEE-UP (BPMN, EPC, ER, UML, Petri Nets) [35] and also available for customised modelling languages such as the one hereby discussed, in the form of an ADOxx plug-in.

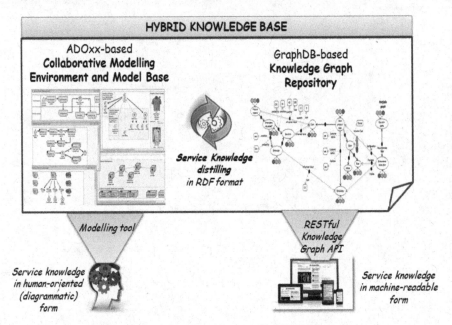

Fig. 6. Deployment architecture for SERVaaS

5   Conclusions

SERVaaS was introduced in the work at hand as a service management framework that makes extensive use of "service knowledge" captured in different forms along a knowledge conversion cycle inspired by the SECI model. A service modelling language was presented as a project-based example of service knowledge externalisation support and complementary references were provided for its methodological framework and technological enablers. In the following, we draw the conclusions in the form of a SWOT analysis:

Strengths: SERVaaS advocates a particular interpretation on serviceology, placing emphasis on its knowledge management aspects which are often obscured by the endeavours of investigating the service-technology interplay. Technical solutions have been developed to support the instantiation of SERVaaS and a proof-of-concept modelling language was presented in this paper.

Weaknesses: The deployment architecture is superficially addressed in this paper as it largely relies on the infrastructure and enablers made available by the Open Models Laboratory for experimentation purposes. (additional details may be consulted in provided references). The focus of the current investigation, subordinated to the EnterKnow project [20] are on diagrammatic semantics and the processing of semantics.

Opportunities: SERVaaS may be a foundational platform for developing "enterprise-aware" information systems that use diagrammatic semantics as back-end, therefore becoming sensitive to the knowledge expressed in models.

Threats: Modelling languages are often perceived as standards (or at least invariant artefacts) aiming for global adoption and cross-domain reusability, with human interpretation being a key factor for establishing the intended diagrammatic semantics. SERVaaS depends on metamodelling platforms and methodologies such as AMME [7] to tailor semantics for domain-specific service descriptions. Otherwise, the opportunities pertaining to SECI's *Combination* phase are drastically limited.

Acknowledgment: The work presented in this paper is supported by the Romanian National Research Authority through UEFISCDI, under grant agreement PN-III-P2-2.1-PED-2016-1140.

References

1. The Society for Serviceology – official website, http://www.serviceology.org/
2. Infor Industrial Manufacturing Perspectives, http://www.infor.com/content/industry-perspectives/serviceology.pdf/
3. Nonaka, I.: The Knowledge-Creating Company, Harvard Business Review 69: 96-104 (1991)
4. W3C, RDF 1.1 Concepts and Abstract Syntax, http://www.w3.org/TR/rdf11-concepts/.
5. Buchmann, R. A.: Modeling Product-Service Systems for the Internet of Things: the ComVantage Method. In: Karagiannis, D., Mayr, H. C., Mylopoulos, J. (eds.), Domain-specific Conceptual Modelling, pp. 417-437, Springer (2016)
6. W3C, The Turtle Syntax, https://www.w3.org/TR/turtle/.
7. Karagiannis, D., Kühn, H.: Metamodeling Platforms, In: Bauknecht, K., Min Tjoa, A., Quirchmayr, G. (eds.), Proceedings of EC-Web 2002 – DEXA 2002, Aix-en-Provence, France, LNCS 2455, p. 182, Springer (2002)
8. Karagiannis, D.: Agile Modeling Method Engineering. In: Karanikolas, N., Akoumianakis, D., Mara, N., Vergados, D., Xenos, M. (eds.) Proceedings of PCI 2015, pp. 5-10, ACM (2015)
9. Kwan, S. K., Yamauchi, Y.: A creed for service designers. In: Sawatani, Y., Spohrer, J., Kwan, S., Takenaka, T. (eds.,) Serviceology for Smart Service Systems, pp. 39-44, Springer (2017)
10. Ueda, K., Takenaka, T., Nishino, N.: Service as artifact: reconsideration of value cocreation. In: Sawatani, Y., Spohrer, J., Kwan, S., Takenaka, T. (eds.) Serviceology for Smart Service Systems, pp. 307-316, Springer (2017)

11. Frank, U: Domain-specific modelling languages: requirements analysis and design guide-lines. In: Reinhartz-Berger, I., Sturm, A., Clark, T., Cohen, Sh., Betin, J. (eds.) Domain Engineering, pp. 133–157. Springer (2013)
12. Karagiannis, D., Mayr, H. C., Mylopoulos, J. (eds.): Domain-specific Conceptual Modelling, Springer (2016)
13. Boucher, X., Medini, Kh., Fill, H. G.: Product-Service-System modeling method, In: Karagiannis, D., Mayr, H. C., Mylopoulos, J. (eds.), Domain-specific Conceptual Modelling pp. 455-484, Springer (2016)
14. Hara, Y., Masuda, H.: Global service enhancement for Japanese creative services based on the early/late binding concepts, In: Karagiannis, D., Mayr, H. C., Mylopoulos, J. (eds.), Domain-specific Conceptual Modelling pp. 509-526, Springer (2016)
15. BOC GmbH, The ADOxx metamodelling platform – reference webpage. http://www.adoxx.org/live.
16. Kelly, S., Lyytinen, K., Rossi, M.: MetaEdit+ a fully configurable multi-user and multi-tool CASE and CAME environment. In: Bubenko, J., Krogstie, J., Pastor, O., Pernici, B., Rolland, C., Solvberg, A. (eds.), Seminal Contributions to Information Systems Engineering, p. 109–129, Springer (2013)
17. The Open Model Initiative Laboratory, http://www.omilab.org
18. Buchmann, R. A., Karagiannis, D.: Domain-specific Diagrammatic Modelling: a Source of Machine-Readable Semantics for the Internet of Things. In: Cluster Computing 20(1):895-908
19. ComVantage Research Project Consortium, Project public deliverables, http://www.comvantage.eu/results-publications/public-deriverables/
20. EnterKnow Project, http://enterknow.granturi.ubbcluj.ro/contact.html
21. Levy, M., Kami, R.: A Web 2.0 platform for product-service system management. In: Mochimaru, M., Ueda, K., Takenaka, T. (eds.), Serviceology for Services, pp.96-106, Springer (2014)
22. Google, Knowledge Graph Search API, https://developers.google.com/knowledge-graph
23. DBPedia Association, DBPedia – official website, http://wiki.dbpedia.org
24. Eclipse, The RDF4J Server Rest API, http://rdf4j.org/doc/the-rdf4j-server-rest-api/
25. W3C, The SPARQL 1.1 Query Language, http://www.w3.org/TR/sparql11-overview/
26. Karagiannis, D., Buchmann, R. A.: Linked Open Models: extending Linked Open Data with conceptual model information, Information Systems 56:174-197 (2016).
27. Buchmann, R., Karagiannis, D.: Modelling Mobile App Requirements for Semantic Traceability, Requirements Enginerring 22(1):41-75, Springer (2017).
28. Buchmann, R. A., Karagiannis, D.: Enriching Linked Data with Semantics from Domain-specific Diagrammatic Models. Business and Information Systems Engineering 58(5):341-353, Springer (2016)
29. Kang, K., Cohen, S., Hess, J., Novak, W., Peterson, A.: Feature-oriented domain analysis (FODA) feasibility study. Software Engineering Institute, Technical Report CMU/SEI-90-TR-021, 1990
30. Gotzinger, D., Miron, E. T., Staffel, F.: OMiLAB: an open collaborative environment for modeling method engineering. In: Karagiannis, D., Mayr, H. C., Mylopoulos, J. (eds.), Domain-specific Conceptual Modelling, pp. 55-78, Springer (2016)
31. Prackwieser, C., Buchmann, R., Grossmann, W., Karagiannis, D.: Overcoming Heterogeneity in Business Process Modeling with Rule-Based Semantic Mappings. Int. Journal of Software Engineering and Knowledge Engineering 24(8):1131-1158 (2014)
32. Ontotext, The GraphDB Server, http://graphdb.ontotext.com/
33. Eclipse, The RDF4J Server, http://rdf4j.org/

34. The Open Model Initiative Laboratory – the ComVantage project page, http://www.omilab.org/web/comvantage.
35. Karagiannis, R., Buchmann, R. A., Burzynski, P., Reimer, U., Walch, M.: Fundamental Conceptual Modeling Languages in OMiLAB. In In: Karagiannis, D., Mayr, H. C., Mylopoulos, J. (eds.), Domain-specific Conceptual Modelling, pp. 3-30, Springer (2016)

From Service Design to Enterprise Architecture:

The Alignment of Service Blueprint and Business Architecture with Business Process Model and Notation

Pornprom Ateetanan

Sirindhorn International Institute of Technology, Thammasat University,
131 Moo 5, Tiwanont Road, Bangkadi, Pathumthani 12000, Thailand
d5722300257@studentmail.siit.tu.ac.th
Japan Advanced Institute of Science and Technology, 1-1 Asahidai, Ishikawa 923-1211, Japan
pornprom@jaist.ac.jp

Sasiporn Usanavasin

Sirindhorn International Institute of Technology, Thammasat University,
131 Moo 5, Tiwanont Road, Bangkadi, Pathumthani 12000, Thailand
sasiporn.us@siit.tu.ac.th

Kunio Shirahada

Japan Advanced Institute of Science and Technology, 1-1 Asahidai, Ishikawa 923-1211, Japan
kunios@jaist.ac.jp

Thepchai Supnithi

National Electronics and Computer Technology Center,
112 Phahonyothin Road, Khlong Nueng, Khlong Luang, Pathumthani 12120, Thailand
thepchai.supnithi@nectec.or.th

Abstract. In this study, we argue that important of strategy, business, design, and technology alignment affecting an organization's ICT enterprise architecture is also reflected by business management perspective and business process model. Enterprise Architecture (EA) is an effective way to develop current and future views of the entire enterprise. EA does this primarily by integrating the processes for strategic, business and technology planning in a way that also integrates with other business and technology process. The seamless collaborate and synergize working between technology and non-technology executives and professionals are needed in the designing and formulating enterprise architecture. Therefore, in order to facilitate this analysis, we propose an approach to relate EA specified business architecture to business process innovation, modeled using Service blueprint and Business Process Model and Notation (BPMN). Our approach is accompanied by a method that supports the process automation of business process model and is illustrated by a Healthcare service practice as a case study.

© Springer International Publishing AG 2017
Y. Hara and D. Karagiannis (Eds.): ICServ 2017, LNCS 10371, pp. 202–214, 2017.
DOI: 10.1007/978-3-319-61240-9_19

Keywords: Business architecture, Business process model, and notation,
Enterprise architecture, Healthcare service practice, Service blueprint,
Service design

1   Introduction

One of the grand challenges that complex enterprises face is to develop a way to holistically see as they are in this current situation and as they want to be in the future. Enterprises also are looking for the way to formulate business and strategic planning that aligns information and communication technology (ICT) with their service and/or business functions that it supports. Since enterprises are facing with two issues which are

1)   System complexity: enterprises were spending more and more money building ICT systems,

2)   Poor business alignment: enterprises get difficult to keep increasingly expensive ICT systems aligned with business and service need and communication gap between ICT and Non-ICT executives and professionals.

To make this possible, a technique is necessary for relating business to ICT or linking service design to enterprise architecture. Therefore, we conclude with the formulation of our research goals:

1)   To relate service design to enterprise architecture through their modeling formalisms and

2)   To explore the relating of business architecture, service blueprint and business process model and notation (BPMN).

The remainder of this article is organized as follows; section 2 covers some background on service design, enterprise architecture, and its applications. Then section 3 and 4, we present the proposed approach for relating the two applications into business architecture. To demonstrate the method and how we relate business architecture, service blueprint, and BPMN, in Section 5, we elaborate an example used in healthcare service practice. We conclude the article with a discussion of the related work (Section 6), a summary of our contribution and with some issues to future work (Section 7).

2   Background

As we aim to explore the relationship between service design and enterprise architecture, we first motivate our selection for these two formalisms and then introduce their concepts and their essential model respectively.

2.1   Service design

The design has several definitions, but at its kernel it is the process of transforming ideas into reality, making abstract thoughts tangible and concrete. Service design (SD) [1-3] is

1) A multidisciplinary area that helps innovate services by bringing new ideas to life through a design thinking approach.
2) Human-centered and holistic, which requires the integration of service science, management, engineering, the social sciences, and the arts through the creation and use of design-based method and tools.
3) All about making services we use usable, easy and desirable.
4) A comprehensive term used in various knowledge domains for solving different problems and it helps enterprises keep competitive and desirable offerings for their customers.

Service design is also a process of creating touchpoints and defining how they interact with each other and the customer or user. Using design tools and methods can deliver an understanding of customer behaviors and needs which can enable new solutions to be developed.

Regarding service research, there are two key methods which are 1) Process-oriented service design method and 2) Interaction design and software engineering methods. Thus, service blueprinting and lean consumption come from service management and use case and activity diagrams from software engineering are applied for the process-oriented method. Unified Modeling Language (UML) provides useful contributions for designing interaction processes respectively.

In industrial practice, the design process is divided into four phases: discover, define, develop and deliver. Tools and methods of each phase [2] can clarify as below

1) Discovery: user journey mapping, user diaries, and user shadowing
2) Define: user personas, brainstorming, and design brief
3) Develop: service blueprinting, experience prototyping and business model canvas
4) Delivery: Scenarios

The service design methods and techniques summarize above provide partial views that should be integrated or synergized with other methods to solve the business and ICT alignment issues in the enterprise.

Service blueprint

Service blueprinting has a long history of service marketing and innovation and is used in understanding existing services or planning new ones [4]. A service blueprint is a detailed visual representation of the total service over time – showing the user's journey, all the different touchpoints and channels, as well as the behind the scenes parts of a service that make it work [2].

The main objective of service blueprinting is to create a solid foundation for service improvement across the service system through enhancement, redesign, or re-engineering [5].

There are five components of a typical service blueprint as Fig. 1 for a diagram of key components [6] which are 1) Customer actions, 2) Onstage/Visible contact employee actions, 3) Backstage/Invisible contact employee actions, 4) Support processes, and 5) Physical evidence.

Service blueprint components	
Physical Evidence	
Customer actions	Line of interaction
Onstage/Visible contact employee actions	Line of visibility
Backstage/Invisible contact employee actions	Line of internal interaction
Support processes	

Fig. 1. Service blueprint components

2.2 Enterprise Architecture

Today, and for the future, EA will help organizations address such difficult terrain by guiding the design of adaptive and resilient enterprises and their information system [7]. EA is a practice and emerging field intended to improve the management and functioning of complex enterprises and their information system [8]. Another commonly referenced definition of the term EA was given by the open group, which considers EA as having two meaning depending on the context [9]: EA is

1) a formal description of a system or a detailed plan of the system at component level to guide its implementation
2) the structure of components, their inter-relationships, and the principles and guidelines governing their design and evolution over time

The simplest form of EA, the idea of EA is that of integrating Strategy, Business, and Technology (EA=S+B+T) which proposed by Bernard, S. [10]. EA is both a management program and a documentation method that together provides an actionable, coordinated view of an enterprise's strategic direction, business services, information flow, and resource utilization.

In summary, EA [10-12] is

1) the authoritative source for reference documentation and standards, making governance more effective
2) repeatable, scalable methodology, making the agile enterprise
3) approach to manage and drive change, in alignment with strategic and business goals, making the enterprise more successful

EA Framework is a discipline or guidelines for defining and maintaining the architecture models, governance and transition initiatives needed to effectively coordinate disparate groups towards common business and IT goals. It also links an enterprise's business strategy to its change programs. There are several independent EA frameworks the most well-known among them are The Open Group Architecture Framework (TOGAF) [11] and the Zachman framework [12].

2.2.1 Overview of TOGAF

TOGAF [11] is a framework for EA which provides a comprehensive approach to designing, planning, implementation, and governance of enterprise information architecture. It provides a high level and holistic approach to design, which is typically modeled at four levels as shown in Table 1.

Table 1. Architecture types supported by TOGAF

Architecture type / Layer	Description
1. Business	The business strategy, governance, organization, and key business processes
2. Data	The structure of an organization's logical and physical data assets and data management resources.
3. Application	A blueprint for the individual application to be deployed, their interaction and their relationships to the core business processes of the organization.
4. Technology	The logical of hardware and software capabilities that are required to support the development of business, data, and application services.

TOGAF uses Architecture Development Method (ADM) for providing a tested and repeatable process for developing architectures. All of the activities are carried out within an iterative cycle of continuous architecture definition and realization that allows enterprises to transform themselves in a controlled manner in response to business goals and opportunities. The basic structure of the ADM [13] which consist of eight phases is shown in Fig 2.

2.2.2 Overview of Zachman framework

The Zachman Framework for Enterprise Architecture (ZFEA) depicted in Fig. 3 as a 6x6 bounded matrix where the columns depict the fundamentals of communication or primitive interrogatives, namely what, how, when, who, where, and why [8]. The intersection between the interrogatives and the transformations in the ZFEA are the framework classifications and primitive elements. Each cell in the ZFEA is a normalized fact so that no one fact can show up in more than one cell. The architecture of an enterprise is the total set of intersections between the abstractions and the perspective and the enterprise itself is the implementation, depicted in the framework as row six.

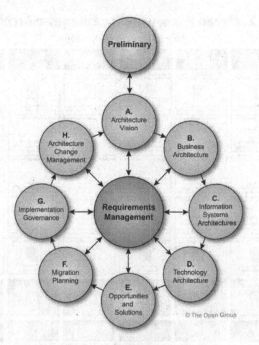

Fig. 2. Architecture Development Cycle

As Fig. 3, the Zachman Framework has six perspectives and six dimensions. The six perspectives are 1) Scope (Planner's perspective), 2) Enterprise model (Owner's perspective), 3) System model (Designer's perspective), 4) Technology model (Builder's perspective), 5) Detailed model (Subcontractor's perspective), and 6) Functional representations (Operator's perspective). Another six dimensions are 1) Data (What?), 2) Function (How?), 3) Network (Where?), 4) People (Who?), 5) Time (When?), and 6) Motivation (Why?).

2.3   Business Process Model and Notation (BPMN)

BPMN [14] is a business process modeling standard and certainly the language most used for diagrammatically representing process [15]. It provides a standard business process model notation for describing and analyzing the business process in detail. It consists of five types of elements: flow, data, artifact, swimlane and connector for visually business processes as shown in Table 2.

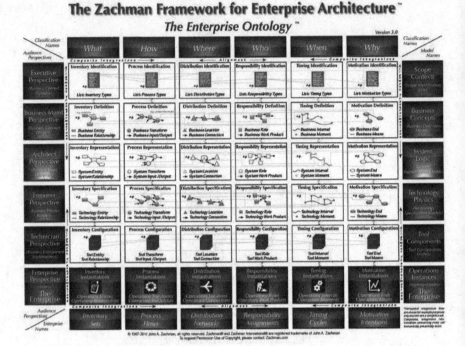

Fig. 3. The Zachman Framework [12]

Table 2. Elements of BPMN

Element	Description
Flow	business process activities, tasks, events, and gateways
Data	business data objects and data stores
Artefact	business process-related textual descriptions, annotations and groups
Swimlane	business process orchestration and choreography patterns by using pool and lane elements
Connector	the association, message flow and sequence flow between different elements

3   Relating Service Blueprint (SB) and Business Process Model and Notation (BPMN)

The relationship of SB and BPMN can be clarified as below [16]

    1) Service blueprinting processes are similar to BPMN's idea of swimlanes. In service blueprint, swimlanes separate customer actions, customer facing employees' actions and functions, and backstage functions, actors, and infor-

mation systems, thereby effectively mandating certain swimlanes for the purpose of analyzing points of contact between the enterprise and a customer.

2) Service blueprinting also intentionally differentiates between different functional areas and roles within each area to highlight and IT systems.

3) BPMN and service blueprinting has physical evidence as front-stage indicators to customers of service quality and to constrain customer actions by carefully designing the servicescape.

In comparison, service blueprinting has a higher capacity to represent user experience and is a suitable process modeling formalism to design customer-provider interface. BPMN can be used when the practitioners aim to depict organizational department, systems, and roles that involved in service delivery process in detail. BPMN has the capability to represent any parts of the service provider organization and their interaction with the customer [4].

Organizational and informational views of BPMN make a preferable modeling approach for information systems and business analyst. BPMN is now applied in the healthcare sector; representing kidney transplantation process in Brazil [15]. It is evidence that service design and ICT can enhance the effective governance for public sectors' service delivery.

4 The relationship among Business Architecture (BA) layer of Enterprise architecture, Service blueprint and Business Process Model and Notation.

The cross-disciplinary research and practice of BA, SD, and BPMN are applied. Regarding BA of EA and TOGAF as shown in Fig. 2, We can look at Phase B: Business architecture, it shows the fundamental organization of a business, embodied in 1) its business processes and people, 2) their relationships to each other and the environment, and 3) the principles governing its design and evolution. It also shows how the organization meets its business goals with the business process. In term of contents, Phase B presents 1) Organization structure, 2) Business goals and objectives, 3) Business functions, 4) Business services, 5) Business processes, 6) Business roles and 7) Correlation of organization and functions

For Zachman Framework as Fig. 3, row 2 represents enterprise model in owner's view which focuses on business process models. The main outcomes are 1) business process models, 2) Business function allocation, and 3) Elimination of function overlap and ambiguity. For combination of row and column, we can describe as follows: 1) Motivation/Why: policies, procedures, and standards for each process, 2) Function/How: Business processes, 3) Data/What: Business data, 4) People/Who: Roles and responsibilities in each process, 5) Network/Where: locations related to each process and 6) Time/When: events for each process and sequencing of integration and process improvements. In common area of TOGAF and Zachman framework, we found that business process change is involved in Phase B of TOGAF-ADM and in Row 2: enterprise model of Zachman framework.

In service design perspective, Service blueprinting visually depict steps in a service delivery process [17]. The aim of service blueprinting is usually an improved understanding of a service delivery system. Service blueprinting support business process modeling that mapping internal processes to service process can be done. Then the Business Process Innovation is one of the key capabilities of the value creation system. The modeling of business processes has become a focused aspect in how business understands and collaborates about their processes. Business architecture (layer) of Enterprise architecture can be modeled in terms of a number if views such as organization view, business capability view and business process view [18]. Three approaches are business architecture, service blueprint and Business Process Model and Notation (BPMN). Service blueprinting supports customer service processes and BPMN supports understand an enterprise's processes with particular focus on how ICT supports process automation.

Although, the scope of BPMN is strictly limited to the modeling of business processes, and the business strategy, organizational structure, functional breakdowns, data, information, and rules models [18] are out of scope. We can use BPMN for modeling each business process details including actor/rules in process swimlanes and pools. Thus, this approach can fulfill the formation of EA starts from Business architecture by illustrating business process model. Inclusion, Business process modeling can support the reinventing business processes, modernizing, re-imagining and digitizing business enterprise. A business process is the key linking point between arena of service design and enterprise architecture which focus on business architecture.

5   Case study: Outpatient department service of public hospital

To demonstrate the usage of the method described in the previous section, we use an example case in healthcare practice with Thai public general hospital. Referring to the Hospital Management System, there are four main systems which are 1) service delivery system, 2) supportive service system, 3) development system and 4) Administration system. The first system, Service system has another four subsystems which consist of 1) Emergency medical service (ER), 2) Outpatient department (OPD) service, 3) Inpatient department (IPD) service and 4) Progressive service. Each subsystem has workflow process since the beginning of the first entry until exit from the system.

We will use the Outpatient department (OPD) service of the public general hospital as the case. From the point of medical provider, there are these following processes; 1) Administrative and documentary services, 2) pre-meet medical doctor services, 3) medical treatment, 4) post-meet medical doctor, 5) medical sciences laboratory services, 6) X-ray services, 7) refer to another clinic, 8) admit services, 9) Refer to other hospital and 10) Pharmacy and payment services. It has the advantage of being familiar and realistic. As patient/customer-centered, service blueprint of OPD is illustrated in Fig 4.

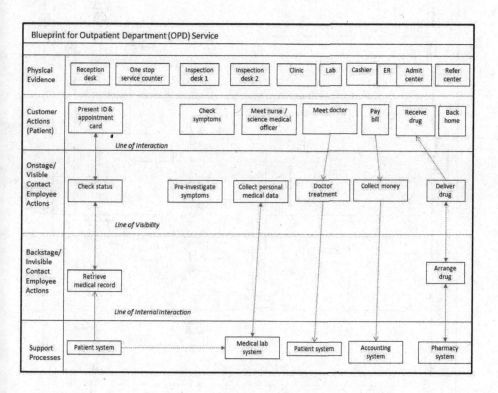

Fig. 4. Service blueprint of OPD service

Service blueprinting as an appropriate method when an enterprise has a customer-centric view toward its service delivery process [4]. An enterprise can utilize service blueprints to bundle a customer focus across the enterprise and enable customer-oriented business practices. Many enterprises have successfully used service blueprinting to increase customer satisfaction and repeat business.

Fig. 5 shows a BPMN diagram of the OPD service that we used in the service blueprinting section. BPMN can be used when the practitioners aim to depict systems and roles that are involved in service delivery process in detail. BPMN can make organizational and informational views as a preferable modeling approach for information system analysts, business analysts, and professionals.

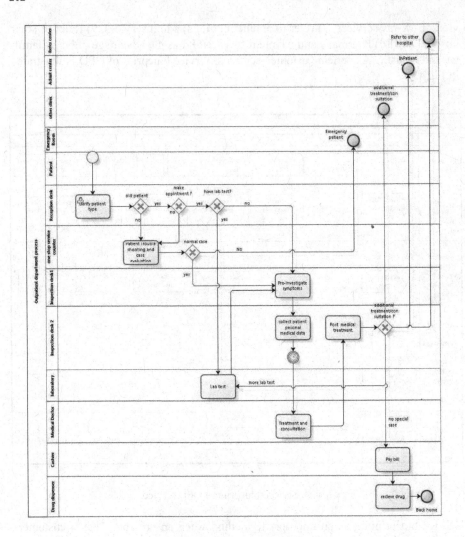

Fig. 5. BPMN Diagram of OPD service

6   Discussion

Although, the idea of relating service design and enterprise architecture through service blueprint and business architecture with BPMN seems to be quite justified and
adopted for ICT and Non-ICT executives and practitioners in ICT and business area.
EA represents a means for achieving coherency and consistency of a business system
for relating strategic elements with business processes [9], for relating the business
mission and goals with ICT mission and goals, and for ensuring more informed decisions about important topics, such as integration with internal and external information systems and business process optimization.

The common language for communicating with ICT and Non-ICT executives and practitioners are needed, to bridge the capabilities gap and enhance competitiveness from their end. Service design tool by service blueprint from the Non-ICT end is selected and align with modeling language by BPMN to fulfill the business process in the business architecture of EA. The ICT tool's clean process modeling engages business and IT from the start with service blueprint concept. Business people are not discouraged as they can visualize the process, make changes and drive the design. Other tools are targeted at developers so they give IT the full control. The business process model is designed to process for value co-creation with customer and stakeholder and can produce good customer experience.

Business process modeling in Business architecture layer is the business process innovation which is one of the key capabilities within the value co-creation approach. It is the approach to reinventing business processes to be modernized, re-imagined, and business digitized. The further study, beyond process modeling, enterprises can turn their process maps into running process applications without programming by advanced software tools and/or with Artificial Intelligence tools.

7   Conclusion

The main contribution of this study is first, we have related the service blueprint and BPMN for business process modeling to business architecture layer of enterprise architecture framework. Second, we have elaborated the method by a case study of healthcare service practice. We also foresee possibility to extend this study. Future work may concern on 1) the approach of digital transformation in the enterprise through EA and 2) the alignment of service design tools with other enterprise architecture layer. Finally, as it can be seen, the linking method presented in this study has been realized using an existing tool that supports business architecture and service design with service blueprinting. However, evaluating the used method is still work in progress.

Acknowledgements

This research was partially supported by Japan Advanced Institute of Science and Technology (JAIST), Japan, the Center of Excellence in Intelligent Informatics, Speech and Language Technology and Service Innovation (CILS) and by NRU grant at Sirindhorn International Institute of Technology (SIIT), Thammasat University and National Electronics and Computer Technology Center (NECTEC), Thailand.

Reference

1. Service design and Innovation: Developing new forms of value cocreation through service. Journal of Service research, 2015. **18**(1).
2. Keeping connected, T.t.s.b. and The design council, Design methods for developing services. p. 23.
3. Chou, C.-J., C.-W. Chen, and C. Conley, A systematic approach to generate service model for sustainability. Journal of Cleaner Production, 2012: p. 15.
4. Kazemzadeh, Y., S.K. Milton, and L.W. Johnson, Service Blueprinting and Business Process Modeling Notation (BPMN): A Conceptual Comparison. Asian Social Science, 2015. **11**(12): p. 12.
5. Radnor, Z., et al., Operationalizing co-production in public services delivery: the contribution of service blueprinting. Public Management Review, 2014. **16**(3): p. 22.
6. Bitner, M.J., A.L. Ostrom, and F.N. Morgan, Service Blueprinting: A Practical Technique for Service Innovation. 2007.
7. Lapalme, J., et al., Exploring the future of enterprise architecture: A Zachman perspective. Computers in Industry, 2016. **79**: p. 11.
8. Lapalme, J., et al., Exploring the future of enterprise architecture: A Zachman perspective. Computer in Industry, 2016. **79**: p. 12.
9. Sasa, A. and M. Krisper, Enterprise architecture patterns for business process support analysis. The journal of Systems and Software, 2011. **82**: p. 27.
10. Bernard, S., Using Enterprise architecture to integrate strategic, business, and technology planning. Journal of enterprise architecture, 2006: p. 18.
11. The Open Group, A.J. TOGAF Version 9.1 Enterprise Edition: An introduction. 2011 [cited 2017 March 5]; Available from: https://www.opengroup.org/togaf/.
12. Zachman, J. The Concise Definition of The Zachman Framework. 2017 [cited 2017 March 5]; Available from: https://www.zachman.com/about-the-zachman-framework.
13. TheOpenGroup. ADM Overview. 2017 [cited 2017 April 23]; Available from: http://pubs.opengroup.org/architecture/togaf9-doc/arch/chap05.html.
14. OMG. Documents Associated with BPMN™ Version 2.0.2. 2017 [cited 2017 March 5]; Available from: http://www.omg.org/spec/BPMN/2.0.2/.
15. Penteado, A.P., et al., Kidney transplantation process in Brazil represented in business process modeling notation. Transplantation proceedings, 2015. **47**.
16. Milton, S.K. and L.W. Johnson, Service blueprinting and BPMN: a comparison. Managing Service Quality: An International Journal, 2012. **22**(6): p. 606-621.
17. Albrecht, J.N., Micro-mobility patterns and service blueprints as foundations for visitor management planning. Journal of Sustainable Tourism, 2013. **22**(7): p. 19.
18. Gill, A.Q., Agile enterprise architecture modelling: Evaluating the applicability and integration of six modelling standards. Information and Software Technology, 2015. **67**: p. 11.

From Software Services to IoT Services: The Modeling Perspective

I-Ling Yen[1], Farokh Bastani[1], San-Yih Hwang[2], Wei Zhu[1], Guang Zhou[1]

[1] University of Texas at Dallas
800 W. Campbell Road, Richardson, TX 75080, USA
ilyen@utdallas.edu

[2] National Sun Yat-sen University
70 Lienhai Rd., Kaohsiung 80424, Taiwan, ROC
syhwang@mis.nsysu.edu.tw

Abstract. Service ontology models have been applied to many application domains to facilitate the semantic rich specifications of various types of services, including the business processes, health care, manufacturing processes, etc. Recently, many service models for the Internet of Things (IoT) domain have been proposed. However, these models are still mostly following the thoughts of software services. In this paper, we discuss some differences of the IoT services from the software services and the requirements in service modeling for IoT services due to these differences. We also extend the existing software service model to support the specification of the IoT services and things.

Keywords. Internet of Things, IoT service model, service computing, service ontology.

1 Introduction

In recent years, Internet of Things (IoT) have gained increasing attentions in research community and industry. It is estimated that there are tens of billions of "physical things" that are connected to the Internet, and the number is still growing rapidly. Various IoT applications are continuously being developed towards the goal of more advanced automation and improved human living.

Many existing IoT systems are statically built. In these systems, the specific IoT devices and control and management software are statically selected and configured at the design time to achieve some predefined tasks and to handle some anticipated events. This type of systems has a similar nature as the conventional embedded systems, except that the constituent components (devices and software) are distributed in a wider area.

The IoT world interconnects a vast variety of capabilities, which can be so powerful if they are properly made use of, in addition to their statically assigned tasks. Consider a dynamic composition example. The police office receives a report of a hit-and-run incident that occurred 10 minutes ago by a red sedan at a location with coordinate

© Springer International Publishing AG 2017
Y. Hara and D. Karagiannis (Eds.): ICServ 2017, LNCS 10371, pp. 215–223, 2017.
DOI: 10.1007/978-3-319-61240-9_20

(x, y). The first task is to collect event related information, so police office will request the recorded videos, if available, from cars that may have been at location (x, y) 10 minutes ago. Then, another task will be to locate the culprit and request the image sensors on cars and on smart roads located within 10 minutes driving distance from (x, y) to detect the culprit. Both of these tasks are dynamic and the set of IoT devices cannot be identified in advance.

Service computing technologies can be leveraged to help with dynamic discovery and composition of the IoT devices to handle dynamically arising tasks. The fundamental technique for service discovery, selection, and composition is the service model. Without proper service specifications, the discovery and composition tasks will not work properly. However, existing service models are mainly designed for software services and may fall short for the modeling of IoT services. Some research works focus on the modeling issues for IoT services, such as encapsulating device control and interaction details and providing high level service interfaces [1] [2] and event based service modeling to manage the interactions among IoT services in an application system [3] [4], etc. Though these models are essential to IoT services, they mostly follow the same thoughts as software services, and do not consider some specific issues that are different in IoT services as compared to regular software services.

In this paper, we consider the insufficiency of existing service models for the IoT domain and discuss what should be considered in the IoT service model that have not been considered important or have not been considered at all in software service models. We then propose the modeling techniques to bridge the gap. The major issues we have identified and the modeling solutions are discussed in Sections 2 to 5. Section 6 surveys the existing IoT service models and discusses their potential problems. In Section 7, we conclude the paper and state potential future research directions.

2   Explicit Model for Things

In existing service models, the specifications of the services focus on their functionalities, not on the devices that can host the services. Also, a lot of research considers Quality of Service (QoS) issues during service composition and these works can address the availability, efficiency and other QoS issues of the service provisioning. But none of these need the specification of the underlying computing facilities that hosts the services. This is because software services are hosted by computing facilities that have sufficient uniformity and can be left out from the picture. On the other hand, the services provided by the IoT devices are mostly device specific and the characteristics of the devices can impact the service it provides. For example, all vehicles can provide the transport service, but each of them has its own characteristics, such as the capacity limit. If the cargo to be transported exceeds the limit of one truck, it is possible to select multiple trucks (different Things) or to select one truck and let it transport in multiple trips. Similar to software services, these issues may be left to QoS considerations. But due to the diversity of the devices, whether the devices are considered at the functional composition time or QoS based composition time, the specification of the IoT devices should be explicit. Thus, besides specifying the services, the IoT service model requires the specific specification of the characteristics of the IoT devices.

There have been specification models proposed to specify devices that may be suitable for IoT systems. For example, OASIS has published the Devices Profile for Web Services (DPWS) [3] which defines the schema for specifying a device and its services. DPWS defines web Service description, discovery, messaging, and eventing for the device. However, there are two problems with this type of models.

(1) This model is device centric and services are defined as a part of the device specification. But frequently, the same service can be provided by a variety of devices. In this case, should we repeatedly provide the same service specifications for each device specification? We can also consider a service centric approach and for each service, define the devices that can provide the service. But this will raise the same issue. A device may be able to provide multiple different services, and the device specification should be repeated for the services.

(2) The specification for devices in DPWS is far from comprehensive. The major fields defined in DPWS schema are the device name, model, maker, etc. The essential properties of the devices are missing. For example, for a car, it is better to know its number of seats so that proper device allocation and scheduling can be performed.

Based on the observations above, we believe the IoT service model requires both the Services and the Things to be incorporated at the same upper level. They can be associated to each other in the upper ontology, instead of having one belong to the other. Also, the detailed specification for the Things should include QoS related properties that may impact the composition decisions. However, different set of attributes are required for different types of Things. Due to the diversity of Things, it is difficult to have a comprehensive model. Thus, domain specific ontology is needed to enhance the specification of the properties and profiles of Things. Fig. 1 shows the upper ontology for the IoT Service-Thing model (ST-model). For time being, the Service class can use the popular service models such as OWL-S, WSMO, etc. Later we will discuss the necessary extensions based on OWL-S for IoT service specifications. The expanded model for Things is shown in Fig. 2.

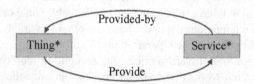

Fig. 1. Upper Service-Thing ontology for IoT.

In the Thing ontology, we try to incorporate the general classes for the specification of Things and leave the details to domain specific ontologies. The General characteristics class is similar to the definition given in the "Characteristics" class of DPWS. The Q&Q properties class is to specify the quantitative and qualitative properties that may impact the service selection decisions. For example, if we need to transport a group of

10 people from one location to another, it is important to know how many seats (quantitative property) are there in each car (Thing) in order to make the correct decision on service and thing selection for handling the transport task.

The Operation profile specifies the attributes that are related to how the Thing should operate. One important element in the Operation profile is the Control model, including the control mechanisms and commands for the Thing. Similar to the encapsulation feature in existing IoT middleware, the Control class can specify the detailed control commands and how the upper level services are mapped to a control mechanism, i.e., the

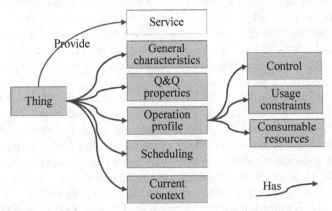

sequence of control commands. Also, Things may be nested. For example, a robotic swarm consists of multiple robots, which are also Things. In this case, the Control class can specify the mechanisms for the coordination of the lower level Things to achieve a certain service of the higher level Thing. These control mechanisms can also be specified in the Control class.

Fig. 2. Ontology for the Thing.

During service provisioning, there may be constraints on the provider Thing regarding how its services can be provided. For example, in most cases, multiple services provided by one Thing will have to be provided exclusively. Some device may have to be operated at a certain temperature range. These and other constraints can be specified in the Usage constraints class in the Operation profile of the Thing.

During the execution of software services, the computing facility would consume power. There are research works that consider how to minimize the energy consumption for services. Similarly, the operation of a Thing may consume some resources. A temperature sensor consumes battery power when providing its temperature sensing service. A truck consumes gas when providing its "cargo transport" service. Also, some Things requiring maintenances can also be viewed as requiring some consumable resources, e.g., a car would consume its maintenance free period. However, the issues of consumable resources for Things are different from the issues of energy consumption in software services. The energy consumption for software services can be handled as a QoS issue, while insufficiency of the consumable resources for the Things may require some external services to replenish them, which is a functional issue. Thus, the resources and the sufficiency of the resources need to be exposed specifically in the specification of the Things. The event model is most suitable for this specification. The Consumable resources class can specify the resources needed and the events for insufficient resources. When such an event is triggered, external services can be activated to execute the replenishing task.

Generally, a software service has an execution context, but it hardly has much importance. In the physical world, the context of the Thing is very critical in service provision. For example, we cannot select a Thing in San Diego to fulfill a service required in Boston within an hour. Thus, the current context of the Thing and the context of the service request should be clearly specified. In fact, there is another important consideration that is not there for software services. Consider that a service consumer requests for a service at location X within a time limit T. A Thing t at location Y can provide this service. Then, we cannot just select t for the task. We also need to compose the transport services to bring t from Y to X within time T in order for t to properly fulfill the request. Here, we define the Current context class to specify the current context of a Thing. Later we will further discuss the issue of contexts in service composition.

A software service can be provided simultaneously to multiple requesters from different geographical locations, while IoT services may have to be provided with a specific context given in a request. Thus, scheduling has a significant role in the Thing-ontology. We define the Scheduling class in the Thing ontology to address the scheduling issues. For example, a plumber (Thing) provides a plumbing service. Several houses may require the plumbing service concurrently. The provider can only offer the service one at a time, and needs to schedule these requests and needs to request transport services to bring itself to these locations. A requester can choose to use another Thing in case one cannot provide a satisfactory schedule. Though scheduling can be considered as a QoS issue, it may trigger functional compositions due to the context issue.

3   Extending the IoT Service Model for the Contexts

We consider the OWL-S model for IoT services, but some extensions are needed to allow the service model to fully support IoT systems. We have already discussed the Apply-to extension in the IoT service model in Section 3. Here we consider the context requirements for the IoT services.

In the OWL-S model, a service is formally specified by its IOPE (inputs, outputs, preconditions, effects), where preconditions are the conditions that have to be satisfied before the service can be invoked and effects are the conditions that will hold after the execution of the service, if the preconditions are satisfied. A service request can be specified as an abstract service with its IOPE being the requirements for match making.

Here, we define "Context preconditions" to support the specification of the context requirements in a service request. Why can't the Context preconditions be specified as the regular preconditions? Generally, preconditions of a service are fixed conditions that stay the same for all service invocations. But Context preconditions are dynamic, and can probably be different in each invocation. Why can't the Context preconditions be specified as an input? The composition reasoning process needs to take the Context preconditions into account, but input values are not considered during composition reasoning. Corresponding to Context preconditions, we also define the "Context effects" class to specify the dynamic effects that impact the states of the service recipients. The extended service model for IoT services is shown in Fig. 3.

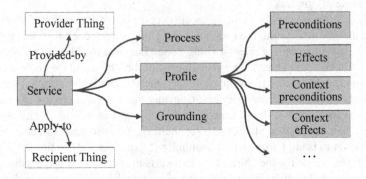

Fig. 3. Extended IoT Service model.

Separation of the regular preconditions/effects and Context preconditions/effects can also benefit staged composition reasoning. For example, consider a disaster site that is hard to reach by human rescuers. To reach the survivor-search goal, the functional reasoner selects a survivor-search service provided by a swarm of robots equipped with life detectors. The service has a Context precondition requiring that the provider Thing (the swarm) should be at the disaster site. To satisfy the goal, a functional composition reasoning is used to get a transport service provided by a truck. The QoS based composition reasoner can then select the truck that is closest to the swarm to provide the transport service. For complex composition problems, such separation can help reduce the complexity of the composition process.

4   Issues in Composition of IoT Services

In a composite service model, various composition constructs need to be provided to allow the services being composed by different execution patterns. For example, OWL-S supports sequence, split, split-join, choice, any-order, iterate, etc. The composition constructs in most existing service models only consider control flow constructs, which are not sufficient for IoT services.

Consider the example of survivor search by a swarm of robots. The robots cannot offer the survivor search service by themselves. The swarm can provide an "explore" service, but the effect of the explore service is traversing a region without any outcome. The robots need to be equipped with life detectors in order to provide the survivor search service. On the other hand, a life-detector Thing can provide the life detection service, but only within a small range. It is necessary to attached the life detector to a robot or a vehicle to fulfill the survivor search service. This type of composition cannot be reasoned if we only consider conventional control flow based composition constructs. We need some composition construct like "Apply", which allows a service x to apply its service effects to its recipient service y, i.e., y's new effects become the aggregated effects of x and its own effects. When the "explore" service is applied to the "life detection" service, the composite service can be "survivor search".

In the physical world, things and their services sometimes need to coordinate with each other to accomplish a certain goal. For example, when a robot and its attached life-detector perform the survivor search service, a survivor is discovered but with some heavy object fell on him. The robot also offers a transport service, which can lift and move away the object. But in this situation, the object is too heavy for a single robot to transport it. The robot can ask another robot nearby to collaboratively lift and move away the object. During this "composed" effort, the behavior of one robot impacts the other and they need to communicate, synchronize, physically interact, etc. to successfully achieve the goal. The composition between collaborative Things and their services can be complex and may have many different patterns. In a more complex collaboration, many Things may have to collaborate to achieve the desired goal and the composition of their services can be even more complex.

Instead of considering each case of collaboration, we consider both example cases given above in a uniform paradigm and provide a collaboration composition construct to support the specification of such compositions. The model for the collaboration composition construct is shown in Fig. 4.

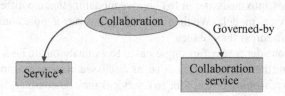

Fig. 4. Upper Service-Thing ontology for IoT.

The collaboration between the services is governed by a collaboration service, which provides messaging, synchronization, event management, as well physical actions required for the collaboration. As can be seen, the collaboration composition may have a little similarity with the conversation model, but is far more complex. It can be used to in place of the conversation model to offer conversational services. For the first example above, the collaboration service should specify that the robot should attach the life detector to itself and define the effects of the collaborative service based on the effects of the collaborative services. For the second example above, the collaboration service needs to provide the synchronization mechanism for the collaborative services and the collaborative services need to define all their synchronization points.

5   Brief Literature Review

There have been several service modeling research directions for IoT in the literature. One direction defines the event model, including event definition, publishing, and subscription, to model IoT service interactions. DPWS [3], SOCRADES [1], SenaaS (sensor as a service) [2], and ED-SOA [4], are example works in this category. Though event model is indeed suitable for IoT services, the modeling concept and mechanism are almost the same as those for software services [5]. Another major direction is designing middleware to support the encapsulation of detailed control of IoT devices and offering web service interfaces to simplify the IoT capability invocation. Representative works include SOCRADES [1], SenaaS (sensor as a service) [2], and ScriptIoT [6] are example middleware for IoT. Encapsulation is essential for the diverse types of IoT devices, but the concepts and designs in these middleware are not much different from conventional middleware for software systems. Some IoT models focus on sensors and sensor data, such as SensorML [7] and SSN-Ontology [8]. These models are data driven, in which services are composed for sensor data processing or for reacting to events detected from the IoT data. None of these existing works can address the issues in service modeling and composition for IoT services that are different from those in software services.

6   Conclusion

In this paper, we take a different approach form other research works in IoT service modeling and look into the issues in IoT service modeling that are different from existing software services models. We then attempt to construct a more comprehensive IoT service model to address these issues.

We plan to consider a set of example cases to evaluate our IoT service model and further investigate the missing issues. Also, as discussed in some examples in the paper, the composition reasoning process for IoT services may be complex and it is better to decompose the composition process into multiple stages, including functional and QoS-based compositions. We are developing automated composition techniques for IoT services based on this decomposition approach.

References

1. P. K. S. Spiess, D. Guinard and D. Savio, "SOA-based integration of the Internet of Things in enterprise services," in International Conference on Web Services, 2009.
2. S. Alam, M. M. Chowdhury and J. Noll, "SenaaS: An event-driven sensor virtualization approach for Internet of Things cloud," in IEEE International Conference on Networked Embedded Systems for Enterprise Applications, 2010.
3. T. Nixon, "OASIS Devices Profile for Web Services (DPWS), Version 1.1," 2009. http://docs.oasis-open.org/ws-dd/dpws/1.1/os/wsdd-dpws-1.1-spec-os.pdf.
4. Y. Zhang, L. Duan and J. L. Chen, "Event-driven SOA for IoT services," in IEEE International Conference on Service Computing, 2014.
5. S. Graham, P. Niblett, D. Chappell, A. Lewis, N. Nagaratnam, J. Parikh, S. Patil and etc., "Publish-subscribe notification for Web services, Version 1,0," 2004. https://www.oasis-open.org/committees/download.php/6661/WSNpubsub-1-0.pdf.

6. H.-C. Hsieh, K.-D. Chang, L.-F. Wang, J.-L. Chen and H.-C. Chao, "ScriptIoT: A script framework for Internet-of-Things applications," IEEE Internet of Things Journal, pp. 628-636, 2015.
7. M. Botts and A. Robin, "OGC SensorML: Model and XML encoding standard," 2014. http://www.opengis.net/doc/IS/SensorML/2.0.
8. M. Compton, P. Barnaghi, L. Bermudez and e. al., "The SSN Ontology of the Semantic Sensor Networks Incubator Group," in Web Semantics: Science, Services and Agents on the World Wide Web, 2012.

Enabling Digital Transformation in SMEs by Combining Enterprise Ontologies and Service Blueprinting

Ahson Javaid[1], Sabrina Kurjakovic[2], Hisashi Masuda[3] and Youji Kohda[4],

Japan Advanced Institute of Science and Technology, Nomi, Ishikawa, Japan[1, 3, 4]
University of Camerino, Camerino, Italy[2]
ahson.javaid@gmail.com, sabrina.kurjakovic@unicam.it,
masuda@jaist.ac.jp, kohda@jaist.ac.jp

Abstract. The goal of every business is to grow in a way to provide better services as per demanding trends. As the 21st century is considered the era of technology, any business that does not adopt and modernize its services, will face the lack of customer interest. Moreover, transforming the services to the digital service, businesses can grow faster than normal. In this research our target is to invite and encourage the SMEs to upgrade their services by using the cloud. Small businesses require high flexibility and have a broad range of service preferences. At the same time SMEs have unique requirements while having limited budgets. Although there are millions of cloud services available, SMEs still struggle to exploit the full potential of the cloud. Decision makers in SMEs often lack the required knowledge about how cloud services can push their business forward. We propose a concept for SMEs which suggests the appropriate cloud service for their (individual) business. For this we use two different tools, service blueprinting (Human interpretable) and ontologies (Machine interpretable). Service blueprinting helps to observe and organize the service processes with respect to customer's point of view. On the other hand, by knowing business nature and service blueprinting technique, ontologies can help to propose an appropriate cloud service for the business owners.

Keywords: Service, Service innovation, Blueprinting, Enterprise Architecture, Cloud Service, Small and Medium sized Enterprise

1 Introduction

Nowadays enterprises operate in globalized, complex and highly competitive markets. This goes along with shorter planning and implementation cycles, rapid environmental changes and distributed work environments. In the era of digital transformation enterprises are forced to continuously rethink and adapt their business strategy in order to maintain their competitiveness. The cloud market for SMEs holds great promise in store. But small and medium sized enterprises (SME) still struggle to take advantage from digitalization by deeply integrating their business strategy with their information technology needs [1]. An essential prerequisite for successful strategy implementation at operational level is a proper alignment of business and information technology [2].

© Springer International Publishing AG 2017
Y. Hara and D. Karagiannis (Eds.): ICServ 2017, LNCS 10371, pp. 224–233, 2017.
DOI: 10.1007/978-3-319-61240-9_21

However, in constantly changing environments business-IT alignment is still a challenge for SMEs [3]. Latter require high flexibility and have a broad range of service preferences. At the same time, they have limited budgets and decision makers do not have the required knowledge about how their business can benefit from the cloud.

This research aims at providing SMEs with a method to find the cloud service they need to run their business more efficiently and to gain competitive advantage. We provide SMEs with a method that allows them to capture their business requirements in a user friendly way and to retrieve appropriate cloud service proposals. The goal is to support service innovation and to enhance the end customer experience of SMEs. This goes along with process digitization, increase in productivity and cost savings. In order to enable a better business-IT alignment we draw upon the approach of [5], [6]. The research describes how ontologies and enterprise architecture modelling can support business-IT alignment by combining both graphical and ontological representations. It is suggested to use a hybrid modelling approach which enables both human interpretation and machine interpretation of enterprise models. The complexity of business-IT alignment will be described using a machine interpretable concept (enterprise ontology).

2 Overview of the Approach

Enabling SMEs to enhance and support their business model through digital services should be achieved by developing a modelling method. Latter consists of a modelling language (syntax, semantics and notation), a modelling procedure (steps that are applied to develop a model) and mechanisms that are applied to the modelling language and procedure [4]. On one hand the modelling method should be human interpretable by providing modelling languages that are understandable for business stakeholders. On the other hand, the method has to be machine interpretable in order to foster consistent business-IT alignment through automation. Because the relationships and dependencies in enterprise architecture are complex, machine intelligibility can help to capture the knowledge and to reason about it. Automation can be achieved by using the concept of enterprise ontologies [5], [6]. Figure 1 depicts the concept of the modeling method.

A graphical modelling environment provides SMEs with a tool that enables them to easily model respectively to capture business requirements. We suggest to draw upon the concept of Service Blueprinting [7]. A Service Blueprint is a process chart that shows the service delivery from a customer focused perspective. It consists of several layers: support processes, invisible contact employee actions, visible contact employee actions, customer actions and physical evidence (e.g. hotel room). Successful business owners and decision makers are familiar with the customer actions and how the enterprise creates value. Therefore, we suggest to enable decision makers to model the customer actions in a simple BPMN notation. The BPMN model should be annotated semantically in order to add extra information about the business that allows machine reasoning. For this purpose, the business Requirements meta model has been developed. The cloud service offers are described in the SaaS (Software as a Service) meta model. Alignment between the business and IT level can be achieved through mapping the annotated BPMN model to the SaaS model and performing queries on the ontology. The results are cloud service proposals which correspond with the needs of the individual SME and fit into its business environment.

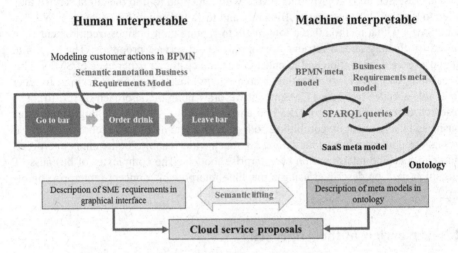

Fig. 1. Modeling method concept

In order to separate the human interpretable models from the ontology we suggest to use the concept of semantic lifting. Semantic lifting is a process that refers to associating content items with semantic objects. Latter are used as meta data to turn unstructured content into semantic knowledge sources. While decision makers are provided with end-user friendly graphical notations, the enterprise ontology is used to specify the semantic objects. Semantic lifting allows to make the human understandable meta models machine reasonable through transformation and vice versa [8], [9].

3   Literature Review

3.1   Enterprise Architecture Management

The discipline of Enterprise Architecture includes all components needed to comprehensively describe an enterprise, such as processes, applications, organizational structure and business and operating models. The goal of Enterprise Architecture Management (EAM) is to support enterprises to achieve their vision and strategy [10]. Over the past decades various Enterprise Architecture Management approaches emerged. They focus on different aspects and subsequently differ with respect to scope and granularity [11], [12]. Aforementioned approaches have been developed by practitioners [13], [14], [15], [16], [17], and [18]. In addition, scientists [19], [20], [21], [22], and the public sector [23]. Business-IT alignment is considered one of the most important topics in

EAM [24], [25], [26]. Most EA frameworks adopted the concept of different layers to classify EA components.

Nevertheless theoretical foundation of strategy in context of Enterprise Architecture Management has not received much attention over the past decades [11], [27]. Common EA frameworks offer various methods for transformation from as-is to a future state (referred to as EA maintenance), but their approaches differ substantially from each other [12], [28]. In general, EA methods that support transformation from EA is-state to target-state are only partially available. There is room for further scientific contribution, in particular with respect to the development of Enterprise Architecture ontologies and tools that support automation [11], [28]. Moreover [5], [6] show how ontologies and enterprise architecture modelling can support business-IT alignment by combining both graphical and ontological representations. In this research we build on that approach. In addition to it we enhance the business architecture layer with concepts from service science.

Service Science aims to explain how value is co-created, how interaction takes place in service systems, and how latter can be classified and explained. [29], describe service systems as "value-co-creation configurations of people, technology, value propositions connecting internal and external service systems, and shared information (e.g., language, laws, measures, and methods). The smallest service system centers on an individual as he or she interacts with others, and the largest service system comprises the global economy." The service-dominant-logic of [30] may serve as "philosophical foundation" for service science, since it provides a theoretical construct – including concepts like vocabulary, assumptions etc. – which can be used as foundation for service science. Service blueprinting has 5 layers which can evaluate the whole service from provider side to the consumer side. Using blue printing approach make the service process method more understandable and effective. As it is more easily understandable and human interpretable.

4   Research Methodology

The methodology followed in this research is based on the design science research approach [31], [32]. In context of this research we performed the two phases: the first one is awareness of the problem, and the second one is suggesting a draft for the solution. We investigated how the business requirements from user perspective can be modeled using concepts from service science. We analyzed service blueprint models of 6 use cases with corresponding cloud services. Once the concept for the modelling method was established, we developed a first version of the ontology which incorporates the meta models and mechanisms.

5   Results and Discussion

The Meta model respectively the ontology consists of three different models. The BPMN model is used as a graphical interface for the user. It allows the decision maker to model the core process of their business model. In order to reduce complexity, we suggest to use only the BPMN process, activity and task (see figure 4). The business requirements model includes all elements required for the semantic annotation of the BPMN model (see section 5.1). It enables the business user to easily annotate the BPMN model with keywords. The SaaS model describes the cloud service from a non-functional perspective (see section 5.2).

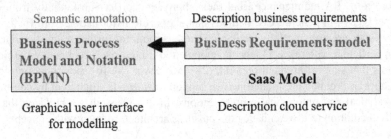

Fig. 2. Meta Model Concept

5.1 Service Blueprint Meta Model

The meta model for the Service Blueprint Model (see Figure 3) draws upon the insights of the case studies. A cloud service is normally related to one or several industries. An industry is, for instance, hospitality, building industry or pharmacy. We call the industry in our meta model "Domain". Furthermore, a cloud service might address a specific target group, which is called "Enterprise" in the meta model. For example, a restaurant management cloud service is used for the optimization of the supporting process in a restaurant. Depending on the features and the pricing model it might be mainly of interest for customers who have at least five employees. By specifying this in the ontology, SMEs with less than 5 employees won't get this cloud service proposal. The key indicators for "Enterprise" are the number of employees and revenues per year. They support the decision whether it makes sense to propose a specific cloud service or not. Process, Activity and Task (highlighted with blue background) represent classes from the BPMN meta model.

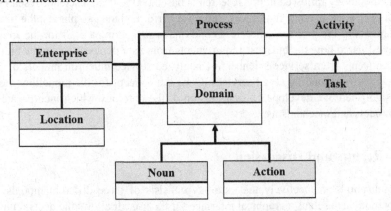

Fig. 3. Business Requirements Meta Model

The process is connected with Domain and Enterprise, since the user can annotate the whole process with this information. Moreover, the user can annotate single tasks of the process with the Action/Noun concept. Figure 4 shows an example of a service blueprint including the semantic annotation. With the concept of Domain, Action and Noun we enable the decision maker to annotate the BPMN model. If the domain is "Restaurant", the decision maker can select verbs and nouns related to a specific industry. For instance, the task "order burger" can be annotated with "Order" (action) and "Dish" (noun).

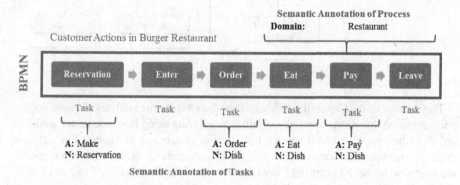

Fig. 4. Modelling and Semantic Annotation of the Service Blueprint

In order to make the annotation as simple as possible for the user, we draw upon a taxonomy and predefined rules in the ontology. The example below depicts the concept. If the user, for instance, annotates a task with the Action "order" two proposals will be shown: Dish and Beverage. The user can select either one or both.

- **Domain > Restaurant**
    - Action > Order
        - Noun > Dish
        - Noun > Beverage
    - Action > Sit
        - Noun > Table
        - Noun > Bar

With this approach we enable the business user to easily model a value stream respectively the actions taken by the end customer. The overall goal is to make the modeling and annotation as convenient as possible for the user.

5.2   SaaS Meta Model

The SaaS Meta Model represents the description of the cloud service. A cloud service is offered in one or several regions (Location). For instance, some cloud services can be used in Europe, but are not available in the USA due to legal restrictions. For the matching of business requirements and cloud services we use the concept of Domain and Cloud Service Capability. A cloud service can be used in one or several domains. For instance, a mobile payment app might be used in restaurant, but can also be used in bars, beauty salons or retail stores.

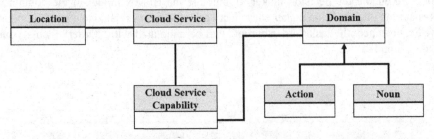

Fig. 5. SaaS Ontology Meta Model

The concept of the Capability has been introduced since the analysis of cloud service offers revealed that most suppliers explain their offering using features. Latter are listed and describe "what" a cloud service can do. For instance, a restaurant management cloud service includes various features: table management, reservation management and payment. In the ontology the Cloud Service Capability has a relationship to Domain and the Action/Noun concept.

5.3   Retrieving Cloud Service Proposals

The major concepts for discovering cloud services are Domain, Noun, Action, and Cloud Service Capabilities. The ontology includes rules which define the relationship between aforementioned concepts. A Cloud Service Capability of a specific Domain is always related to a set of Actions and Nouns. The ontology includes a predefined set of Cloud Services Capabilities that are mapped to one or several Domains and corresponding Actions and Nouns as depicted in Figure 6.

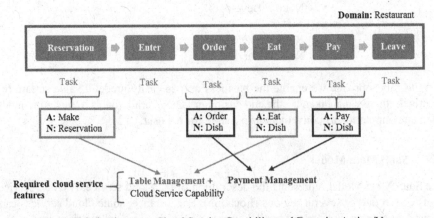

Fig. 6. Relation between Cloud Service Capability and Domain, Action/Noun

For instance, if the decision maker annotates a process with Pay/Dish and/or Order/Dish then the ontology knows, that the Cloud Service Capability Payment is relevant. Pay/Dish means that the end customer has to pay a dish in a restaurant. It requires the capability payment. Order/Dish assumes that the customer is going to eat the dish and therefore the customer has to pay for the dish. Also in this case the ontology knows that the capability payment is required. The example below shows the concept of the ontology queries:

IF (Domain = Restaurant)
and
(Action = Pay and Noun = Dish) and/or (Action = Order and Noun = Dish)
then
Cloud Service Capability = Payment Management

Another example is the restaurant table management. We start from the assumption that a restaurant requires the feature table management to efficiently manage all table reservations, and seating capacity as well as table turns in the restaurant. If the BPMN model is annotated with Make/Reservation and/or Eat/Dish the ontology knows that the capability table management is required.

IF (Domain = Restaurant)
and
(Action = Make and Noun = Reservation) and/or (Action = Eat and Noun = Dish)
then
Cloud Service Capability = Table Management.

6   Conclusion and Research Significance

With the described approach we make first steps towards a service oriented selection of cloud services that can support SMEs to use digital technologies to enhance their business models. The described concept allows bridging the gap between business and IT. It provides both decision makers and cloud service providers with a tool to describe their needs respectively offers in a language that is understandable for them. Machine intelligibility helps to capture the knowledge and to reason about it.

Over time we will refine the ontology and further develop the annotation concept. Once the concept for the ontology is finalized we will develop a software tool which enables decision makers to model and to retrieve cloud service proposals.

This research enables SMEs to face the challenges of digital transformation in order to stay competitive in the long term. With the help of ontologies we establish a modelling method which can be generalized and used for various business environments.

References

1. Big business in small business: Cloud services for SMBs. No 25 Recall. February 2014 Copyright © McKinsey & Company, Inc.
2. Henderson, J. C., & Venkatraman, H. (1993). Strategic alignment: Leveraging information technology for transforming organizations. IBM Systems Journal, 32(1), 472–484.
3. Simon, D., & Fischbach, K. (2013). An Exploration of Enterprise Architecture Research, 32(1), 1–72.
4. Karagiannis, D., & Kühn, H. (2002). Meta modelling Platforms. In K. Bauknecht, A. Min Toja, & G. Quirchmayer (Eds.), Proceedings of the Third International Conference EC-Web. Aix-en-Provence: Springer Berlin Heidelberg.
5. Hinkelmann, K., Gerber, A., Karagiannis, D., Thoenssen, B., van der Merwe, A., & Woitsch, R. (2015). A new paradigm for the continuous alignment of business and IT: Combining enterprise architecture modelling and enterprise ontology. Computers in Industry.
6. Kang, D., Lee, J., Choi, S., & Kim, K. (2010). An ontology-based Enterprise Architecture. Expert Systems with Applications, 37(2), 1456–1464.
7. Shostack, G. Lynn (1984), "Designing Services that Deliver," Harvard Business Review, 62 (1), 133-139.
8. Hrgovcic, V., Karagiannis, D., & Woitsch, R. (2013). Conceptual modeling of organisational aspects for distributed applications: The semantic lifting approach. In Proceedings - International Computer Software and Applications Conference (pp. 145–150).
9. Kappel, G., Kapsammer, E., Kargl, H., Kramler, G., Reiter, T., Retschitzegger, W., Wimmer, M. (2006). Lifting Metamodels to Ontologies: A Step to the Semantic Integration of Modeling. In Model Driven Engineering Languages and Systems (pp. 528–542).
10. Ahlemann, F., Legner, C., & Schäfczuk, D. (2012). Introduction. In F. Ahlemann, E. Stettiner, M. Messerschmidt, C. Legner, & G. Hobbs (Eds.), Strategic Enterprise Architecture Management (pp. 81–110).
11. Aier, S., Riege, C., & Winter, R. (2008). Enterprise Architecture – Literature Overview and Current Practices. Wirtschaftsinformatik, 50(4), 292–304.
12. Buckl, S., & Schweda, C. M. (2011). On the State-of-the-Art in Enterprise Architecture Management Literature. Language, 144.
13. Dern, G. (2009). Management von IT-Architekturen: Leitlinien für die Ausrichtung, Planung und Gestaltung von Informationssystemen.
14. Keller, W. (2012). IT-Unternehmensarchitektur: Von der Geschäftsstrategie zur optimalen IT-Unterstützung. dpunkt.verlag.
15. Niemann, K. D. (2005). Von der Unternehmensarchitektur zur IT-Governance. Bausteine für ein wirksames IT-Management. Vieweg+Teubner Verlag.
16. Schekkerman, J. (2008). Enterprise Architecture Good Practices Guide: How to Manage the Enterprise Architecture Practice. Trafford Publishing.
17. The Open Group. (2011). TOGAF® Version 9.1. Van Haren Publishing.
18. Zachman, J. A. (1987). A framework for information systems architecture. IBM Systems Journal, 26(3), 276–292.
19. Frank, U. (2002). Multi-perspective enterprise modeling (MEMO) conceptual framework and modeling languages. In Proceedings of the Hawaii International Conference on System Sciences (HICSS-35). Honolulu.
20. Hafner, M., & Winter, R. (2008). Processes for Enterprise Application Architecture. In Proceedings of the 41st Annual Hawaii International Conference on System Sciences (HICSS) (pp. 1–10). Hawaii.

21. Lankhorst, M. (2005). Enterprise Architecture at Work - Modelling, Communication and Analysis. Berlin: Springer-Verlag.
22. Ross, J. W., Weill, P., & Robertson, D. C. (2006). Enterprise Architecture as Strategy. Creating a Foundation for Business Execution. Harvard Business Review Press.
23. Department of Defense. (2009). The Department of Defense Architecture Framework (DoDAF), v.2.0.
24. Kappelman, L., McGinnis, T., Pettite, A., & Sidorova, A. (2008). Enterprise architecture: Charting the territory for academic research. In Proceedings of the Fourteenth Americas Conference on Information Systems (p. 11). Canada.
25. Valorinta, M. (2011). IT Alignment and the Boundaries of the IT Function. Journal of Information Technology, 26(1), 46–59.
26. Winter, K., Buckl, S., Matthes, F., & Schweda, C. M. (2010). Investigating the State-of-the-Art in Enterprise Architecture Management Method in Literature and Practice. In Mediterranean Conference on Information Systems.
27. Teubner, R. A., & Pellengahr, A. R. (2013). State of and perspectives for IS strategy research: A discussion paper.
28. Fischer, R., Aier, S., & Winter, R. (2007). A Federated Approach to Enterprise Architecture Model Maintenance. Enterprise Modelling and Information Systems Architectures, 2(2), 14–22.
29. Maglio, P. P., & Spohrer, J. (2007). Fundamentals of service science. Journal of the Academy of Marketing Science, 36(1), 18–20. http://doi.org/10.1007/s11747-007-0058-9
30. S.L. Vargo and R.F. Lusch, "Evolving to a New Dominant Logic for Marketing/ Journal of Marketing, 68/1 (January 2004): 1-17.
31. Hevner, A. R., March, S. T., Park, J., & Ram, S. (2004). Design Science in Information Systems Research. MIS Quarterly, 28(1), 75–105.
32. Peffers, K., Tuunanen, T., Rothenberger, M. A., & Chatterjee, S. (2007). A Design Science Research Methodology for Information Systems Research. Journal of Management Information Systems, 24(3), 45–77.
33. S.H. Haeckel, L.P. Carbone, and L.L. Berry, "How to Lead the Customer Experience/ Harvard Business Review, 12/1 (January /February 2003): 8-23.
34. Wagner, C. (2004). Enterprise strategy management systems: Current and next generation. Journal of Strategic Information Systems, 13(2), 105–128.

Applying Semantic-based Modeling to the Domain of Services Using the SeMFIS Platform

Hans-Georg Fill

University of Bamberg, 96047 Bamberg, Germany
hans-georg.fill@uni-bamberg.de

Abstract. Semantic-based modeling refers to the combination of conceptual models and ontologies via semantic annotations. In this way, the semantic representation and semantic analysis scope of conceptual models can be extended without requiring changes in the underlying modeling language. This is beneficial when existing models need to be semantically processed in new ways or when changes in the modeling language may lead to uncontrollable side effects. The approach of semantic-based modeling has been implemented in the SeMFIS platform which is provided for free via the OMiLAB initiative. For applying this concept to the domain of services use cases on the business and the technical layer are described.

Keywords: Services, Conceptual Modeling, Semantic Annotation

1 Introduction

The high dynamics in today's business and technical environments requires well-structured methods for supporting decision makers. In service-oriented technology and management, conceptual modeling has been found as an adequate means for bridging business and IT aspects [1]. Thereby, a large variety of service aspects can be represented and analyzed such as the structure of service offerings in the form of process models, the composition of services from a business and a technical perspective or the simulation of service offerings. For this purpose, different kinds of modeling methods are available and may need to be adapted to meet particular representation and analysis requirements. The approach of semantic-based modeling offers a new approach for extending the semantic representation and analysis scope of such modeling methods by combining conceptual models with ontologies.

2 The SeMFIS Approach

The approach of SeMFIS (Semantic-based Modeling Framework for Information Systems) realizes semantic-based modeling via distinct semantic annotation models [3,7]. With these models, relations between the elements contained in a

© Springer International Publishing AG 2017

Y. Hara and D. Karagiannis (Eds.): ICServ 2017, LNCS 10371, pp. 235–236, 2017.

DOI: 10.1007/978-3-319-61240-9

conceptual model and elements in an ontology can be established. This permits to dynamically add semantic information to conceptual models without having to adapt the underlying modeling language. The SeMFIS approach has been implemented using the ADOxx meta modeling platform and is provided for free via the OMiLAB initiative [9,8,7][1].

For applying SeMFIS to the domain of services, approaches have been developed both for the business layer as well as for the technical layer. On the business layer this includes for example the analysis of risk aspects in processes and the benchmarking of existing processes[5,4,6]. On the technical layer, the approach has been used for realizing semantic service discovery and for service-based interactions with modeling environments [2,7].

3   Conclusion and Outlook

Semantic-based modeling offers a loosely-coupled extension of the semantic representation and analysis scope for conceptual models, which can be applied in the service domain. The approach is currently extended to include also visual rules for processing the semantic information in conceptual models.

References

1. Demirkan, H., Kauffman, R.J., Vayghan, J.A., Fill, H.G., Karagiannis, D., Maglio, P.: Service-oriented technology and management: Perspectives on research and practice for the coming decade. Electronic Commerce Research and Applications 7(4), 356–376 (2008)
2. Fill, H.G.: Design of Semantic Information Systems using a Model-based Approach. In: AAAI Spring Symposium. AAAI (2009)
3. Fill, H.G.: On the Conceptualization of a Modeling Language for Semantic Model Annotations. In: Salinesi, C., Pastor, O. (eds.) CAiSE Workshops 2011, pp. 134–148. Springer (2011)
4. Fill, H.G.: Using semantically annotated models for supporting business process benchmarking. In: Grabis, J., Kirikova, M. (eds.) BIR Conference. pp. 29–43. Springer (2011)
5. Fill, H.G.: An Approach for Analyzing the Effects of Risks on Business Processes Using Semantic Annotations. In: ECIS'2012. AIS (2012)
6. Fill, H.G.: Semantic Evaluation of Business Processes Using SeMFIS. In: Karagiannis, D., Mayr, H., Mylopoulos, J. (eds.) Domain-Specific Conceptual Modelling. Springer (2016)
7. Fill, H.G.: SeMFIS: A Flexible Engineering Platform for Semantic Annotations of Conceptual Models. Semantic Web 8(5) (2017)
8. Fill, H.G., Karagiannis, D.: On the Conceptualisation of Modelling Methods Using the ADOxx Meta Modelling Platform. Enterprise Modelling and Information Systems Architectures 8(1), 4–25 (2013)
9. Fill, H.G., Redmond, T., Karagiannis, D.: Formalizing Meta Models with FDMM: The ADOxx Case. In: Cordeiro, J., Maciaszek, L., Filipe, J. (eds.) Enterprise Information Systems, pp. 429–451. Springer (2013)

---

[1] http://semfis-platform.org

Author Index

Printed in the United States
by Bookmasters

Printed in the United States
By Bookmasters